A Year
with
Chaplain
Cheatham

Sermons by Richard B. Cheatham

ISBN: 1482648547
ISBN-13: 9781482648546

Honor your father and your mother, that your days may be long in the land which the LORD your God gives you.

—Exodus 20:12

"Draw near to us, and bless us, O God, and cause
Thy face to shine on us, that Thy ways may be known
upon the earth, Thy saving help to this generation."
Amen

FOREWORD

This book is a memorial to my father, Richard B. Cheatham, PhD (1916-2004).

Most of the sermons were given at Fairfax Christian Church in Fairfax, Virginia, during the mid 1960's. The ones that are marked *A Williamsburg sermon* were written in the late 1990's after he and my mother Louise Cheatham retired to Patriots Colony in Williamsburg, Virginia.

I have selected a year's worth of sermons roughly following the Julian calendar. There are 54 sermons including ones for Maundy Thursday, Good Friday, and Easter. There are two Father's Day sermons simply because I felt they were worth including.

All of the quotes from the Bible are from either the King James or the Revised Standard Version.

I would like to tell you a little about my father's life. He was born in Nashville, Tennessee, January 16, 1916, and given the name *Dick Beauregard Cheatham*. His father said, "They're going to call him Dick anyway, so let's just name him that." In school however, his teachers insisted he put his *real* name on his papers, so he started using the name Richard for school and official papers.

His mother was Sarah Pearl Faris. Her first husband, who had the last name of Frost, died young leaving her with five children. In order to make ends meet she started taking in boarders. One boarder was Fisher Allen Cheatham, who married her and became my father's father.

Sarah Pearl was a very strict disciplinarian. If she felt her son needed disciplining she would say, "Go cut me a switch." She would switch the back of his legs and, he told me, it really stung. When he was a little boy his father used to hold his hand every night until he fell asleep. He had three teddy bears, Teddy, James and Bugger.

When my dad was about 8 or 9 years old his family moved to Florida. He rode the whole way in the rumble seat of the car. For those of you who aren't familiar with rumble seats, it was a seat that opened out where the trunk of a car usually is today.

In Florida my father had a friend named Sam Bailey who had a pet alligator. The alligator bit him on the lip and didn't let go for three days, so the story goes. Dad also had a Sunday school teacher who swallowed a fish bone and couldn't speak normally for weeks. She said in a hoarse whisper, "I can't speak any louder because I have a fish bone stuck in my throat."

As a boy one of my Dad's gifts was a pair of stilts. I know this because in the 1980's when my husband Ken and I had small children, my mother and dad visited us in Michigan. We went to Huckleberry Village (it's one of those historical reenactment places) where Dad, as a man in his 60's, amazed everyone by walking around on the stilts they had there.

When the Great Depression hit, Dad had to quit high school and go to work in New York City where his sister Elizabeth found him a job delivering vegetables to a restaurant. As he was driving down 5th Avenue he noticed that the potatoes were rolling all over the road. So, he stopped and scrambled around picking up as many potatoes as he could. When he took the basket of potatoes to the entrance of the restaurant, the man thought the basket didn't look quite full. So my dad said, "It's a large basket." Luckily the man didn't make an issue of it saying, "Well, all right." Another job was working as a bank page where the boys did errands for the bankers, and made sure they had fresh glasses of water on their desks. The bankers sat way up high and the pages sat on benches below.

He also worked in a drug store behind the soda fountain. One day a guy with a thick New York accent came in and asked him for what he thought was *home brew*. Even after numerous repetitions, he just couldn't understand what the man was after. Finally, Dad realized that what the guy wanted was a *phone booth*!

When times got better Dad's family went back to Florida. He finished high school and graduated from the University of Florida where he was in a great fraternity. One of his fraternity brothers was very gassy. Well, one winter evening this man had his back to the fire in the fireplace. The young man had gas and it caught on fire and burned a hole right in the seat of his pants. I never knew whether to believe this story or not.

Dad went on to the College of the Bible, now Lexington Theological Seminary, where he graduated first in his class. It was there that he met my mother, Louise Robertson, the niece of his Old Testament professor and Dean, Charles Lynn Pyatt.

When he was baptizing people in the river, as a young minister in Kentucky, things went well until he tried to baptize a rather heavy woman. Every time he tried to tilt her back and dunk her under the water her feet would rise up. He tried several times but finally gave up and just sprinkled her instead.

Another experience he had as a young preacher in Kentucky was gaining the friendship of parishioners where he preached. At first the people didn't like him because he didn't eat very much when he was invited to peoples' homes for dinner after church. He got wind of the ladies' feelings and started eating more. Then he was well accepted and liked.

World War II found him in the Aleutian Islands as an Army Chaplain where his famous story of the finger sandwich took place. My brother and I loved this story, probably because Dad was such a good story teller. It was very cold and desolate up there in the Aleutians and some soldiers would cut off a finger so that they would be sent home. A soldier he knew cut off two fingers while chopping wood. No one knew if it was a true accident or not. As they were in the boat, taking the soldier with the missing fingers over to the mainland, one of the medics decided to play a little joke. He got some bread, and mayonnaise, and a little lettuce and offered a nurse a sandwich with the fingers in it. She laughed and passed it on to someone else.

When Dad met someone new he would extend his hand, smile at the person, and say, "Cheatham is my name." There was a strength and warmness about him. He always enjoyed the *Cheatham* jokes, like the one about the law firm of Ketchum, Holdem, and Cheatham.

As a Chaplain he was stationed at Fort Meade, Maryland; Germany; the Chaplain school at Fort Slocum, New York; South Korea; the Presidio of San Francisco, California; and the Pentagon.

The Fairfax sermons were written at an important juncture in his life. He had wanted, for a long time, to learn more about psychology, for he felt that he could be of more help to people in a counseling situation rather than in the pulpit. Spurred on by an unpleasant incident at work, he decided to retire from the army and complete his PhD in psychology. Now a Colonel working in the Office of the Chief of Chaplains in the Pentagon, Chaplain

Cheatham had served for 20 years, so he was eligible for retirement.

My parents rearranged their lives, and lived on the stipend from his Georgetown University counseling internship, his earnings from Fairfax Christian Church, his military retirement pay, and my mother's teaching salary. The majority of the sermons in *A Year with Chaplain Cheatham* were written at this very pivotal time. You can see the influences of both his religious views and psychological insights.

He completed his PhD at American University in Washington, D.C. My parents moved to California where he taught at the Pacific School of Religion in Berkeley. Later, he opened his own private counseling practice and taught several teachers' classes in psychology. The Cheathams stayed in California until they retired to Patriots Colony in Williamsburg, Virginia, where they died.

May his words be helpful to you and light your way.

Sara Lynn Cheatham Meuchel
January 2013

CONTENTS

CONTENTS

CONTENTS

1

KEEPING AND NOT KEEPING VOWS

The New Year

Ecclesiastes 5:5 It is better that you should not vow than that you should vow and not pay.

A theme that consistently appears in the writings of the Old Testament is that a person's promise or vow is serious business. Jewish custom dictated that a vow made could not be broken. Even when Isaac gave his final blessings on his death bed to Jacob who he thought was Esau, Isaac could not change his promise. Jacob even deceived his father, and had tricked him into believing that he was his brother Esau; yet, the blessing given to Jacob was inviolate: it could not be taken back or in any way altered. The writer of Ecclesiastes, that grand old cynic, also gives testimony to the seriousness of a promise. His position is that it is wiser not to make a vow than to make a promise and then to break it. *"It is better that you should not vow than that you should vow and not pay."*

What one of us would disagree in principle with this ancient teaching of Israel? Surely, when we consider the matter seriously, we must admit that, in a sense, when a person makes a promise, he is revealing what he is at the core of his personality. If the vow is kept, the person puts himself on record as responsible and dependable. If the vow is not kept, the person also places himself on record as one who cannot be counted on, and at once, his sincerity and integrity are in jeopardy. If we agree, then, with Ecclesiastes that a vow is serious business and that vows made should be kept, why is it that we often find that keeping a promise or a resolution is so difficult? This is the question I propose for us to face this morning.

First of all, a vow is frequently broken because it is not intended that it should be kept. Vows that are made to be violated go on all of the time and I am not so sure the practice is healthy.

I suspect that one of the reasons so many New Year's resolutions are broken so often is that they were made without any serious thought of keeping them. Persons get caught up in the festivities at the beginning of a new year, and in a moment of weakness they resolve to give up a bad habit, or to go to church every Sunday, or to start something they believe they ought to be doing but are not doing. These kinds of promises provide, I suppose, certain emotional release for the person. Such promises we might call *emotional binges*, periodic upheavals a person goes through every now and then to feel better. They may be emotionally releasing but they are not constructive in developing new behavior patterns. In all probability, they are more damaging than beneficial, for a promise constantly made and broken develops moral flabbiness and instills in the self a lack of respect for integrity as well as for one's self. Ecclesiastes was not talking nonsense when he wrote: *"It is better you should not vow than to vow and not pay."*

A word of caution ought to be added at this point for those who are responsible for teaching and training children. A young person is sensitive to honesty and consistency. The young thrive best on a diet of dependability from those they look to for guidance. An adult sometimes makes a promise in a moment of weakness to make a child feel better but without any intention of keeping the promise, thinking that the child will forget later on. The promise may not mean a thing to the adult, but to the child it means a trustworthy world in which to live; therefore, a promise ought never to be made unless there is a serious intention to follow through. Broken promises to a child are about as serious a crime as an adult can commit.

This was brought home to me in a very personal way in 1960 when I was on duty at the Presidio of San Francisco and received orders to return to the Pentagon. Our son was fourteen at that time, an age when friendships are perhaps more important to a young person than at any other stage of development. He had made many friends where we lived in San Rafael. He was attending his first boy-girl parties and he had his first real girl friend. Life was at its best for him. I broke the news to him as gently as I could but still it was a blow and he cried, something he seldom did. After he had recovered from the initial shock, he came to me and asked if I would allow him to return to San Rafael in our little Morris Minor when he was sixteen. Like the adults I have been describing who make promises to children to make them *feel better* without thinking through the implications as well as never intending to keep the vow, I said, "of course, you can." I remember the thought going through my mind at the time that in two years he will forget San Rafael and will be involved with new friends in our next home. But, when those two years were about over, he began to talk about returning to San Rafael. I discouraged the idea but he reminded me of the promise. I was what you might call *caught*, right in the middle of a rash promise and a hazardous trip across country by a boy of sixteen. I really did some sweating and lived through some anxious moments trying to decide what to do. I was like Hamlet – "to be or not to be, that is the question". Well, many of you have heard the story. Dad decided *to be* and confirmed the vow made two years previously. The trip was made by my son and a friend. It all turned out fine, thank goodness. Some tell me it was good experience for a boy of 16, that he learned many valuable lessons. Either way, I am not sure who learned the most, the father or the son, for certainly this father learned that it is the mark of wisdom to give careful consideration to one's promises. It is much better to allow a person to suffer pain when he is disappointed and to assist him to live with it than to glibly make a promise to ease the pain but knowing full well the promise will not be kept. The results of broken vows are far more devastating than the anguish of unpleasant experiences.

The second observation regarding our frequent inability to keep vows is that we often make promises, not because we believe in the vow, but because we feel we have to please another person. Promises made to satisfy the desires of someone else for our lives are difficult to keep because there is always the possibility that the vow is made with anger and resentment and decisions made in bitterness are decisions made half-heartedly.

Some years ago I served with an army officer who had lost his *go power*. Once he had been an aggressive, resourceful person, filled with ambition, pride, and determination. After five or six years, however, he began to run down, spend too much time at the bar, and not enough doing his job. He began to be late for duty and to be tardy getting his reports in to higher headquarters. Several times he was called *on the carpet* by his superior. He would make promises to improve. They would last for a while but then he would lapse back into irresponsible conduct. About this time, we had several long talks at his request and the more he spoke of his life and the personal problems he was having, the more it became evident that his failures to function well and his seeming inability to keep his promises were related to his basic dislike of his profession.

"Why don't you resign, then?" I asked him. "That would never do," he replied, "I could never bear to face my family, for the men of my family have been military men for five generations and it would break my mother's heart and disgrace my father if I left the service. You don't understand," he went on pitifully, "that I have to serve in the army whether I want to or not. I will make it somehow." I left that unit sometime after this conversation and I never knew what happened to the young captain. One cannot but admire such devotion to family tradition but what a price one often has to pay to do what others expect but what one does not actually want to do.

Now, this does not mean that a person ought never to do what others would like for him to do, even though he is opposed to doing it. It is indeed a tight rope one has to walk at times between what one wants for himself and what others want for him. What destroys the best of us and keeps us from keeping our vows is not that we perform an act because others demand or desire the particular behavior of us, but because we are not aware of our behavior and do not consciously understand what is going on. There is really something magnificent, I think, about the person who performs a deed for another individual he deeply loves or admires, although he does not necessarily enjoy what he does or believe in it. One does not always have to resent what he does for another. He can still carry out an undesired or unpleasant act for the other person in an attitude of understanding, appreciation, and love, as long as he knows what he is doing.

I once knew a man who attended a weekly worship service I conducted every Sunday with his wife. Naturally, I thought he was a man of deep faith, but one day in a chance conversation we had together at an informal party, I was astonished when he told me he disliked going to church and felt church going was a waste of time. "But I don't understand," I replied somewhat shocked. "I see you at church services every Sunday." "Oh", he said, "my wife receives much personal satisfaction from religious services and I go with her because I know it means a great deal to her for me to go with her. Also, I believe it is my place as a husband to support my wife in her interests just as she supports me in my interests. Who knows," he said laughing, "one of these days I may wake up to find out that religious faith is what I really need to make my life complete. See you next Sunday at church!"

I don't know your reaction to this man's attitude or to his logic. I believe, however, he did not have a problem of keeping a promise because he was doing something to please another person, although he did not necessarily believe in what he was doing. This man impressed me as a person who was at peace with himself, and was at the same time in love with his wife, because he was fully aware of his behavior. He was a mature, integrated, real person. He could keep vows because he was acquainted with his motivations and because his love for another person was stronger than his prejudices or his personal beliefs.

Now I do not mean to suggest that all of our behavior or our vows should be conducted on the basis of pleasing or of not pleasing another person. Answers at this point are not that simple. The answer depends on the extent of the involvement, our awareness of what is at stake, and the degree of generosity we are able to muster. For example, consider the two examples just related. There is a world of difference in the decision faced by the army captain and the man going to church with his wife. In one instance, a vocation was at stake and this means one's very existence, for surely one's work is largely a person's way of life. Also one man was coerced or driven into doing what someone else wanted for his life. Here you have a perfect condition for resentment and poor performance. In the other instance, the choice is not so critical – going to church to please another for an adult is not a matter of life or death. Also, the man made his choice because he was allowed to be generous. He was not driven but was allowed to do what he thought best. He could afford to be generous because he was permitted to be generous. He could keep a vow though he did not necessarily believe in it because he was free to make the decision. The other man could not keep his vow because he was not permitted to make his choice. And here is one of the critical areas in this business of keeping or not keeping our vows.

We do have much to learn about living. Religious faith is belief, but it is not all belief. Part of our religious faith is to keep our vows in regard to our relationships with ourselves, with our children, with each other, and with the cause of Christ and His Church. We do need to dream dreams, and to establish goals to live by and purposes to live for. But at the same time, there is a necessity of maintaining the honesty of our word, the consistency of our vows and the integrity of our promises. We can keep our vows if we surround our words with caution, our behavior with awareness, and realism. Jesus still provides us with the last and final suggestions, *"Let what you say be simply 'Yes' or 'No',"* and do not forget to *"be as wise as serpents and as harmless as doves."*

2

THE EVIDENCES OF A LIVING FAITH

Hebrews 11:1 Faith is the assurance of things hoped for;
the conviction of things not seen.

One of the demands that is required of a claim is proof. If a person says that he owns an automobile or a piece of property, he must show a certificate of title to prove his ownership. If a manufacturer of electrical appliances makes a claim that a motor he makes will last for five years without replacement, the only way he can verify his claim is for the article to last five years. *The proof of the pudding is always in the eating.*

This same reasoning is also applicable to religious faith. It isn't quite enough for a person to say he has faith. In order for his statements to have any validity, his faith must be demonstrated. It isn't as easy, however, for a person to show he possesses faith as it is for a manufacturer to prove his motors will last five years. The criterion for a motor to give satisfactory performance for five years is completely uncomplicated. It only requires that the appliance operate effectively for a period of five years. But what criteria are available by which to measure faith? What is required of an individual to indicate that he does have faith?

This question seems important to ask for surely one of the real needs of the church today is to have some standards by which to judge the quality of faith claimed by its adherents. Too much does the church talk about faith without describing what is meant. Too many of us make loosely diffused statements concerning our faith without giving testimony to its operational properties. Let us look, then, at the evidences of faith as it is lived.

The writer of Hebrews gives an excellent statement concerning faith. He calls the reader's attention to faith as it was demonstrated in the lives of faithful people in the history of the Jewish nation. Then, he draws a conclusion from these acts of the people about whom he writes, *"Faith, then, is the assurance of things hoped for; the conviction of things not seen."* In this concise, direct proclamation, we discover certain distinct properties concerning faith.

First of all, we are made to understand that in faith all is not known. The writer of Hebrews makes clear that when one has religious faith, he does not possess all knowledge. He is assured that what he hopes for will come to pass. He is convinced of the truth in which he believes. But he does not know what will come to pass. The pilgrimage of faith is similar to a man going on a journey to a strange and distant country. He is assured and convinced that the city is there but he does not know the city. Knowledge can only come through experience. Faith is assurance without experience.

Now, it ought to be said at once that faith is an act that is not stupid. The text does not claim that faith does not know anything. Faith has assurances and faith has convictions and these qualities do not appear without some grounds for their appearance. Assurances and convictions do not develop without something occurring that causes them to emerge. The point is that faith emerges to permit one to go on beyond that which one knows.

Sometimes persons become disturbed in matters of religion because they are unable to know for sure everything there is to know about life, heaven, and hell. They demand answers, and are irritated when they cannot get answers. They go to this church and to that church and to some other church looking, searching for a church that has all the answers tied up neat and orderly in a pretty package. There are churches, too, that have these nice neat answers to hand out. They claim to know exactly where hell and heaven are. They have carefully worded interpretations of every Bible passage. They have the whole plan of salvation devised in a formula ready to serve on a platter. This is a comforting approach but it robs religion and life of richness, freshness, and challenge. There are no final answers to any problems. We know much, yes, but most of all, we know little. When we come to religion with faith, we delight in life with all of its mystery and with all of its awe. We come not to dissect, to analyze, or to hypothesize. We come to appreciate and to listen and to hear what we can learn. How rich life can be when we accept it and cherish it with all of its beauty, its awesomeness, and its mystery.

Next, faith has the quality of making it possible for one to go on from where he is. Sometimes I think this is perhaps the most profound evidence of faith and if someone would ask me to give what I think is the best indication of faith in the life of an individual, I am sure I would reply that it is the resource or the permission one grants himself to go on from where he is. Faith in some respects is related to a creed. It can be expressed in a theoretical doctrinal statement. But such a faith is dry, sterile, without life. When a person, though, is stopped dead in his tracks by disappointment or by some great tragedy, and has the capacity to give himself permission to get up and to go on to meet another day, that is real faith, that is faith that lives.

When I first entered the military service some years ago, I was somewhat horrified when I attended my first military funeral. A pilot had been killed and members of his unit had come to his funeral to pay their last respects. The service was reverent and the ceremonies going from the chapel to the grave were solemn and serious. However, as soon as the rites at the grave were finished, the volleys fired, and the bugler had blown taps, the members of his organization took their places in formation and marched out of the cemetery, preceded by the band playing and their singing, *Off We Go into the Wild Blue Yonder*. I say this horrified me when I first heard it. It all seemed so disrespectful to play such a rousing tune after the funeral of a deceased airman. But after a while I began to understand it made good sense and demonstrated the realities of faith. It mourns with those who mourn. It weeps with those who weep. It cries with those who cry but faith permits us to rise from our knees, to dry our tears, and to move out once more into life and to get along with the business of making the most out of what is made available for us to use.

My observation leads me to believe that faith is more in evidence than we sometimes think. A minister sees more of the victories that people win than most people. I am always amazed at what people can take and still keep on at the job of living and I find that what makes the difference is that which we call faith – not to look back but to go on from where one is.

Then a living faith is also known by the freedom one has to give of himself. The author of the epistle we are using today as a background for our sermon tells of Abraham who went out not knowing where he was going. Some Biblical interpreters believe that Abraham lived in a land whose religion was sterile, archaic, and completely immoral. These practices were alien to his nature and he felt the call to some higher way of life and belief for his family and himself. He was not afraid of what lay before him because he was able to give of himself in response to the call of something higher and something better. What a difference it makes when one can cut old ties and break old rigidities and give oneself to others or to something outside of one's own personal interest.

A young woman went to a counselor because her life seemed always to be uneventful and unhappy. She had made a fine record scholastically in school and was doing well in her job as a secretary in an important business. Still, she felt life was not quite right somehow. She felt tense and tight and was having trouble sleeping. The counselor found that she was a rather rigid person in her living. She lived by herself and had no friends. Her only outside interest was going to church each Sunday - and her job. She seemed to think she could not make any friends because they might impose on her routine of living and ask her to do things she didn't want to do. These matters were discussed quite frankly with the counselor and he asked her did she ever do anything for anyone. Well, she couldn't remember. So the counselor suggested perhaps she ought to make an effort. One day she came in for a talk and related how one of the girls at the office was going home for Thanksgiving and had asked this young woman to drive her to the airport after work the day before Thanksgiving. Otherwise, she would not be able to make the plane. She told her she didn't know but would let her know. Her first reaction she told the counselor was to say no because she didn't want to be imposed upon, but she remembered his question and it got her to thinking. Finally she said, "I think I'll try". Well, she did take the girl to the airport and the next time she saw the counselor she was all smiles, something had happened. That something was a new faith – to give up protecting, defending, holding back - and giving oneself to others. This one act for this young woman was the beginning of a whole new pattern of living. She had discovered the dynamic and existential level of life – what it means to give oneself to Christ. *"In as much as ye have done it unto the least of these my brother ye have done it unto me."*

This month you and I are beginning a new year. We have brought over from the past all of our ancient prejudices and rigidities. We have been living with old creeds and clichés. We have omitted many from our household of friendships. We have not tried to make new friends. We have held on to our little household gods and our little rituals and precious trinkets. But a new year is with us. A new beginning is possible. We are never too old to learn new ways and to accept new attitudes. God is calling each one of us as he called Abraham to give up the old patterns and the old gods that cramp our lives and deprive us of being at our best. We don't always have to be sour and self-centered and little children who have to be pampered and made over. It is time we became identified with the Christ we proclaim and to accept into our lives the living words of faith, *"If anyone hears these words of mine and does them I will liken him to a wise man who built his house on a rock. And the rains fell and the floods came and the wind beat upon that house and it fell not because that house was established on a rock."* How firm is your faith in the words that Christ proclaims as his gospel?

3

IS HONESTY THE BEST POLICY?

Judges 11:35 And when he saw her, he rent his clothes, and said, "Alas, my daughter! You have brought me very low, and you have become the cause of great trouble to me; for I have opened my mouth to the LORD, and I cannot take back my vow."

The story of Jephthah and his daughter is a study in honesty. Jephthah was one of the courageous military leaders of the tribe of Gilead who won many battles for the Israelites in their conquest of Canaan early in the 11th or 12th century B.C. One of the stories by which Jephthah was remembered was put down in writing several hundred years after he lived. It is found in the book of Judges. Jephthah was having his military troubles with the Ammonites. In desperation, according to the written account, he requested divine help. He promised the Almighty that if he won his campaign over the Ammonites, he would offer to God the first person who appeared in the doorway of his house after his return from battle. Jephthah wins the engagement, returns to his home, and the first person who comes out of the door of his home to welcome him is his only daughter. Jephthah, of course, is shaken and cries, *"Alas, my daughter! You have brought me very low, and you have become the cause of great trouble to me; for I have opened my mouth to the Lord, and I cannot take back my vow."* His daughter sizes up the situation, realizes the predicament of her father, and insists that he keep the promise he has made, and allows herself to be sacrificed. Such devotion to a promise causes one to shudder, for it seems much too severe. Yet, we see in this story what is sometimes involved when we begin to talk about truthfulness, keeping a promise, or honesty.

For some of us, I suspect the honesty of Jephthah and his daughter may cause us to question, even from a standpoint of ethics, the advisability of strict honesty. In brief, this ancient story lifted from the pages of the Old Testament may tempt us to question the time honored adage of Benjamin Franklin and to ask, "Is honesty the best policy?"

Not only in the case of Jephthah, but also in numerous situations in which people find themselves today, honesty is a questionable commodity, even when it is expected. For example, on the front page of last Sunday's *Washington Post,* an article appeared entitled, *Student Leaders Alarmed at Cheating.* The article is an account of a survey made by student leaders in 100 Virginia high schools to find out the attitudes and opinions of high school students regarding cheating in the classroom.

The survey reports that 19 percent of students do not think it's wrong to cheat and 13 percent cheat occasionally. Also, in about 70 percent of the schools cheating is a serious problem. Those students who said they cheated stated that they cheated because of pressure from parents to make good grades and because of the necessity of having to make high grades to get into college. These students also reported that they found it easier to cheat than to prepare themselves for tests and quizzes in advance.

Students who I have talked to concerning this report tell me that the only defect in the report is that the incident figures of cheating are too low. They believe, in other words, that those who answered the questionnaires did not make an honest report concerning their own cheating habits.

These students with whom I discussed this article may be correct in their individual impressions. Allowing, however, even for an increase in the figures, I am encouraged that, at least 75 % or perhaps even more, of our high school students in Virginia believe that cheating is wrong and do not practice dishonesty in their school work. I wonder if we would get as high a percentage of adults who send an honest tax report into the Internal Revenue Service before April 15th.

Although the figures of those who do not cheat or who do not practice dishonesty either in school or in other situations far exceed those who are dishonest, it is a problem in our society and there is a sizable segment of persons who do not believe that honesty is the best policy, for hardly a day goes by that a situation doesn't come to our notice of persons indicted for income tax evasion, athletes suspended from teams for violating the rules against betting on the outcome of games, business officials brought to trial for price fixing, labor leaders tried in courts for charges of misappropriating union funds – these and other incidents that come to public attention plus instances we know about personally remind us that not all believe in and practice honesty. Not everyone agrees that honesty is the best policy.

This morning, however, I am not so much concerned regarding flagrant displays of dishonesty, which really is a minority movement, as I am about the subtle acts of dishonest behavior with each other which I believe are far more serious in their consequences than dishonesty that is obvious and clear cut. Let us consider several instances of dishonesty of the subtle, personal type that eats away and destroys personal and human relationships, which are really our most precious treasures.

One type of subtle deceit that destroys is that which gives dishonesty a good name. Sometimes, a person will break a law and justify his lawlessness by saying, "The law is no good and it is all right to break a bad law." This was the attitude of many during prohibition days. Perhaps, it was a bad law but that didn't give persons a right to break it. If a person is going to break a law, let him admit he is breaking it, take the consequences if he is caught, but not justify breaking the law because he thinks it is no good. Personal inconveniences can never be an excuse for breaking any law. We need some of the stuff of Socrates who was sentenced to death by a court. His friends suggested he escape and live in another Greek city. But Socrates was wiser. He informs his friends he cannot deny the law because it is unfavorable to him. He tells them that he has lived in Athens all his life enjoying the fruits and benefits of its laws and regulations. Now that Athenian law, he goes on, does not suit him, this does not give him the right to violate it. So Socrates stayed in prison, drank the hemlock, and died. His life is much like that of the story of Jepththah and his daughter. Neither felt that one is ever justified in violating his word. Each believed in honesty, whether it suited his personal interest or not. Such sacrifices do cause us to ponder our temptations toward casuistry and deceit.

A second display of subtle fraudulency is our tendency to interfere with a person's efforts to be honest. Sometimes a child will say, "I don't like Aunt Mary!" A parent will say, "You mustn't feel or think that way about Aunt Mary. She is a nice person." At once, the child becomes confused in his feelings. He feels one way but is told by someone he respects and loves to feel a way that he doesn't feel. So he isn't sure how to feel. If such a practice continues, the child becomes unsure of his feelings, is afraid to be honest, and learns the fine art of unconscious deceit within himself. No wonder persons become adults and are heard to say, "I don't know what I believe or how I feel," and feel completely split within themselves. It seems wiser to allow a child to say how he feels, to find out why he feels as he does toward Aunt Mary, to help him to discover the cause of his feelings, and to point out that Aunt Mary may have her faults, but that she also has many fine qualities that one can learn to love and appreciate. The key here is to allow persons to be honest with their feelings while not feeding their prejudices, and to allow them to discover the positive as well as the negative ingredients in their relationships with other persons.

The third defect sometimes found in this matter of honesty is in the poor ways we teach honesty. Few persons learn honesty by being told to be honest. This quality of character, like all others, is not really taught; it is caught. Early in the 1920's Hartshorne and May made the most thorough and complete studies of honesty in children that has yet been carried out. They used excellent methodology and conducted their experiment under the most rigorous scientific conditions. They found that honesty is not a trait that a child manifests in every situation. He is honest when it is convenient to be honest. Those children who went to Sunday school cheated as much as those who didn't go. The children who cheated least were those whose friends cheated least and who came from homes where cheating was not required or a part of their life. Here we see that children *catch* honesty. It is not taught as we ordinarily think of teaching.

Now what I am saying is that if we want our children to respect and practice honest behavior, we ourselves must be honest. If we are undercharged by a store, we must see that the difference is paid. If we are home and someone wants us at the door and we do not want to see who is there, we cannot tell Johnny to go and tell the unwanted caller that we are not at home. Neither can we talk about the importance of religion and the church to the child and expect him to believe it if it is not a serious part of our lives. Children are quick to detect deception and are quick to learn deception. But they are also quick and apt to learn honesty and believe in it if we ourselves are its supporters and practitioners.

We may find the story of Jephthah and his daughter repulsive. We may say the story is much too terrible to practice today and so it is. But we will miss the whole point of the story if we reject it because of its horrible aspects. A key point about this story is that the daughter of Jephthah was schooled and educated in the importance of honesty and trustworthiness. She knew the word of her father could not be violated, regardless of personal consequences to herself. Where did she learn such devotion to the principal of honesty and truth? I suspect that she had *caught* this way of life and faith from her father. The traits of character are developed in an amazing way and human life is enriched when children are blessed with parents who provide them with those firm beliefs and practices that surround their lives with certitude, stability, and a love for truth and honesty. When this happens, the question *Is honesty the best policy?* becomes superfluous, for then honesty becomes not a policy, but an actual way of life.

Sermon

4

A CONSIDERATION OF AN ANCIENT LEGACY

Micah 6:8 He has showed you, O man, what is good; and what does the LORD require of you, but to do justice, and to love kindness, and to walk humbly with your God?

One of the characteristics of our age is discovery. At this moment, a rocket is on the way to the planet Mars. The results of this adventure, we hope, will bring us new knowledge concerning outer space and provide us with more information to assist us in sending men to the moon. We are not satisfied with where we are or what we know. We are interested in newness, discovery, and adventure.

I do not mean to underemphasize the importance of forging ahead. In fact, I personally approve of every effort to know more and more about our world and to uncover better procedures for accomplishing our tasks. Yet, there is always danger as well as folly in moving ahead when we are not acquainted with what we already have. Sometimes we are so intent on getting on with new methods and novel experiments that we do not take the time to have full knowledge of what has been given to us by those who have preceded us.

This morning, therefore, instead of urging us to move ahead, I want to turn our attention to a legacy provided for us by an ancient prophet who spoke in the name of Jehovah over 700 years before the birth of Jesus. The prophet's name is Micah who lived and spoke in the latter half of the 8th century B.C.

The people in his day were asking questions about religious faith just as people are asking them today. What is important in religion? What is essential in the life of a person for him to be well pleasing in the sight of God? These questions are not answered exactly in the same way by men today, for people are not really so concerned about God's views of their conduct. Their questions are phrased like this: What is my life? How do I get the most out of life? What am I here for? What is there in life worth living for? These are really the same questions, only with a different turn. The answers are similar, too, only slightly turned.

Instead of looking for new answers to the ultimate questions, let us consider the meaning of the answers to these questions given as a legacy to us by an ancient and wise prophet.

First of all, Micah states his problem in the form of a question. He asks, *"What doth the Lord require of thee?"* What does God want you to do? Did you ever ask yourself that question? Exactly what is it that I am supposed to do in life to make my life meaningful and to realize the most of which I am capable?

Micah answers the question he poses by showing what the answer is not. He points out quite forcibly that God does not want offerings, burnt or otherwise. Ancients believed that their God enjoyed the aroma of meat cooking. The smell was pleasing to them, so it was, of course, pleasing to Him. God was not interested in this kind of sacrifice. This is indeed a departure from the elaborate ritual system one finds in Leviticus and Deuteronomy where there are explicit instructions given concerning the way sacrificial offerings are to be prepared and placed on the altar. Micah, however, objects to such practices.

Now, we do not have ritualistic practices today in our church. We do not slaughter animals or bring rams, or jars of oil to worship our God. So perhaps these statements are inapplicable to us.

Yet, in a way they are, for you and I, in a way, believe we can satisfy our religious commitments by *giving something* to gain God's favor or that of someone else. We give old clothes to the Community Chest or to Goodwill. We give our money or a part of it to the church. The wealthy man gives a check to a hospital or an educational institution or even to the church. This is modern day parlance for thousands of rams or 10,000 rivers of oil. Yet, if this is all that is brought and given on the altar of life it is evidently not sufficient according to this ancient legacy.

The next suggestion for pleasing God offered by Micah is giving up one's first born child for the transgressions of one's own soul. In the ancient East among many peoples, it was a custom for the first child to be offered in sacrifice, believing that if the first child was given to the gods then the gods would favor the parents with additional children. Archeological diggings in recent years among the ruins of ancient villages and cities of the East have turned up the bones of infant children in the cornerstones of houses. It is believed these skeletons are the remains of the first-born, given by parents to honor the gods.

The Jewish people from time to time also practiced child sacrifice but the mainstream of religious observance rejected this practice. The incidence in Genesis of Abraham's willingness to slay his son Isaac but of God's refusal to accept the sacrifice of a child gives us insight into Jewish life that they did not as a people practice this sacrifice officially. Evidently, however, it was done, else why does Micah refer to it? He seems to settle the matter completely: God does not want a child for the mistake of a parent.

We do not offer children today in our culture as a religious observance, and anyone caught in such an act would be punished by law. Yet, it is true that we discover that parents do sacrifice their children for the sins of their souls. We see this phenomenon often.

A father sometimes has an ambition for himself, perhaps he wanted to be an engineer but he was too lazy or too something to make such a sacrifice. Yet, he insists that his son do what he did not do or could not, whether his son wants to be an engineer or not. He wants the boy to atone for his mistakes.

Again, we are not perfect but we want our children to be perfect. A parent lies but if the child lies, he gets a whipping when the child was only doing what the parent was doing. Somehow we punish the child for what we do not like about ourselves. He has to suffer for the sin in our soul.

Once I remember I was caught in such an act – criticizing my child for what I did not like about myself. Some years ago one summer when my son was 13 or 14, I told him before I left the house in the morning to cut the yard that day. When I came home about 5 or 6 that evening the grass was not cut. When he came home from playing ball, he was hit by some rather stern and overly strong words. He told me he was sorry he had not cut the yard, but he had forgotten. That wasn't enough for me. I let go with more words of admonition. Finally, he looked up at me sharply, and looking at me with a tear, "Dad," he said, "didn't you ever forget anything?" And he walked off. He knew I had forgotten things I had promised him

I would do many times. I disliked this quality in myself. I was really the one who was admonished. I became angry at myself when I forgot. Here, in this episode with my son I was taking out on him what I really dislike about myself. I was punishing my son for the fruit of my transgression. It happens all the time. Micah admonishes us that such behavior is unacceptable. Only a man himself can atone for his mistakes.

What then does God require if not *giving something* to him or transferring our misdeeds off to another, especially on our children? He replies, *"He hath showed thee O Man what is good."* In other words, *you ought to know.* The answer is within you – God makes himself known in the deep places of our spirits.

The answers to life's imponderable and perplexing questions are within us, if we will only take time to be quiet and look within.

First of all – we are to be just, honest with ourselves and with each other. A just man pulls his share of the load, whatever the load is that has to be shared. He does not *give something* whether it is an animal or oil, or rams or money to the church, or clothes to the Salvation Army or to the Goodwill, or his time or abilities or anything else to please God so God will like him, or so that he will gain God's favor. He gives because he knows he is on a team and he wants to do his share or his part. He does not sit back and allow others to do the job while he gets all the benefits and all the enjoyments of life. Rather a just man is a good sport. He gives what is required to get the job done, because he wants to pull his load and do his share, anything else is less than fair play and justice.

Second, according to Micah, the man who does what God expects of him loves kindness or rather he is kind. He makes allowance for the mistakes of others, not that he approves of what others do, no more than he approves of what he always does, but he recognizes that no person can do a good job all of the time. Justice assists us in not being lax, but kindness helps us in not becoming too rigid and demanding. Rules must be enforced and laws obeyed, but always there are extenuating circumstances, and allowances must be made for individual differences. A chance is given, if deserved, for getting started again. This applies to our attitude toward ourselves as well as toward others.

Micah then comes to the end of his famous interpretation of religion by suggesting that the third ingredient in God's grace is for you (man) to walk humbly with your God. Sometimes I wish that his phrase could be interpreted by an artist on a canvas – a man walking humbly through life with God, the source of all life and the friend of all men. I am sure the man would not be groveling in the dirt as though he were worthless. I am sure he would not be crawling behind God, shy or afraid. I am certain he would not have his face down as though he were ashamed to be a man and humiliated because he was not God. Rather, somehow, I think the man's face would be strong, brave, courageous, emanating an impression of an individual who felt he was glad to be alive, excited because he was expectant of things to happen, pleased to be a man, joyful that he had responsibilities and problems that were challenging, serene because he was confident and sure that life was good, but whose eyes would be as trusting as those of a little child because he knew that he was in partnership with his Father in whom he had complete and implicit confidence and trust and would never let him down.

At least, that is the way the picture in rough outline would appear to me.

Micah does leave us a rich inheritance doesn't he? Your job and mine and that of all others who believe in Jesus Christ as God's Son is to understand our legacy and make it a living force in the life of our world.

Sermon

5

THE CHANCE TO BE GRACIOUS

Luke 7:36-50

36 One of the Pharisees asked him to eat with him, and
he went into the Pharisee's house, and took his place at table.
37 And behold, a woman of the city, who was a sinner, when
she learned that he was at table in the Pharisee's house,
brought an alabaster flask of ointment,
38 and standing behind him at his feet, weeping, she began to wet his feet
with her tears, and wiped them with the hair of her head, and
kissed his feet, and anointed them with the ointment.
39 Now when the Pharisee who had invited him saw it, he said to himself,
"If this man were a prophet, he would have known who and what sort of
woman this is who is touching him, for she is a sinner."
40 And Jesus answering said to him, "Simon, I have something to say to
you." And he answered, "What is it, Teacher?"
41 "A certain creditor had two debtors; one owed
five hundred denarii, and the other fifty.
42 When they could not pay, he forgave them both.
Now which of them will love him more?"

43 Simon answered, "The one, I suppose, to whom he forgave more."
And he said to him, "You have judged rightly."
44 Then turning toward the woman he said to Simon, "Do you see this
woman? I entered your house, you gave me no water for my feet, but she
has wet my feet with her tears and wiped them with her hair.
45 You gave me no kiss, but from the time I came
in she has not ceased to kiss my feet.
46 You did not anoint my head with oil, but
she has anointed my feet with ointment.
47 Therefore I tell you, her sins, which are many, are forgiven,
for she loved much; but he who is forgiven little, loves little."
48 And he said to her, "Your sins are forgiven."
49 Then those who were at table with him began to say
among themselves, "Who is this, who even forgives sins?"
50 And he said to the woman, "Your faith has saved you; go in peace."

Graciousness is one of those words in the English language that is charged with all sorts of delightful expressions. When we hear the word, we at once call to mind such words as charming, good manners, courtesy, politeness and kindness. If a person is attentive in looking out for his friends, is warm in his manner, cheerful in greeting and meeting people, makes you feel welcome when you go to his house, is considerate of what other people are up against, is glad when others succeed, and grateful for his blessings, such a person is gracious. He gives out of the abundance of his heart. Perhaps, no higher compliment can be said of another than to say, "There goes a gracious person."

Jesus praised the quality of graciousness. As Luke tells us, Jesus came to a village, probably Capernaum. Simon, a citizen of the village invited Jesus to his home for a meal. There were no restaurants, of course, in those days. Strangers to a town were invited by a citizen to his home for food and lodging. Perhaps Simon was annoyed because he had to invite a wandering teacher to his house. He felt he had to extend his hospitality because perhaps he was the wealthiest man in the village but he may have extended his invitation reluctantly. He gave Jesus none of the courtesies usually given a distinguished visitor, such as provisions for washing his feet, a kiss of welcome, no oil to sooth his tired feet after walking for miles in the heat of the Palestinian sun and in the sandy and rocky roads of the Palestinian countryside.

Whenever a visitor came to a village in those days and was entertained in one of the homes, it was common practice for the people of the village to gather around the house to watch the people eat and to listen to the conversation. When Jesus sat down in Simon's house and stretched out on a couch, a woman watching the proceedings from the crowd evidently noticed that Simon was not at all hospitable to the Galilean visitor. She may have been embarrassed for her own countryman as well as moved by the presence of this unusual person; so all at once, she rushed from the crowd and knelt at the feet of Jesus. She washed his feet, crying as she did so, kissed his feet, wiped them with the tresses of her hair, and rubbed them with expensive ointment or oil.

Some might call the behavior of this woman a vulgar display of emotion. We would say that a person ought to contain her feelings and not make a public scene. Such behavior is not acceptable in our society, but for that society in that day, such signs of affection were common and acceptable. Furthermore, this woman was in all likelihood a prostitute. When she saw her life in the light of the character of Jesus, she was overcome with feelings of deep remorse and she sought relief from her feelings by tears and by acts of humility and thoughtfulness for Jesus. She performed an act of graciousness that was criticized by Simon but praised by Jesus. He says to Simon, *"Do you see this woman? I entered your house, you gave me no water for my feet, but she has wet my feet with her tears and wiped them with her hair. You gave me no kiss, but from the time I came in she has not ceased to kiss my feet. You did not anoint my head with oil, but she has anointed my feet with ointment."*

Surely, this dramatic incident tells us that it is important in the lives of persons to be given the chance to be gracious. Simon and the village classified this woman; they hung a tag on her. She was a prostitute, a person unworthy to perform any act but to serve the sexual passions of men. That was her role in life and it could not be changed or altered. But, Jesus did not label people. He saw beyond the exterior. He understood that prostitutes and other outcasts were persons with feelings and needs like every other person. He believed that people could change; and when they showed signs of wanting to change – tears, remorse, self-criticism, self-understanding, a desire to talk about their predicaments – Jesus believed that they should be given every chance and encouragement to become a different person. This woman, perhaps for the first time in her life, saw a man she really admired and respected. He treated her with respect. He gave her the opportunity to be gracious and to display in tears and acts of kindness that she was sorry for her transgressions and desired a better way. Jesus trusted her and said, *"Your faith has saved you; go in peace."*

I suppose there is no greater kindness that we can bestow upon another person than to present him with the chance to be gracious.

Persons – you and I – need very much to be offered the opportunity to do a kindly deed, to perform a worthy service, be considerate and helpful, or to give expression to our feelings of gratitude. These are spiritual needs of the soul that have to be expressed in order for individuals to grow in the life of the spirit. A person is never fully grown until he has experienced the blessedness that comes from acts of kindness and thankfulness, not required or demanded, or done to get something in return, but that issue from the heart in spontaneity and freedom. This virtue cannot be verbally taught, it has to be experienced.

Sometimes, we unconsciously deny persons this chance and their lives are hurt because we are not aware of our error. When I was a young man just beginning in the ministry, an older clergyman friend of mine and I were discussing once whether or not ministers should accept fees for funerals. I contended that such fees should not be accepted. He disagreed and made his point with a personal story. A few years previously he told me, his wife had died and a minister friend of his had conducted the funeral. After the funeral was over, he sent his friend a note of thanks and enclosed a check for $25, not as payment for a service performed, but as an expression of gratitude. The minister friend returned the check, stating he was embarrassed that his friend had sent a check for a service he appreciated being able to perform. And my friend, in telling me this story, said, "I have never really felt right about my gift being returned, for I was not allowed to do something I really wanted to do, in appreciation for a kindness shown me." The minister who said the service for the deceased wife of his friend did not mean to hurt his friend. He thought he was being kind; but in being kind, he was being unkind, for he was not allowing a person to be gracious. Our conversation ended by my friend saying to me, "Don't ever deny persons an opportunity to show kindness. You do not have to spend the fees for funerals persons give you if you feel uncomfortable in using the money for yourself. You can always turn the money over to the church or give it to someone who is needy, but be careful in not allowing people to do what you say people ought to do from the pulpit." These are words that stay with you as the years go by.

There is a lesson here I think for us in training and educating our children. We are so prone to demand that children perform chores around the house or we do not require they do anything. Either way by itself is a mistake. Children do need to be required to accept responsibilities for chores around the house. Still, I feel confident there are certain jobs that we expect them to do which they should not be made to do in order to allow them to do something helpful without being told, coerced, or forced. Graciousness springs not from demand but from desire. When a person is allowed to be gracious, the act becomes far more beneficial to his development than if he is made to do it and practice in being gracious should be promoted, encouraged, and praised. A mother once described to me with tears the feeling of deep satisfaction she felt when her twelve year old daughter one evening after dinner unexpectedly said, "Mother, I will wash the dishes tonight. You go sit down and read the paper." These moments of inner growth do not come often in the lives of most children but it may be they would emerge more frequently if we allowed children more opportunities to be gracious.

Now, I do not mean to imply that you and I ought to go around making ourselves the object of charity and insisting that people favor us in various ways so that they may have the chance to be gracious. Such behavior is more damaging to human relationships than not allowing persons to be generous, for no one cares to do anything for the person who almost demands that others provide him with support or assistance. This matter of giving and receiving is a sensitive area in human relationships and can be so easily damaged by over-demanding, over-grabbing persons as well as by those who refuse to help others at all. A society woman, who lived more by the values of social status than by gracious friendship, called several of her friends to tell them that her daughter was going to be married. During the telephone conversation, she asked those she called, "Now, you are going to give a shower or a tea for Mary, aren't you?" One of the women she telephoned, in telling me of this incident said, "I was furious and hurt at the same time. While she was telling me of the wedding, I was thinking that I would have a shower for Mary; but when she asked me, in fact demanded, that I have a shower, she destroyed my feelings of wanting to entertain her daughter. I told her, "Yes," I would have a shower, "but I don't want to and I am sorry now I said that I would!"

Graciousness cannot be forced, demanded, or hurried. It can only occur from a relationship that is born out of trust, respect, and deep regard of persons for each other. One reason I like to be associated with this church is that I feel that we are related to each other in an atmosphere of trust and respect. We are not made by law or rules to give our time, our efforts, or our money. What we do, we do because we want to.

Let us truly be grateful for the chance to be gracious, for herein lies the secret of what life is all about and what it means to be a Christian.

6

FINDING STRENGTH THROUGH CHRIST

*Philippians 4:13 I can do all things through
Christ who strengthens me.*

Anyone who has lived any time at all knows that life is no bed of roses. The events of this past week in a part of the world we can hardly pronounce – Vietnam – remind us that we live in a time of crises. We no sooner get over one close call, and before we hardly get settled down again and draw a deep breath, we are in another difficult situation. Well, who of us in life these days doesn't need extra strength to draw on to keep us going?

Paul, the Apostle of Jesus, had his ups and downs, too. He went from one crisis to another. He barely escaped from Thessalonia with his life. In Athens he had absolutely no success in gaining accept-ance of his message concerning the Lordship of Christ, and during his visit back to Jerusalem he ran headlong into Jewish authorities who denied him the right to speak on the Supremacy of Christ. When he refused to accept their decision, he was placed in irons, shipped off to Rome for trial, and landed in a Roman prison. Concerning his hardship, he wrote to the Corinthians:

"Five times I have received at the hands of the Jews the forty lashes less one. Three times I have been beaten with rods; once I was stoned. Three times I have been shipwrecked; a night and a day I have been adrift at sea; on frequent journeys, in danger from rivers, danger from robbers, danger from my own people, danger from Gentiles, danger in the city, danger in the wilderness, danger at sea, danger from false brethren; in toil and hardship, through many a sleepless night, in hunger and thirst, often without food, in cold and exposure. And apart from other things, there is the daily pressure upon me of my anxiety for all the churches." (II Corinthians 11:24-28)

Here was a man whose whole life was one crisis after another and he needed strength to keep going, too. He found he couldn't do it alone. We discover the source of his extra strength in a sentence of one of his letters to the Philippians — *"I can do all things through Christ who strengthens me."* Well, how can you and I find strength through Christ for the inner and outward adversities and crises that confront us? How can we find strength that Christ offers to get us through these days?

The power that Jesus provides is not mystical or magical. We draw strength by utilizing his approach, his beliefs, and his attitudes to crises. Paul knew Christ because he faced his crises as Christ faced his crises. We know him as we learn his secrets of dealing with his problems. What are his ways?

First, face your situation head-on. As we observe the life of Jesus, we notice that he never skirted or shirked an unpleasant situation or drew back and hid from an enemy. When the scribes or

Pharisees came to a village looking for him, he did not hide or run. He met them head on. He did not sidestep their questions but dealt with them directly. When it came time to meet his biggest test by going to Jerusalem, his disciples tried to divert his attention. They even insisted he stay out of Jerusalem. But he knew better. He carried the attack to the enemy for he knew the issues had to be faced there or they would not be faced at all.

True, he withdrew from the conflict occasionally to rest, to regain his prospective through prayer or the companionship of his friends, but these periods of retreat were not to hide, but to gain new strength to go out again.

I suspect sometimes we lose energy by trying to avoid or circumvent our predicaments. Some try to avoid problems by pretending they really do not exist, like Mr. Macabe in Charles Dickens's *Pickwick Papers* – something will turn up and everything will be all right. Others try sleeping away their difficulties. Tiredness and headaches are diversionary tactics to avoid a difficult job. Some use liquor to hide from a bad situation. Even religion is sometimes used to avoid conflict using pious phrases and singing pretty songs.

A girl in college didn't do her work, but started praying and attending chapel. She came to the chaplain about difficult passages in the Bible, and started talking about being a missionary. Luckily the chaplain saw her maneuver. She was using religious exercises as excuses to avoid doing her work. He told her, "Do your work, and then we'll talk about your other interests."

Religion's purpose is not to avoid a crisis or conflict, but to put one in the middle of the fray. There is an old spiritual that says, "So high you can't go over it, so wide you can't go around it, so low you can't go under it, you've got to go through that door!" If Christ is to strengthen us we have to face what has to be done head on. Paul could say, *"I can do all things,"* because he did not run away.

Second, discover some higher meaning in the task that the difficult situation requires. Every circumstance requires that some kind of task be performed to deal with the situation. If shelter is needed one has to build a house. The hungry have to have food. A rotten political and religious system had to be dealt with. In Jesus' time religion had become sterile, and man's relationship to God was on a mechanical and legalistic level. Man's relationship to man was on the basis of race and nationality. Jesus decided to attack these evils by offering his life. Surely Jesus was strengthened when he saw the task against a larger background – the reconciliation of man with God. His task was to reveal the mind and heart of God to the mind and heart of man. He prayed, *"Father forgive them, for they know not what they do."* and *"Into thy hands I commit my spirit." "I am doing thy will."*

7

FACING UP TO THE DEMANDS OF LIFE

*Luke 9:62 Jesus said to him, "No one who puts a hand
to the plow and looks back is fit for the kingdom of God."*

Some years ago during World War II, a clergyman in uniform, a chaplain in the Navy, reported for duty on board a large battleship. He was escorted to the office of the commanding officer. After a few amenities, the commanding officer said to the chaplain, "Chaplain, I want to be perfectly honest with you. I don't want you on my ship but I have to let you stay because Navy regulations require that I have a chaplain on board. These are my instructions to you - Don't let me catch you interfering with any rules the men of this ship are expected to follow. Do not ask for any special favors to be given to any sailor. My men are here to fight and I don't want you and your *Come to Jesus* religion making sissies out of my men! Religion, I suppose, is all right for children and the elderly, but it has no place in the lives of fighting men! Good-day, Chaplain, and please make yourself scarce."

These plain words said to a startled and shaken chaplain are not peculiar to a battle-hardened naval captain. They are believed by a large segment of realistic men and women, people who get things done, for they think of religion as an influence that makes weaklings out of people. They consider religious belief and practice as an escape technique that excuses persons from doing their duty, indulges them in their failures, encourages them to become weaklings and cowards, and prevents them from facing up to the demands of life. Many agree with Karl Marx, that religion is an opiate of the people.

I regret the naval captain never really knew what Christian faith was all about. He was only familiar with a caricature of Christian teaching, for Jesus never indulged in avoidance of any task, but insisted that men and women measure up to the responsibilities of life. Here is the way he insisted that life be lived, *"No man having put his hand to the plow and looking back is fit for the kingdom of God."*

What does it mean then, to face up to life's demands?

First of all, it means that each person has to answer for his own life. A person may be faced with a decision that is of serious moment. He may get information from friends or from professional sources. He may talk over the pros and cons of the issue that confronts him, but the decision, if it is worth anything at all, must finally come from within his own soul. He alone must decide. His answer alone is decisive.

The life of Jesus is a life of personal decision. As you read the gospel account of his life, you can almost feel the tension mounting as Jesus considers going to Jerusalem. Peter and the disciples make an effort to dissuade him. His family makes an effort to persuade him to return to Nazareth. He listens to what they have to say. But once the decision is made to go to Jerusalem, there is no turning back. Luke says, *"He steadfastly set his face to go to Jerusalem."* There is finally the agony in the Garden of Gethsemane. He made an effort to reason himself out of his mission, but at last, he rises from his knees and declares, *"Not my will but thine be done."*

The problem that you and I face in so many of our dilemmas is that we want somehow to find a way to get out from under the demands placed upon us. We ask another person, "What shall I do?" Or we try to find an easy out by saying, "Oh, I can't do that. Ask someone else." Or again we may watch television, take a drink, read a book, eat more candy, go to sleep, or get sick, or a hundred other things – even pray – to avoid meeting head-on what we know we have to do. The devices we employ to avoid meeting the obligations of life are nothing short of ingenious.

We need the inspiration to assume what is rightfully ours to do, that we discover in Lillian Hellman's play, *Watch on the Rhine.* Kurt returns to his home from Germany after participating in the underground movement to overthrow the Nazis in the days preceding World War II. He is visiting his family, thinking his time of sabotage activity is completed when he receives a note unexpectedly requesting his return. His family prevails on him to stay. They remind him that he has done his duty and he is needed at home. He considers their comments but finally says, "Every man can find an excuse for not doing his duty and I can find one, too. Still, I know what I must do. I must return to Europe." And he leaves, never to see his family again. This is the kind of stuff Christian faith puts in our veins when we take it seriously. This is the kind of vitality Jesus gives to life, not escape but responsibility. This is the stuff you and I need to make a go of our campaign to construct a new building for our church. Each must face squarely, not the other fellow's responsibility, but solely and absolutely, his own.

Now, what Jesus does is to make it very clear that in whatever position we assume for ourselves we must perform the requirements of that position to the best of our ability. One man in the gospel story said to Jesus, *"Lord, first let me go and bury my father."* Another said, *"I will follow you, Lord, but let me first say farewell to those at my home."* But Jesus infers that excuses for not doing the job one has accepted are not good enough. When one has taken on a job, he is expected to do it. If he can't do it, then it is better not to accept than to agree and not do it. This, I believe, is what is said to us in the symbolic admonition of our text, *"No man, having put his hand to the plough, and looking back, is fit for the kingdom of God."* A requirement of good faith is performance and commitment. The sternness of the gospel is sometimes quite frightening. What a contrast to how the exalted captain of the ship understood the crux of *Come to Jesus* religion!

8

WHY RELIGION IS SOMETIMES REJECTED

*Acts 17:18 Some also of the Epicurean and Stoic philosophers
met him. And some said, "What would this babbler say?" Others said,
"He seems to be a preacher of foreign divinities"— because
he preached Jesus and the resurrection.*

How well do you know and understand your faith? Do you know your faith well enough to explain it to a person who believes that what you believe about your faith is foolish and ridiculous? If you have never had an occasion when you had to defend your faith against a person who thought your faith was ridiculous, then you have been denied an experience which every Christian at one time or another ought to face, for when you are driven into a corner to answer the arguments of a doubter, you really come to grips with the question: Am I grounded in my faith or is my faith something that I have accepted and lived with because it has seemed nice and comfortable or because I have merely gone along with it to please my family and my friends?

Well, whether we have had to answer critics of faith or not, not one of us wants to be ignorant of his religious faith, or why he believes it and what its basic teachings are. One way we can discover how much we actually understand about the faith to which we give our loyalty is to hear the arguments of those who reject and have nothing to do with religion. If we can answer the remarks of those who do not accept Christianity to our own satisfaction, then we can state, at least, with a fair degree of certainty, that we do know what our faith is all about.

This morning, therefore, I propose to present to you very briefly, three or four of the major arguments against our religious faith that are used frequently by those who reject our faith. You go over these in your minds and see what you would have to say in reply. I will give what I think are reasonable answers, and perhaps, by you and I working on these answers together, we will not only be able to answer the critics, but we will also have the opportunity to strengthen our own faith.

One of the statements made by a person who rejects Christian faith, or any faith for that matter, is that man is sufficient; he does not need a Supreme Being to complete his life. In a sense, then, this means that religion is unimportant and unnecessary.

This is basically the thinking that Paul confronted when he came to Athens in about the year 52. He did his best to persuade the Jews that Jesus was the Messiah but his efforts met with only minimal success so far as numbers were concerned. Also he became associated with a group of Greek Athenians with whom he discussed religious matters. These Athenians were interested in Paul's views concerning the nature of the world and his beliefs regarding God and His Son, Jesus Christ and evidently introduced Paul to the scholarly philosophers of the city who were divided into two main groups, the Epicureans and the Stoics. These philosophers were cordial to Paul but the account in Acts causes the reader to conclude that they considered the views of Paul ridiculous. Outwardly they were polite and respectful; but, inwardly, the writer of Acts indicates they really laughed at him and did not take him seriously. Luke, the author of Acts, has them ask, *"What does this babbler have to say?"*

If you were trying to describe the attitude of many fine, good, but skeptical people toward religion today, you would be unable to discover a more accurate description of their feelings concerning those of us who do take religious seriously than you find in Acts concerning the attitude of the Epicureans and Stoics toward Paul, *"What does this babbler have to say?"* Polite, yes, on the outside, but they often look at us in jest.

There are Epicureans today, though that name is no longer used, as there were in the first century. The Epicureans, both then and now, believe that happiness, not necessarily sensuous pleasure, is the goal of life. Happiness is sought for its own sake. Whatever you do, you do to be happy and you avoid any behavior that causes pain or suffering. Another objective is to make the existence or need of the gods unnecessary. Life is entirely mechanistic and material. There is no spiritual dimension to life, only body and mind and they operate by laws over which man has little or no control. Does this not seem strangely modern?

The Stoics represent another popular view of life, both ancient and modern. Stoicism conceives of the world as having a God but he is impersonal, cold logical reason, and without separate existence. He is a kind of a blind cosmic force similar to life in an organism that is alive but without awareness. Reason, intelligence, facts, and efficiency were honored by the Stoics. They are admired for their moral sincerity and earnestness but there is little feeling in their system. They are devoid of humanity, suffer in silence, and offer no comfort. Death is not feared. It is accepted and not in any way considered a loss. Does this approach remind you of the views of people you know? Stoicism is closely akin to our modern non-theistic existentialism that has had such a profound influence on the continent of Europe as well as in this country.

But we do not have to turn to academic philosophers to get a test of either Epicurean or Stoic thought. We find it in people we meet and know every day. They are good people. They pay their debts and taxes, live in fine homes, hold down responsible positions, are loving and affectionate parents, and are honest in their relationships with others. They are fun to be with and are ready at any moment to be of help to anyone who is in trouble. Yet, they frankly admit that they do not need religion. They get along all right without the Church, so why be bothered? What answer do you make to these people, so similar in life and thought to the men Paul faced at Athens, those who say they do not need religion, and who in a sense, say of us who do hold a religious view and believe in the church, *"Now what do these babblers have to say?"* They say it in jest, but there is no deeper rejection of a person than to make fun of his beliefs. What do we say? Let us try to offer some answers.

First off, I think we ought to offer our admiration to any man who can look at the harsh facts of experience — tragedy, suffering, death — and not be moved and who can accept the death of his loved ones and himself as final. It takes a strong person to look at the grave and declare, "That is the end. There is nothing more." Furthermore, it seems admiration is due a man who has a high regard for honesty and fair play and who assumes responsibility for the good of the community and his world, believing in his heart that there is no judge, no God to whom he owes allegiance except what he demands and requires of himself.

Yet, there are several answers that can be given after we have paid our respects and admiration to the Epicurean and to the Stoic.

The first comment is that a man of faith does not say a person absolutely has to have religious faith. Life can be lived without religion. People do it all of the time. The man of faith also states that people can live good and honest lives without religion. People do it all the time. Religious faith, therefore, is not a matter of need. It is a matter of belief; it is a way of looking at life. It has nothing to do with arguments to prove the existence of God. It is a matter of looking at the universe as a blind, mechanistic, system going lickety-split, without any reason or purpose, following certain laws that accidentally come into being, or looking at the universe as an on-going process that is created and maintained by an intelligent Supreme Being who has a deep, and abiding concern in the works of his creation. Disbelief sees the world as devoid of a maker, unfriendly, even hostile and cruel. Belief looks at the world as having a Maker, who is friendly and gracious. Arguments for either position can be offered that are logical reasonable, and persuasive. The tenets of religion are not arrived at by proof. They are arrived at by faith, the decision as to whether one will accept or reject faith is one that each individual has to make for himself. Religious faith is never a matter of argument. It is always a leap, a hunch, a conviction that carries the self from mechanism to purpose, from chaos to order, from unfriendliness to friendliness, from cold impersonal intellectualism to warm, personal human ties and feelings.

The supreme reply that Christian faith offers to irreligious man, however, is Jesus Christ. We stake our claim on his life, his person, his revelation, his death, and his resurrection. That is the argument that Paul presented to the philosophers of Epicureanism and Stoicism that day in Athens at the Areopagus.

Jesus never developed a neatly woven argument for God's existence. For him, God is, he needs no proof. He is his own proof. Jesus merely called him Father and invited men and women and children to live together in peace and goodwill because they all had one Father in heaven. He pointed to the lilies of the field, the birds of the air, the laughter and happiness of little children, the gaiety of people at a party, the love of a father for a son who had left his father's home but who had returned. He asked, *"Do you not see God, O ye of little faith?"* And pointing to himself he said, *"Ye who have seen me have seen the Father also,"* and then one of his biographers has him say to his followers, *"In my Father's house are many mansions. If it were not so I would have told you. I go to prepare a place for you and if I go to prepare a place for you, I will return again and receive you unto myself, for where I am there ye may be also."* These are statements or symbols of faith. They stand for what Jesus had to say about the nature of the world and the force that is behind it all.

Well, with this much said, this babbler has said about all there is to say other than we make an effort to serve Him and to make His way of life a living force in the life of society. We offer no panacea, no utopias, no guarantees of safety or protection, no rewards, not even happiness. We only offer a faith in a God who we believe is known in Jesus Christ, and we believe that he is the author and finisher of our faith and He is the same yesterday, today, and forever.

9

WHAT RELIGIOUS FAITH PROVIDES

Psalm 27:1 The LORD is my light and my salvation; whom shall I fear?
The LORD is the stronghold of my life; of whom shall I be afraid?

Several of you have spoken to me concerning my statement in last Sunday's sermon that religion is unnecessary or not needed. You have wondered how this is possible. I wish to begin today by elaborating briefly on your concern. When we say something is needed, we mean, in the strict sense of the term, that persons, all persons, are unable to survive without that something. All persons need air to breathe, food to eat, warmth, water, freedom from disease; otherwise, they would be unable to exist. What I meant last Sunday is that you cannot put religion in the category of these basic needs. This, however, does not mean that religion is not beneficial. Persons can get along perfectly all right without keeping themselves clean. "What is the use of washing," says a healthy 10 year old boy to his mother, "you just get dirty again." Though we can exist without cleanliness, we know how much better we feel living in a clean house, wearing clean clothes, or after taking a hot bath. Cleanliness is beneficial and so is religious faith. Let us consider a few of the values that religion does provide.

Allow me to say at the outset that I personally always feel somewhat squeamish talking about what religion can do for us, for such an approach makes religion an article of clothing or a cake of soap and makes it associated with the sick advertisement one hears these days on television. You buy hair oil, not to keep your hair in place, if you have any *(alluding to his bald head)*, but so an artificial blonde girl will pat your face and coo in your ear. Now religion, at its best, is not accepted to get anything – happiness, friends, or even eternal life. Religion is accepted to explain mystery, to discover meaning, or to provide a loyalty, an ultimate loyalty, to which a person can commit his life. To accept a religious faith, in order to gain or get something is to violate at once the very premise on which faith is founded – the giving of one's self in loyalty to life as we know it in Jesus Christ. Any other motive is pharisaism – *"they pray,"* said Jesus, *"on street corners to be seen of men."* They pray to be praised and therefore lose that which prayer makes possible. No saint ever started out in the religious life to be a saint; otherwise, he would never have become a saint. Such rewards as sainthood are never sought. They may only be given by not seeking.

Now, you see why I live in horror of ever preaching religious faith in order for people to gain or get anything. Yet, religious faith does provide much when it is accepted, believed in, until it becomes the source of one's being, not to gain anything, but when it is that to which one's life is given. What then does it provide?

You probably will not find in all the Bible a statement that answers this question better than the first verse of Psalm 27: *"The Lord is my light and my salvation; whom shall I fear? The Lord is the strength of my life; of whom* shall I be afraid?" This is not an invitation, a plea, or a demand that one accept faith. The Psalmist, whoever he might have been, was merely expressing a condition of his life that was made possible by his religious faith. Here is what his faith provided for him, a state or a dimension of his life that made him unafraid, courageous, capable to deal effectively with any contingency – *"The Lord is my light and my salvation; whom shall I fear? The Lord is the strength of my life; of whom shall I be afraid?"* Well, what does it mean?

We are safe, I think, to say that this almost calm, unpretentious comment of the Psalmist means that a person's religious faith shows the right paths or directions for life. God is the source of illumination and we who are Christians find our ultimate illumination in Jesus Christ. *"I am the light of the world."* John, one of his biographers, writes that, *"He is the light that shineth in darkness and the darkness has not put it out."* In other words, when a person knows the path he should walk in life, he is steady, firm, committed, and he is not likely to become afraid, confused, or bewildered. *"The Lord is my light and my salvation; whom shall I fear?"* Now, let us enlarge this concept to see how it really does make sense and how it actually does work out in life.

First of all, what about society? Does religious faith make any difference here? There is evidence, it seems to me, that it does make a difference. Biblical faith holds that there are certain inexorable or immutable laws of conduct, made by God, not man – man discovers – that are necessary for a stable and orderly social community. In Hebrew-Christian tradition, we find these laws set down in the Ten Commandments. Follow these, says religious faith, walk in these paths, provided by the Lord of light, and your society shall be stable from within. Break these laws, however, and there is danger of disintegration and confusion.

You see, these are laws by which to play the game. Everyone has to follow the rules, do his part, assume his load; else the whole system is weakened. It is built upon honesty, trust, and personal integrity.

These laws are above the personal interests and desires of the individual. They have their foundation in the source of light, in the very structure and nature of the universe itself. If this were not the case, then everyone would have their own way and there would be no center of authority. Even kings and princes, says Biblical faith, are subject to these laws as are the common people. What is imposed upon one is imposed upon all.

Remember the account of David, Bathsheba, Uriah, and Nathan. David, the king, was overcome with lust for the beautiful Bathsheba who was married to Uriah, a Hittite. He ordered Uriah into battle and made sure he was killed. David then took Bathsheba as one of his wives. David fulfilled the legal law but he had broken the moral law of God – *Thou shalt not covet thy neighbor's wife!* Well, David was faced by the stern prophet Nathan and reminded of his evil deed and he was forced to repent and the Biblical account says he suffered much because of his evil deed.

What religious faith provides then is the stuff that holds a society together and no man has a right to be a member of that society and enjoy its benefits if he breaks faith with his fellow members.

The next attribute of religion is that it provides directions for the family. It is no accident that marriage begins with a ceremony before a minister who represents God. People who never attend church usually want a ceremony held in a church. They somehow feel they want to get started off on the right foot and they believe the values that the church represents will somehow help them to make a first step that is right.

Russia, after the Bolshevik Revolution in 1917, decided that marriage laws and the sanctity of the home were old-fashioned, ridiculous, and represented a way of life that upheld religion. When they decided to outlaw religion, then they insisted the rules concerning marriage should go, too. People could get divorces by only submitting a written statement on a slip of paper and handing it to a magistrate. Men and women were encouraged to have children out of wedlock. Free love was the order of the day. Now that God was dead, you could pull out the stops and live it up. It didn't take Russia many years, however, to discover that they had opened a Pandora's Box. Delinquency on the part of children went to unknown figures. They had no homes; many lived in barracks; and others roamed the streets. Women were left with children without anyone to provide support or affection. Not many years went by, however, before the state clamped down and reinstituted its old laws concerning marriage and the family. The moral enforcements that had previously been provided by the church now had to be insisted upon by the state. Today Russia has tight laws governing marriage and I predict it will not be too many years before religion again will return officially to Russia.

We ought to be seriously concerned about some of the changed attitudes in our country toward marriage and family life. We need to keep in mind that the moral codes we have been given by religion are not something invented by man. They are laws we have discovered in God's universe. They have stood the test of time and I dare say are far superior to anything we see in *Playboy* or some of our so-called sophisticated literature. If the Lord is our life and our salvation, then let us walk in his ways. That is the way toward family integrity and stability.

Next, I want to mention the light that religion brings on the person. One fact we must know is that a man or a woman cannot live in isolation. We really cannot exist without each other. Only the mentally sick person lives without personal contact with other people and he probably is ill because he has cut himself off or has been cut off from others. Still, we know that even the unfortunate person suffering from a psychosis, even though he does not communicate in reality with another individual, does live in a world of persons he has manufactured for himself. If we do not have others, we seem to make them up. We find it hard to live without the benefit of other people.

But moments of loneliness come to us, nevertheless, when we are by ourselves and no other person can help, no matter how much we wish they could. Not one of us can really bring comfort to another person who has lost another who has been near and close to him or her. These moments are hard to bear and no one enjoys going through them. Or who can really help a person who is suffering depression or a severe emotional disorder.

When Dr. Harry Emerson Fosdick, who is for me the greatest Christian preacher of this generation, was a young man in seminary he suffered a severe mental condition. He was unable to sleep or to work. He tells in his autobiography, *The Living of These Days*, of finally going to England and stopping to visit with friends at Stratford-upon-Avon. For most, says Dr. Fosdick, Stratford-upon-Avon is known as the birthplace of William Shakespeare but for him that lovely town is always remembered as the place where he slept all night for the first time in many weeks. During this nightmare, he said that he found out what it meant to pray. Here God became truly real to him and much of his book, *The Meaning of Prayer*, which he wrote years later, and is indeed a classic, came out of this trying experience. Religious faith can provide a man comfort and strength and hope when all other hope seems gone. Surely, Dr. Fosdick knew what the Psalmist meant when he wrote, *"The Lord is my light and salvation; whom shall I fear? The Lord is the strength of my life; of whom shall I be afraid?"*

Well, these are only a few of the many values that religious faith can provide. But one does not come to religion seeking or demanding them. One only finds and receives these benefits as he gives himself in complete devotion and commitment to the God of our Lord, Jesus Christ. Paul expressed it this way: *"For I am persuaded that neither height nor depth, nor angels, nor principalities, nor death, nor things present, nor things to come nor any other creature shall be able to separate us from the love of God, through Jesus Christ, our Lord."* If a person can believe these words and hold on to them, he too can say with the Psalmist, *"The Lord is my light and my salvation – whom shall I fear? – The Lord is the strength of my life - of whom shall I be afraid?"*

Let us pray: O God our father, we need clear heads and right minds. Life becomes confused at times for each of us. We are not sure of what is right and what is wrong. We don't know whether to be honest or false. We are unsure of what to tell our children concerning their association with others or concerning standards of decency and morality. Even in our business dealings, we are uncertain whether to make a huge profit and lose our integrity or to make a small profit and maintain our belief in honesty. Sometimes we don't know whether we should or should not become a part of the church and support its program. We are disturbed about whether freedom is only for those who are like us or for all people, whether they are like us or not. We are disturbed about our relationship with other nations – should we support less fortunate nations or keep what we have for ourselves. Like Hamlet – should we be or not be.

So we enter into Thy House, this day, O God and we find ourselves in prayer, for we very much want to know what is proper for ourselves, our families, our friends, and our nation. O God, help us in our divided minds that we may know how to distinguish between good and bad, right and wrong. This we ask in Jesus name.

Amen

10

LENT AND THE MEANING OF SACRIFICE

Matthew 7:13-14

*13 Enter by the narrow gate; for the gate is wide and the way is easy, that
leads to destruction, and those who enter by it are many.
14 For the gate is narrow and the way is hard, that
leads to life, and those who find it are few.*

Last Wednesday the Christian world began its observance of the sacred season of Lent. The season will last for 40 days plus Sundays and extends this year from Ash Wednesday, March 3rd, to Easter, April 18th. These days of Lent coincide with the days Jesus spent in the wilderness when he fasted, searched his soul in prayer and meditation, and hammered out his mission. As Jesus fasted and sacrificed in the wilderness for 40 days and 40 nights, so Lent urges all Christians to observe 40 days of denial and personal sacrifice.

We are not really certain how the word Lent came to be used to designate this occasion, but we believe it derived its name from an old Latin word for the spring season of the year. Since Easter came in the spring, the spiritual season before Easter gradually took over the word for spring, so the time was called Lent or the Lenten Season.

Lent is observed in various degrees by various Christian churches. Roman Catholics are required to eat very lightly for breakfast and lunch, and for supper, to eat not more than was eaten during the two meals earlier during the day. The requirement does not hold for Sundays. Lutherans and Episcopalians have no requirement for fasting, but are encouraged to accept some form of denial. Our church gives the season only slight attention – we are holding special Bible classes each Sunday evening during Lent. Although it is not our custom to urge special personal sacrifices during Lent, it does seem to me it is appropriate to begin this first Sunday in the pre-Easter season by considering the meaning of sacrifice, a concept that is really what Lent is all about.

What does sacrifice mean, then, for those of us who have accepted sacrifice as a way of life? In one sense, sacrifice is what the Christian faith emphasizes.

Let us begin by saying that sacrifice means to deny or deprive ourselves of something we want. We do not need to belabor this point, for all of us are very much aware that we are here today because of sacrifice. We have our lives because somewhere in the years of yesterday our father and mother, or someone else who loved us, spent time and patience taking care of us, watching out for us, so that today we are able to take care of ourselves. And now those of us who are parents are spending time, patience, and effort making it possible for our children to move out into the world to take care of themselves. Also we enjoy not only our life and its resources because of family and friends, but we also have the benefits of political freedom because brave men – statesmen, diplomats, and military men dared to oppose and win out over tyranny, oppression, and men of evil design and violence. We also are in debt to men and women of endurance and courage for the freedom of worship and faith we are proud to represent today. We are grateful to men like Bishop Cranmer, Latimer, and Ridley of England who struck a blow for religious freedom in the 16th century under Queen Mary when she tried to stamp out Protestantism. We read with excitement as well as gratitude the words of Bishop Latimer to Bishop Ridley as the flames shot up around them as they were burned at the stake. Said Latimer, "Be of good cheer, Master Ridley, we shall this day light such a candle in England as by God's grace shall never be put out." These and other sacrifices are largely the reasons why we can worship here this morning in freedom. Lives of faith are built on the foundation of sacrifice, that eternal quality applied by persons who believe in giving up something, even life itself.

We recognize and admit, at once, however, that sacrifice does not mean denial or deprivation merely for the sake of giving up something. It means denial of something of real value, for some gain of real worth.

This means sacrifice is of little value if it is made only because we think sacrifice is good for us. Not often, but sometimes, I hear of a person who has become somewhat over zealous about his faith. He has heard that Christianity teaches sacrifice, and persons ought to deny themselves. The person gets aroused and goes around trying to find something for which he can make a sacrifice. Every once in a while a person comes to a minister and says, "A man has to sacrifice to be a Christian. Tell me how I can sacrifice or I am afraid God won't like me." Well, this is unhealthy, for the purpose of sacrifice isn't to gain anyone's approval. It is done because something of value is required.

Sacrifice does not mean giving up something to satisfy some requirement or to observe some rule, unless it is related to accomplishing some higher good. A young woman once remarked that she was giving up Coca Cola for Lent and was going to drink Pepsi Cola instead. We laugh, not because the story is so clever, but because it is so ridiculous. Actually, though, the poor girl is really more to be pitied than laughed at because she was serious. This is not sacrifice. This is merely satisfying a rule of her faith which says during Lent you have to make a sacrifice. Sacrifice cannot be required or demanded. If it is, it only becomes an insipid mechanical act that has about as much depth to it as walking down the sidewalk backwards and seeing if you can avoid going off the walk.

We do not sacrifice because Jesus lived a life of sacrifice or because we think we have to walk in his steps. He would laugh at us for being copy-cats and imitators. When he said, *"Follow me,"* he meant that if there is a job of value to be done that serves the benefit of mankind or the purposes of God, then step up and do it, and do not be concerned about losing your life. Surely, he did not fast in the wilderness because he wanted to gain the approval of God or because he enjoyed it. He fasted because he wanted to keep his mind and spirit clear of distracting influences. He wanted to be alone with his God. He felt fasting would help him face his moment of truth and find his mission in life. Sacrifice in the desert had a purpose. It was related to a definite, specific, concrete life situation. Sacrifice must be that for us if it is to have any vital function in our Christian witness.

Sacrifice, then, is an act we perform when we give up something at the moment to realize some higher value, either for now or later. Jesus denied himself food, comfort and companionship in the wilderness to give him the necessary spiritual resources and mental keenness to become a faithful Son to his Father. This is a symbol which means he strengthened himself by sacrifice to accomplish his mission in life or to fulfill what he understood to be the purpose of his life. He gave up immediate pleasures to realize future goals.

This procedure – giving up something now for realizations of greater value – seems to be a consistent pattern of his life. Eventually, this "something in the now" which he gave up was his life. He firmly believed that the issues around which he so assiduously conducted his life could not come to pass unless he sacrificed his life. Men had to be redeemed, men had to be shaken from their sin and lethargy, and he felt the only recourse was the cross. So almost without hesitation, he offered himself on Calvary – giving up *something now* – his life – for a greater good. This is ultimate sacrifice.

Certainly, you and I are seldom called upon for such extreme sacrifice as Jesus was called on to make. Yet, there is a principle here that seems to me to tell us much about life at its deepest and life at its best. Isn't it true that the values that count the most in life, I mean the things we prize and deeply cherish, have only been realized and attained as we had the opportunity and the strength to sacrifice for them? What we most highly prize we have usually won by giving up some immediate pleasure and concentrating on the work that made it possible to attain the goal. A boy wants to be on the track team – he only makes it by training, giving up time with his friends, denying himself hours of play, not eating sweets, but rather spending long hours working at his activity – until one day, providing he has the ability, he makes the team. Education itself is a grind sometimes but few can make it today without it. Many boys and girls who have dropped out of high school are now coming up and getting that diploma because they have learned by the hard and painful road of experience that to get along in most instances today you have to know something as well as be able to do something.

From beginning to end, life is a series of sacrifices that we all must make if the best we want to happen is to happen. Some are fortunate enough to learn this fact of life early. Others do not learn it until later and others never learn it at all, and as a consequence, are always problems to themselves as well as to others. When Jesus went into the wilderness to fast, he was teaching us, perhaps not deliberately but we see through his example, that those who make the most of life and get the most out of life are those who have learned the difficult but profitable practice of discipline and sacrifice. The world does not belong to the impulsive and the undisciplined. It is only for those who have the fortitude of self-control. Jesus reminds us, *"Enter by the narrow gate; for the gate is wide and the way is easy, that leads to destruction, and those who enter it are many. For the gate is narrow and the way is hard, that leads to life, and those who find it are few."* This Lenten season can be a time to go through the narrow gate and to travel the hard road. May it be a time of profitable and wholesome sacrificial living for us all!

11

THE DEAD SEA SCROLLS

This afternoon those of us who are studying the Gospel of Mark each Sunday evening during Lent are going to the Smithsonian to see the Dead Sea Scrolls. Any other persons interested in making the trip with us are invited. We will leave the church at 2:00 p.m. These scrolls which have been on display at the Smithsonian for two weeks will be available for viewing for one more week.

The question naturally arises in the minds of many - what are these scrolls? and why are they so important? Because of the significance of these documents for understanding our early religious history, and because they are in our city for public viewing, this morning would be a pertinent time to discuss them.

These scrolls were found at several different places between 1947 and 1956 near the Dead Sea. The earliest finds were in the spring of 1947. Several Bedouins, while exploring caves on the western shore of the Dead Sea at the northern end, came across several large clay jars. They found in the jars several manuscripts that were musty and brittle with age. They, of course, did not know their value, but looking for an easy way to make money, sold them to book dealers in Bethlehem. Finally, by a series of transactions, the manuscripts found their way into the hands of the head of St. Mark's Syrian Orthodox monastery and library in old Jerusalem. The metropolitan, whose name was Athanasius Yeshue Samuel, recognized the probable worth of the manuscripts, and brought in various paleontologists to examine them. Some felt they were extremely valuable; others were not so sure. Finally, photostatic copies were made of portions of the manuscripts, and shipped to Professor William F. Albright of the Johns Hopkins University in Baltimore, perhaps the foremost authority in the world on Semitic and other oriental languages as well as ancient biblical manuscripts and archeology. Professor Albright declared the documents "to be the greatest manuscript discovery of modern times."

The world of Biblical scholarship, of course, became electrified. Carefully controlled excavations were made of this area where the original documents were found. After almost 10 years of exploration, some eleven caves were discovered as well as the ruins of buildings occupied by an ancient religious community. In these caves were found coins, pottery, and many other manuscripts. These documents contain one or more copies of the books of the entire Old Testament except for the Book of Esther, commentaries on several books of the Old Testament, some books of the apocrypha, and Jewish hymns. Also found were manuals containing rules and regulations of the religious community at Qumran. This group had lived in the area at various times over a period of almost 300 years from about 200 B.C. to about 100 A.D. Some of the writings were on papyrus, some on leather, and others on copper. It is believed that what was found is part of the library of a primitive

Jewish Community known as the Essenes and the monastery where they lived.

What is the importance of these scrolls for the Christian Church? Let us mention only four items briefly.

First, they are the oldest Biblical manuscripts in existence. Until the Dead Sea Scrolls were found, the oldest Old Testament manuscripts we had dated from about the 9th century A.D. The Dead Sea documents were written or copied not earlier than the 3rd century B.C. or 200 B.C. and not later than 100 A.D. In other words these Old Testament writings found in the Qumran caves are approximately 1000 years older than any present manuscript. One interesting and amazing feature is that there are no major differences in the text of the Old Testament books between the Dead Sea Scrolls, copied somewhere between 200 B.C. and 100 A.D., and 9th century A.D. texts. Thus, we are able to say that the scribes who copied these manuscripts through the years were faithful and sincere in making new copies of the Scriptures. This is what we mean by working under the control of the Holy Spirit.

The second contribution of the Dead Sea Scrolls is that they give us invaluable information concerning the Essenes. Hitherto, we have known very little about this group of Jewish people who had such an influence on religious thinking among the Jews and the Christians during the years preceding and following the birth of Jesus. We knew there was such a group but they are not mentioned by name either in the Old Testament or in the New Testament. Several historians mention them – Philo of Alexandria, Josephus, and Pliny the Elder, but their description of them is not extensive. The Scrolls, however, tell us much about the Essenes for they were the people who constructed the monastery and preserved the manuscripts discovered at the north end and western side of the Dead Sea. Among the scrolls found in the jars is a Manual of Instruction for new members of the sect and also a Book of Discipline, explaining what Essenes did and what they didn't do.

The community of the Essenes, we believe, came into existence during the years when Palestine was under the Greeks, a period that began with the annexation of Palestine by Alexander the Great in 337 B.C. and continued to about 143 B.C. During these years, many Jews adopted the culture and customs of the Greeks. But a number of the Jewish people felt their faith would be swallowed up by the culture of Greece if the melding of Greek and Jewish culture continued. A number of Jews withdrew to preserve the ancient faith and ways. They were purists who believed the way to preserve the best of tradition was to withdraw into an exclusive community. Here we have the beginning of the Essenes. Later these people put their faith in the Maccabean rulers who defeated the Greek Seleucids and established Israel as a free and sovereign state for some 80 years from 143 B.C. until 63 B.C. They thought these new rulers would restore the ancient Jewish order but they were disappointed, for the Maccabees became almost as corrupt as the foreign rulers had been. These strict, exclusive Jews, therefore, gave up all hope of Israel ever becoming a full and independent nation and restoring the kingdom of David. They withdrew from society, lived in monasteries according to strict rules of life and looked for God to restore to Israel its rightful place in the world. They were a good deal like Jehovah Witnesses are today, hoping, praying, preparing for the end of the world, and an intervention of God into the world to make things right, especially for them. These were the Essenes who we believe lived in a monastery near the Dead Sea. They were evidently wiped out by the Romans when they destroyed Jerusalem in about the year 68 A.D.

The scrolls tell us, then, about the Essenes and it may be that John the Baptist was a member of this group earlier in his life or he was strongly influenced by their teaching. They practiced baptism. John may have learned this rite from them. Furthermore, the Essene emphasis on *repent for the end is at hand* by the Essenes sounds very much like the preaching of John. Also, his strict and ascetic way of life is similar to the life led by the Essenes. Some have even suggested Jesus belonged to this rigid party of 1st century Puritans.

Another asset of the Scrolls from the Dead Sea is that they enlighten us concerning teaching in the New Testament that has been difficult to understand. One teaching strain, to which we have already alluded, is what we call by a technical word today – apocalypticism. It means a way of looking at history. Briefly, this approach held that there is a fight going on between evil and good, the evil seems always to have the upper hand, but eventually the good will win out. According to Jewish thought – emphasized by the Essenes – God would intervene in the world by some miraculous feat, set up his kingdom with a new David at the head, and the Jewish followers of the law would be in charge of things. This other worldly view of history crept into Christianity. Some believe it was taught by Jesus. Others say it was taken over by the followers of Jesus and tailored to their beliefs concerning Jesus. They believed, then, that he was the Messiah who would return to earth and establish a new heaven and a new earth. They believed this would happen in their lifetime. But this ancient apocalyptic view of history is still in the church today and some Christian groups spend time and effort deciphering symbols in the Bible trying to find a clue for predicting when Jesus will return. This particular view of history and its end has its roots in the Essenes, about whom we read in some of the Dead Sea Scrolls.

The Scrolls make clear another teaching that has troubled schol-ars through the years. In one of Jesus teachings, he says, *"You have heard said of old times, that you should love your neighbor and hate your enemy, but I say to you, love your enemies and pray for him who hates you."* Nowhere in the Old Testament is there any commandment to hate one's enemy. Interpreters have wondered who the persons were that Jesus had in mind who believed the enemy should be hated. One of the documents found in the Dead Sea Scrolls seems to clear up the mystery. The Manual of Discipline, a rule book for members of the Essene community, for example states: "It is the duty of the member of the community to love all whom God has chosen and hate all whom he has rejected." Perhaps Jesus was contradicting the teaching of the Essenes when he suggested love for one's enemy.

These then are some of the contributions that the Scrolls make to our thinking. It must not be thought that these ancient writings found near the Dead Sea change or modify the Biblical understand-ing of our faith. They do, however, enrich our understanding of the Bible, giving us information concerning that little known period before, during, and following the birth of Jesus. It will be years before all of the materials can be translated and evaluated; in the meantime, however, we are grateful for the manuscripts and for the devoted persons who devote their time in studying such docu-ments and providing us with the information they contain. May we afford ourselves the opportunities to learn more about them. You will find excellent paperback books on the Scrolls in any good book store.

12

WHEN WE COME TO JESUS

John 12:20-23

*20 Now among those who went up to worship
at the feast were some Greeks.
21 So these came to Philip, who was from Beth-sa'ida in
Galilee, and said to him, "Sir, we wish to see Jesus."
22 Philip went and told Andrew; Andrew went with
Philip and they told Jesus.
23 And Jesus answered them, "The hour has come for
the Son of man to be glorified."*

A characteristic that distinguishes the person who is on top of life from the person who is having a hard time making a go of life is awareness. The healthy individual may not always do the right thing but he knows he is not doing right and he knows why. The unhealthy person, however, seems to be driven by forces within him over which he seems to have no control. His behavior is unconscious, uncontrolled, and not understood. It does seem important, therefore, for the health of ourselves and others, particularly those with whom we are closely associated, that we have a fairly clear understanding of the reasons behind most of our behavior. We must admit, of course, that it is not entirely possible to understand all of the reasons for all of our behavior. So much of what we do is hidden from our consciousness. This we have to admit and accept. But one fact seems certain: the more we are able to account for our behavior the better we are able to function in life, and the less we are aware of our conduct, the less effective is our living.

This observation is particularly pertinent in the religious area of our lives. Religious exercises can be detrimental if they are employed irrationally or without awareness. Sometimes, a religious person may have a grudge against someone else, so much so that he hates the other person. He feels guilty about his hate feelings so he prays that God will remove the hate but the hate still remains. Sadly, the more he prays the more intense the guilt. So he reasons that God is to blame because he hated the other man, for he has prayed to God to remove the hate. Since God will not cause it to disappear, then the hate is God's fault and not his. His religion, then, is detrimental because it ferments the hate rather than lessening the hate. Naturally, the problem is that he has misused prayer. He has used the wrong approach in absolving his hate. He fails to understand that the only real cure for hate is to go to the person who is hated and make amends. Get the matter straightened out with the other person, then hate will disappear. How easily religious exercises such as prayer can be used to cripple life when one is not aware of what he is doing when he prays and why. When we understand what we are doing in our religious behavior, only then can it serve to strengthen rather than cripple.

Consider also this crucial matter in our lives of coming to Jesus Christ and participating in the Christian community which we call the church. Do we ever really stop to ask ourselves this question: Why do I come to the church every Sunday, or in some cases, most every Sunday or, in other cases, perhaps once in a while? It really isn't a bad idea every now and then to assess our reasons for our religious behavior.

Your first reaction to this question may be one of disgust. You may ask, "Do we have to analyze everything we do?" You may also ask, "Can't we merely live and die in the church – in the bosom of Christ, as some have expressed it – without asking why?" You may also add, "Persons in the first century, in the New Testament churches, did not analyze their reasons for sharing in the Christian movement and they got along all right." Well, if we read the development of the Christian community as we find it in the New Testament with a kind of romantic half-blind naivety, we may arrive at the conclusion that everyone who came to Jesus came with complete sincerity and out of pure motive. On the other hand, if we read the account critically, such was not the case. What is more important, the reasons people came to Jesus were of crucial importance to him, for the record seems to imply that Jesus knew that if people followed him for the wrong reasons, his cause would be crippled. He showed his disapproval when he was aware that people became his disciples for ulterior motives. He was pleased when they came for sincere reasons. Amazingly, if we can take the record as an accurate sample of what really happened in the beginning years of the church, we find that more came for reasons other than those which appear noble. Let us briefly examine, if we may, some of the motivations behind the actions of persons who came to Jesus, and if possible, view the reactions of Jesus.

First, there were those who came to him because they were curious, and wanted to see what would happen when they tried to embarrass or trap him. In Mark, the 12ᵗʰ Chapter, we read that the Herodians approached him while he was in Jerusalem. These were men who were anxious to restore the kingdom of Herod Agrippa to power. They had heard of this strange man and they wanted to taunt him, really to find out how he would reply to some questions that were of concern to the Jews. A burning issue was whether or not a Jew should pay a tax to the Romans. They had a position and they wanted to push their propaganda. They acted like they wanted to learn from Jesus, but learning a new approach, was the farthest thought from their minds. Their interest in Jesus was purely one of curiosity. Notice how they try to ingratiate themselves, put on a false front, give him a *snow job* as the young folks today call it. Listen: *Mark 12:13-17*

13 And they sent to him some of the Pharisees and some of the Hero'di-ans, to entrap him in his talk.
14 And they came and said to him, "Teacher, we know that you are true, and care for no man; for you do not regard the position of men, but truly teach the way of God. Is it lawful to pay taxes to Caesar, or not?
15 Should we pay them, or should we not?" But knowing their hypocrisy, he said to them, "Why put me to the test? Bring me a coin, and let me look at it."
16 And they brought one. And he said to them, "Whose likeness and inscription is this?" They said to him, "Caesar's."
17 Jesus said to them, "Render to Caesar the things that are Caesar's, and to God the things that are God's." And they were amazed at him.
"Teacher, we know that you are true, and care for no man: for you do not regard the position of men, but truly teach the way of God. Is it lawful

to pay taxes to Caesar, or not? Should we pay them, or should we not?" Notice Jesus' reaction as recorded by Mark: *But knowing their hypocrisy, he said to them "Why put me to the test? Bring me a coin, and let me look at it." And they brought one. And he said to them, "Whose likeness and inscription is this?" They said to him, "Caesar's." Jesus said to them, "Render to Caesar the things that are Caesar's, and to God the things that are God's."* He answers politely, but yet he doesn't answer. He knew they really had no desire to learn from him, only an interest in sort of playing a game. They were detached, removed, set and rigid in their beliefs. How nice to sit back and observe what is going on, but afraid to become involved: yet somehow fascinated by it all, but critical and detached. Some do come to Jesus, even today, because of curiosity, afraid though, to become a part of his community.

Some, too, seek Jesus because everyone else is doing it and, well, one has to climb on the band wagon and do what the best people do, so we had better do it, too. The best example, of course, in the New Testament, is the throng that lined the streets when he entered Jerusalem. Yet, a few days later he wept over Jerusalem because of the blindness of the people, going this way and that, driven by everything that came along, but unaware of their behavior, not committed to any purpose of depth and meaning. These same, however, that greeted him were no where to be found when the crucifixion came. The one who comes because it seems nice and therapeutic to go to church, and well one's children ought to go to church – it's the decent thing to do you know – will not be around when stern demands are made and the going gets tough. May I say here that I have always deeply admired the congregation of this church who brought this church into being. About a year or so ago, the going wasn't easy. Some of you have said to me that you weren't sure then whether the venture was going to live or not. But it did live and is now a going and growing family because people, except for a very few who left, were not here because church going was merely a nice thing to do. It kept going because people were here because they were blessed with deep, not shallow, motives.

Well, a third cause for persons coming to Jesus in the earliest days was to see him and to get something for themselves. People came to be healed, and were healed, and never were heard of again. They had gotten what they wanted, so why worry about what happens to the cause of Christ? Ten lepers were healed but only one came back to give thanks. You can feel the hurt and disappointment in the reply of Jesus to the man who did return, "*Were there not ten who were healed? Where are the other nine?*" Even two of his most trusted disciples, James and John, early in their association with Jesus appear only interested in Jesus because of what he could do for them. They put their demand to him almost like children who only see their parents as objects of satisfying their wants: *(Mark 10)* "*Teacher, we want you to do for us whatever we ask of you.*" "*What do you want me to do for you?*" *Jesus inquired. They replied,* "*Grant us to sit, one at your right hand and one at your left, in your glory.*" Jesus must have felt disgusted with them for their shallowness. He must also have felt sorrow, for here were two of his friends, close to him, whose only thought was – what do I get out of this? But he was patient and gave them only a slight pat on the wrist. He tries to get them to understand that in his kingdom there is no such thing as one being over another and offices and trappings, carpets on the floor and nice desks and fixtures. The important consideration is service. Here is the way Jesus explained it: "*Whoever would be great among you must be your servant, and whoever would be first among you must be slave of all. For the Son of man also came not to be served but to serve, and to give his life as a ransom for many.*"

Those words need to be repeated again and again today, now, in our time. How confused we become in our thinking when we come to Jesus! One would think the reason we come to Jesus from some of the religion I hear advertised and preached is that we come to Jesus to gain a home in heaven, to save our necks for eternity, or for some other personal reward. He seems to tell us that these self-ish and self-centered considerations are wrong but for centuries the church has taught and preached it. Yet, Jesus tells us that we come to him because we want to learn from him and to serve in His Name. Whatever else following in his steps does for us are merely fringe benefits or by-products as Mrs. K expressed it in a recent session of the adult class.

One of the few times that Jesus seemed really glad and excited when people came to him is found in the gospel of John. (John 12) It was the Feast of Passover. The Jews came from everywhere to celebrate this great annual festival in their religious life. Jesus was there, evidently off by himself, studying and thinking. Some Greeks came to Philip, one of the disciples, and asked if they could see Jesus. We do not have the entire conversation, only a glimpse into what took place. They made a deep impression on Philip for he probably had instructions that Jesus was not to be disturbed, but he decided that these men were serious and Jesus would surely like to see them. Philip went to Andrew. They discussed the situation and finally decided to tell Jesus. We have no record of Jesus' conversation with them but we do have his reactions. He was overwhelmed, joyful, pleased that here were men who wanted nothing from him – no curiosity seekers, no social prestige oriented people, no persons who wanted to be healed or desired any favors, only men who were anxious to learn what he had to teach them that their lives might be enriched and made more meaningful. Here were men who came to him out of motives that were real and honest and certain.

The gospel accounts indicate that Jesus was so impressed that he announces that now he can die because his real message has at last been understood, it is getting across, and he has no fear that what he has lived and taught will not continue and his gospel will be spread throughout the world.

Our prayer today is that Jesus will be pleased with our motives for coming to him and that we shall join that great host of men and women who throughout all the centuries have rightly understood him and have served him because they truly believed in his gospel and have made an honest effort to be faithful.

13

ON TAKING OUR CRITICS SERIOUSLY

Luke 19:1-10
1 He entered Jericho and was passing through.
2 And there was a man named Zacchae'us; he was a chief
tax collector, and rich.
3 And he sought to see who Jesus was, but could not, on account
of the crowd, because he was small of stature.
4 So he ran on ahead and climbed up into a sycamore tree to
see him, for he was to pass that way.
5 And when Jesus came to the place, he looked up and said to him,
"Zacchae'us, make haste and come down; for I must stay at your house today."
6 So he made haste and came down, and received him joyfully.
7 And when they saw it they all murmured, "He has
gone in to be the guest of a man who is a sinner."
8 And Zacchae'us stood and said to the Lord, "Behold, Lord,
the half of my goods I give to the poor; and if I have defrauded
any one of anything, I restore it fourfold."
9 And Jesus said to him, "Today salvation has come to this
house, since he also is a son of Abraham.
10 For the Son of man came to seek and to save the lost."

The most painful experience for most persons is to be criticized. It is easy for most to find fault with others but it isn't at all pleasant for most to be on the receiving end of fault-finding or criticism.

A person doesn't like to be criticized because it damages one's self-esteem. It makes one feel so uncomfortable, embarrassed, and ashamed. These are feelings we do not enjoy having, so what a person usually does, then, when some one speaks critically of him, to throw off these feelings of inferiority is to strike back. The tail feathers turn up and become ruffled and the defenses go into action. Then remarks like these are heard, "Who's stupid? You are stupid yourself!" Or this, "You don't know what you are talking about. You have no right to criticize me. What you do is worse than I ever do. I don't want you ever to make a remark like that again." These words do sound strangely familiar, don't they? Criticism is distasteful. When we hear it, we want to strike back.

Our lesson from Luke today, however, brings us in contact with a man who evidently, from what we read in the record, reacted differently than most of us do to criticism. Instead of becoming angry and defensive, Zacchaeus took criticism of himself seriously. Jesus came to Jericho. In this prosperous Palestinian village, Zacchaeus was employed by the Roman authorities to collect taxes from the Jewish people. The tax he extracted from the people was not large but it was resented by the people, not because they minded paying a tax but because it was paid to one of their own countrymen who turned it over to the Romans. Anything he got over and above the regular tax, Zacchaeus could keep for himself. He must have done pretty well for himself and his methods, according to Luke, the writer of the narrative, were not of the highest order. He probably took more than was proper, so he was despised by his townspeople.

Yet, when he was confronted by Jesus, he became a different man. We do not possess a record of the conversation between Zacchaeus and Jesus but one fact is certain - he took seriously what Jesus had to say to him. His life changed completely. Here is the way Luke describes his reaction to Jesus' criticism of him, *"Behold, Lord, the half of my goods I give to the poor; and if I have defrauded any one of anything, I restore it fourfold."* No getting one's feathers ruffled here but acceptance of criticism and making it serve one's usefulness and contributing to new behavior. Is it possible that you and I can learn from this account of Zacchaeus so that we can react differently to criticism? Instead of striking out at our critics, we can listen, evaluate their remarks, and perhaps profit from their comments. What are some of the factors that can assist us in taking our critics seriously?

For one thing, we can learn to listen to criticism and not feel threatened by it. We can realize that we are not perfect and that criticism is due us as much as praise. Anyone who has lived any time at all knows he makes mistakes and does not perform at top level all of the time. This is our condition as men and women. If we were always perfect in every thought we had, every move we made, every act we performed, well, we would become gods and cease to become creatures. Personally, it helps me to know I do not have to be perfect in everything I do because I am unable to be perfect. By recognizing this fact, I am not overly troubled by mistakes or failures, for I realize they are as much a part of me as are my successes and things I do right. Naturally, I am happy when things turn out right and I feel badly when they do not turn out right. Still, I have no right to expect all of one or of the other. This is my condition, my state, myself, and I must realize that because of my inability to be perfect, I will be subject both to praise and criticism. If I think, otherwise, I will become miserable, mean, and arrogant, and have around me walls of defenses that keep me in ignorance and living in a false tower of fantasy. Paul hit it about right when he said, *"We see through a glass darkly."(We see in a mirror dimly.)* All cannot be known. Everything is relative and subject to wrongness. This I must accept if I am to be an adult.

Another thing. We can make the most of criticism by using it to evaluate and improve our performance. Now, it takes a pretty strong person to be grateful for his critics and to seriously consider their evaluations. Zacchaeus must have had a lot of stuff in him. Some scholars say this was really Luke or Matthew who later became one of Jesus' closest associates. If this interpretation is correct, we can see the wisdom of Jesus in beholding in this man spiritual qualities that could be utilized for his mission, personal characteristics so deep that he could stand up to criticism of his life, apply the comments to him personally, recognize their validity, and then to make a change. That is really the stuff that we all wish we had!

You know, actually, when we think about the situation in earnest, we will have to admit that criticism is a factor in our favor, for it helps us to correct our errors and to improve our performance. I think one of the most profitable experiences I ever had in theological seminary was in 1951 and 1952 when I was doing my masters work at Columbia University and Union Theological Seminary in New York. I had been out of seminary 10 years by that time and I thought I knew about everything there was to know about preaching. Well, just for kicks I took a course called *The Bible and Preaching* from Dr. Robert J. McCracken who was teaching at Union and who was the senior minister at the Riverside Church in New York. What I learned was that I didn't know as much as I thought I knew. Every week we went to the Chapel and heard each other preach a sermon. Then the other students and Dr. McCracken would kindly but sternly tear us apart. It was an agonizing ordeal but I can truly say it was one of the most profitable educational experiences I have ever had. Why? Not because we were told how skillful we were as preachers and not poor either but because we were positively criticized for what we did. Each of us, I hope, learned to take our critics seriously.

This brings us to say, then, that in all of life; it may be wiser to listen to our critics than to our admirers. Not always but many times our critics are more our friends than our admirers, for our critics think enough of us to help us improve ourselves. Jesus thought enough of Zacchaeus to say *"come down from that tree Zacchaeus, I want to have a word with you."* He wasn't interested in gaining Zacchaeus approval or adding him to his list of friends. He wanted to help him and he helped him by assisting Zacchaeus to face himself in honesty and in truth.

Certainly, some of the most serious mistakes in history have been made because people did not listen or profit from their critics. Jesus was critical of the religious leaders of his day. He said they were leading the nation up the wrong tree. He realized revolt against Rome, even hatred of the foreigner was no solution to their predicament. He insisted that moral earnestness and purity of heart were the required essentials, but they would not listen. Finally, Rome grew tired of the behavior of the Jews and obliterated Jerusalem in the year 68 A.D. Conditions might have been different had they taken the criticism of Jesus seriously.

Another illustration may prove useful. Luther and the other reformers of the 16th century pled with the Roman Pope and other church officials to take a new look at religious faith. Luther did not want to leave the church. His interest was reform and reexamination. But the leaders were so blinded by their own self importance and sense of omniscience that they would not listen; so Europe was bathed in blood and the church became divided. For over 400 years, the Roman

Church became stiff, rigid, and inflexible to change. Now after all of these years, signs of flexibility are showing. Even some of their own theologians are admitting that Luther should have been taken more seriously and they are beginning to appreciate his criticisms. Not only in this, but in most instances you can think of, it is a mark of wisdom to listen to our critics. We may be able to learn some new approach that will add to the common good or our personal betterment.

Naturally, we need to say that not all critics are of the same quality. One of the essential points to remember in listening to criticism is to consider who the person is who is doing the criticizing. Not all persons who are critical are qualified to judge. Two questions then need to be asked regarding criticism: Is the person doing the criticizing competent to judge? And second: Why is the person criticizing? Until the two questions can be answered satisfactorily then criticism ought not to be taken seriously. So if persons make a judgment of you, consider carefully the source and ask these two questions. Is the person qualified to judge? What is his reason for criticism? If he isn't qualified forget it. If he is criticizing to hurt you or to make himself look good, forget it, for he isn't interested in you but only in himself.

Let us close then by saying that Christ is the person we can be sure of and on whom we can depend for fair criticism of our lives. He is preeminently qualified to judge our behavior and our motives. I know of none who is more capable or who has more completely proven himself. Furthermore, he criticizes because he has no axe to grind, nothing to sell, no personal ambition. His only concern is your welfare and mine. He tells us what is wrong with us because he loves us and gave himself for us. No wonder Zacchaeus did not get his dander up when Jesus had something to say to him. He took the Master and his criticism seriously and became a new man. How about it? Are you as wise as Zacchaeus?

14

A REASON TO SHOUT HOSANNA

Palm Sunday

Mark 11:9 And those who went before and those who followed cried out, "Hosanna! Blessed is he who comes in the name of the Lord!"

The crowds shouted *"Hosanna to God in the highest, blessed is he who comes in the name of the Lord!"* These stirring words were on the lips of many when Jesus entered the gates of Jerusalem almost two thousand years ago beginning a celebration we now call Palm Sunday and in which you and I share today.

Today, Palm Sunday, we join with those who were in Jerusalem with Jesus, and with Christians all around the world by singing, *"Hosanna, blessed is he who comes in the name of the Lord!"*

We welcome Jesus because he provides us with a way of life that focuses on a concern for others, thereby reconciling us to God, to others, and to ourselves. An emphasis on concern for others permeated almost all of the teachings of Jesus, only love of God had a higher claim.

He not only taught a concern for others as a focal point of his teachings but he demonstrated it in his own life. A reading of the four gospels tells us that Jesus spoke seven statements from the Cross. Of these seven, four of them were concerned with the predicament of others. The most profound of all was, *"Forgive them Father for they know not what they do."*

One day not so long ago, I was having lunch with a Jewish friend of mine. She told me that she wanted to learn more about the Christian religion and that she was reading the New Testament. In reading the account of the Crucifixion, she was so overcome that she burst into tears. She said that she could not imagine anyone expressing such love, asking forgiveness for those who had hung him on a Cross. She was overwhelmed. It is the substance of which our faith is made.

Few of us, of course have to have our faith tested to that extent but concern for others can be expressed in varied ways and each of us has to discover the way that is appropriate for her or for him.

Remember, too, what I learned from a man in a wheel chair - that concern for others cannot be forced, demanded, or coerced. It must be freely given as it was with Christ.

Sixty years ago, when I was a fledgling seminary student, I was sent by the Dean of the school to conduct a worship service for a small rural church. The day happened to be Palm Sunday. As I greeted the people leaving after the service, an elderly gentleman pleasantly shook my hand – I noticed he was using a crutch to walk – and said to me, "Young man, it is easy to sing praises to Jesus when things are going well but how can you when you are in pain most of the time?" He passed on, not waiting for an answer. In a way, I am glad that he didn't wait for an answer, for as inexperienced as I was at that time I hardly think I could have given him an answer.

Since that Palm Sunday so many years ago, I have thought many times about his question. That question may be in the minds of some of you, "How can I sing Hosanna when I feel so bad, or hurt, or as I am going through some sort of misfortune?"

Let us see if we can sing Hosanna when life seems to have let us down. As in all matters of serious import, it seems to me we look to Jesus and his life for an answer. He too was in pain and anguish as he hung on the Cross. His reaction to his condition was similar to ours. He felt that God had let him down. The biblical account reports him crying, *"My God, my God, why hast Thou forsaken me?"* Here we see his humanity in his divinity.

But note that his feelings of rejection were momentary. His divine capacity enabled him to rise above his pain and to turn his attention away from himself and to think about others, even of those who had nailed him to the Cross, *"Forgive them Father for they know not what they do."* Surely these words helped in relieving some of his intense distress.

In those astonishing words, I have a hunch that we find an answer to the gentleman's question, "How can we sing Hosanna when we are struck by adversity, are in pain or are bearing a serious misfortune?" When we have gotten over the initial reaction and we are in a position to ponder our predicament, we can find some relief from our distress by finding a way to consider another person, thus a reason for shouting hosanna.

Pain is not always physical. Pain often comes in the form of mental anguish. One of the most devastating of mental or emotional distress is resentment that permeates our entire being, rendering us functionally unable to go about the usual business of living.

I think of an excruciating experience that happened to the early 20th century poet Edwin Markham. He had a friend who let him down. He was so angry that he was unable to write his poetry. He must have thought of all kinds of possible responses: give him a tongue lashing, call in the press so as to publicize what a terrible person this man was, or pay him back with some sort of nasty deed. But, Markham rejected these responses and took the path Jesus offered. The poet had concern about his friend's predicament as well as his own. He went to his friend and told him how disappointed and hurt he had been because of what had been done to him, and asked forgiveness for his resentment and anger toward him. His friend apologized, asked forgiveness, and they became reconciled. Markham was able to be relieved of his distress and return to creating his useful poems. As a result of that experience, Edwin Markham wrote the little poem *Outwitted*:

> He drew a circle that shut me out-
> Heretic, rebel, a thing to flout,
> But love and I had the wit to win;
> We drew a circle that took him in!

Surely, we find in this story a reason to shout Hosanna! Our bodies and minds do not tolerate bitterness and ill will toward others. They have a tendency to produce all sorts of physical and emotional symptoms and only a meeting with the other to reconcile the enmity can really cure the distress.

Then there are incidents that few people hear about of a person who expresses a concern for others that is unthinkable. The story of a small boy who was dying is told by Dr. Robert Coles. The boy said, "My parents will feel less sadness about my dying than they would if my sister died, for she is their favorite."

Jesus seemed to have recognized this outgoing love in little children when given proper care and attention, for he said to those who wanted to deny children access to him, *"Suffer the little children to come unto me and forbid them not for of such is the kingdom of heaven."*

How is it with your life? Are you carrying around some pain or distress? Perhaps you may be relieved of some of the discomfort, if you are able, by finding some way, ever so small; to render some thought or deed that would be useful to another.

When we do so, then we can sing *"Hosanna in the highest, blessed is he who comes in the name of the Lord!"*

15

THE SADNESS AND GLORY OF FAREWELLS

Maundy Thursday

Anyone who has said farewell to family members or friends before going to another place to live or to start a new adventure knows the sadness that accompanies such an experience. The emptiness and loneliness that one feels at such a time can be quite severe and upsetting, even to the person who is usually calm and composed.

Farewells begin early. We may say with safety, I think, that life is literally a series of *goodbyes* and *hellos*. The child comes into the world saying goodbye to the warmth and comfort of his mother's body and hello to the strange world of noise and confusion. Otto Rank suggested some years ago that birth is such an emotional upheaval in a person's life that he never really gets over the shock and unconsciously yearns, throughout his life, to return to that state of bliss and contentment he knew before he was born.

The trauma of birth symbolizes our existence, for life is a process of saying goodbye and hello. After a year or so, the child says farewell to crawling and hello to walking. He soon begins to leave his parents and plays with those outside his family. Soon he takes the hurdle of saying goodbye to Mamma and walks down the street or takes the bus to begin the long adventure of going to school which might some day take him completely away from home for months and years at a time. Then, the time comes when he must leave his parents' home and venture out to establish a home and a life of his own. For all, these moments of leaving have regrets and heartache and for some they are more intense than for others.

Then, there are those times when we have to say goodbye to friends and places where our roots have been deep and life has been good. Because of circumstances, persons have to leave the familiar community where they have lived for many years and move to a new locality to start all over again. One man, in explaining such an experience that had happened to him, said, "When I moved here I thought I was cut in pieces. I was in Fairfax but most of me was back in Ohio. Even after ten years, I still feel at times that I left a part of me back there." Farewells are not easy.

War-time also demands farewells. Perhaps, those of us who have lived through long wars will never forget the emptiness we felt when we said *goodbye* to our families or our sweethearts and were gone sometimes for years. Many servicemen have said to me after many long months away from home, "I always have a little lonely feeling down inside." And now, with our engagement in Vietnam and with our other military commitments around the world, we notice that farewells are increasing.

Jesus felt sadness when he had to say *goodbye* to his disciples. They had enjoyed three good years together. They had experienced many trying times but they had many exciting days, sharing their joys and lives with each other. Now all of this was drawing to an end. They did not know it would soon be all over but Jesus did and he was sorrowful.

He wanted to spend his last hours with his friends so he arranged for them to share a meal together. He did not want to be forgotten, which perhaps is one of the deepest fears of one who is going away. No one likes to be forgotten. Jesus, therefore, ate and drank and talked with his friends, and, at the close of their meal together, he asked tenderly that they not forget him. He suggested that after he was gone and when they gathered together for a meeting, that they remember him by eating bread and drinking wine. After he was gone, they remembered what he had asked; and when they came together on the first day of the week, they remembered their Lord by eating bread and drinking from a cup. Tonight, you and I, as his followers, still recall the request of Jesus when he said *farewell*. We remember him by joining together around this table and by receiving the loaf and the cup.

Farewells may be sad but they also have their lights of glory. Farewells are essential for personal growth. A person would always be a child if he never left the arms of his mother, took his first step across the floor, went off to school, or left the contentment of his parents' home to find a life for himself. No one ever made a positive contribution either to himself or to the life of another person without the capacity to say *goodbye* to the comfortable and *hello* to the strange, the new, or even the dangerous. What wars would ever be won without the bravery of men and women to endure farewells and separation. No discoveries would ever be made without the adventurous spirit of men to give up and say goodbye to the old and move on and say hello to the untried and the unplowed. There is no glory without farewell.

Surely, this observation of life is made clearer to our vision when we consider the life of Jesus Christ. His life was one event of farewell and hello after another. At the age of twelve, his family took him to Jerusalem for the Passover, the same ancient feast that is now being celebrated by the Jewish community. On their return to Nazareth, his parents discovered he was not with them. In haste, they returned to Jerusalem and found him discussing weighty matters of existence with wise and scholarly men. *"Why have you made us anxious?"* his mother asks. He replies, *"I must be about my Father's business."* In essence, Jesus informs his parents, not in rudeness or disobedience, but in a spirit of high adventure and purpose, that he must now leave, say farewell to the authority of his father and mother, painfully perhaps for him but moreso for them, and give his life over to the authority of God, to that which was highest and best for his life. In saying farewell to the comfortable and pleasant circumstances of his home, he was saying, at the same time, hello to the terrible demands that he believed were necessary for his life. The climax of it all was, *"Glory to God in the highest and on earth, peace, goodwill to all men."*

Life, indeed, does have its occasions of tragedy for all of us and none are more prominent than in this matter of saying farewell. Yet, these moments of farewell must be faced and goodbyes must be said if there is to be growth and salvation for any of us. This is one of the truths that emerges out of this service we share tonight around this table. There can be no glory without pain.

16

THE PAIN OF LONELINESS

Good Friday

Matthew 27:46 & Psalm 22:1 My God,
my God, why hast thou forsaken me?

Some years ago Otto Rank wrote an enlightening book with the intriguing title, *The Trauma of Birth*. In this book, Dr. Rank advanced the theory that when a child leaves the comfort and serenity of his mother's womb, he experiences deep discomfort and pain, and forever after, he longs to return to this blissful state of his prenatal life.

Rank may have overstated his case; nevertheless, he does have considerable evidence to support his thesis. The little child does not like to be alone. He likes mamma or daddy to lie with him before he goes to sleep. He fights off going to bed, not because the child dislikes sleep, but because he does not want to be alone and wants to stay up to be with his parents and other members of the family.

How many of us remember that little boy or little girl we once were and that strange and ominous feeling that came over us when the door was shut and we were left alone. We were supposed to be brave little people but down deep there was that hollow feeling. Then soon, do you remember, that toy, that blanket, that thing we learn to snuggle up to? We gave it the power of real presence and it returned that power to us blessed with comfort and contentment. I still remember that little boy who once had the same name I now have, who each night collected his little bears – Bugger, Teddy, and James – and off they went to sleep in peace and contentment together.

These fetishes of youth, however, we finally discard and find our lives in our relationships with others – members of our family, playmates, school and church friends, later with that special boy friend or girl friend, then marriage and family for some, business associates, or adult friends if we do not marry. In substance, we discover who we are and find the meaning for our lives in wholesome relationships with others. In a sense, we are made to live with each other. Rank would say that this state of contentment with others is a replacement for the nirvana we knew before birth.

Now when we are *thrown out* on our own by various circumstances of life, often over which we have little or no control, and find ourselves without meaningful relationships, we often feel that same uneasiness and loneliness we felt when we went to bed as children in the dark alone. A romantic song describes this sentiment rather well,

> "Me and my shadow, not a soul to tell our troubles to....
> Just me and my shadow, All alone and feeling blue."

I suppose there is no more devastating feeling than to be separated from others. Loneliness is painful. I think you know what I mean. Have you ever lost someone for whom you deeply cared? Have you ever been to a large city, crowds everywhere, but you were by yourself and knew no one? Have you ever been to a social affair, everyone having a wonderful time, but you knew no one and you felt all alone? Ever been to a new church looking for someone to say *hello*, but no one did, and you left sad, sadder than before you came? Perhaps Rank was right when he wrote that birth is traumatic, especially when there is nothing to take the place of that prenatal blissfulness.

Now, I wish to move our thinking to a different level and advance the idea that one of the reasons that Jesus Christ has such an attraction for all of us is that he was so much like ourselves. I agree with Gustaf Aulen that we discover his durability in his humanity. He enjoyed and suffered the same emotions that are common to us all. He laughed and cried, was happy and angry, was hopeful and downhearted, was cheerful and sad. He also endured the pain of loneliness. The writer of Matthew's gospel caught this feeling of desolation within Jesus as he hung on the cross in the words of the Psalmist, "*My God, my God, why hast Thou forsaken me?*" This would lead us to infer that Jesus not only felt isolated from his friends – they all deserted and left when he needed them the most – but he also felt that even God had forgotten him. There is hardly any statement in all of the New Testament that carries with it such sorrow and desolation as these words of Jesus on the cross – "*Eli, Eli, lama, sabach thani…*" "*My God, my God, why hast Thou forsaken me?*"

But Jesus did more for us than merely express his loneliness. He comes close and tells how we can face loneliness and deal with it.

First, he helps us by experiencing loneliness. He did not deny it, run away from it, or take something to keep from feeling his loneliness. They offered him vinegar but he refused it.

Sometimes, I feel we deny ourselves the privilege of loneliness when once it starts to occur. We run from it – turn on a radio, take a sleeping pill or a tranquilizer, have a drink, give a big party, or become a burden to others. Now we do need others – we are dependent on others – but at the same time, it is harmful to avoid being by one's self. Going through loneliness or feeling lonely is not altogether bad. It helps us to become aware and acquainted with ourselves and it gives strength for other moments of loneliness that are bound to come along.

Jesus loved his friends and he seemed to find joy and contentment in the company of little children and trusted companions. Other times, however, he withdrew to be by himself. He enjoyed the quietness and companionship of himself. Often he suffered in loneliness, but the experience seems to have provided him with renewed strength and vigor. If he had not experienced the pain of loneliness before his crucifixion, he probably could not have endured the intense loneliness during his crucifixion. Jesus teaches us that the experience of loneliness has value.

Secondly, our Lord helps us in our loneliness by discovering ways to relate ourselves to others through service and trust. I do not mean to imply that Jesus went about doing good so he would not be lonely, for such an approach would be using persons for one's own personal gain. Rather, he went about in a spirit of concern and helpfulness because he genuinely cared about others as persons.

Now you and I, or at least most of us, have all sorts of ways by which we can establish meaningful relationships with others rather that sitting around all day fretting about our moments of loneliness. There are elderly people who would enjoy a visit from an outsider.

There are young mothers with little children who would welcome a half day shopping if someone would watch their children. There are persons in nursing homes or hospitals who would enjoy a visit. Go not to tell them your problems, but go to listen and care. You may find new resources for dealing with spiritual pain.

Next, Jesus assists us in dealing with the loneliness that accompanies death. The thought of not being is desolation in itself and brings moments of despair and dread to many. Jesus, of course dealt with death in the ultimate sense. He staked his life not only on the ultimate victory of his life over death, but also on the ultimate victory of God over all forms of tyranny and unrighteousness.

For himself, he said, *"Into thy hands I commit my spirit."* His belief in the victory of God over all the earth appears in the last verses of the 22nd Psalm from which he quoted the verses that have concerned us this evening. He started out, *"My God, my God, why hast Thou forsaken me?"* Surely he ended his meditation in the words of the Psalmist - *(Psalm 96)*

> *10 Say among the nations, "The Lord reigns!*
> *Yea, the world is established, it shall never be moved; he will judge*
> *the peoples with equity."*
> *11 Let the heavens be glad, and let the earth rejoice;*
> *let the sea roar, and all that fills it;*
> *12 let the field exult, and everything in it!*
> *Then shall all the trees of the wood sing for joy*
> *13 before the Lord, for he comes, for he comes to judge the earth.*
> *He will judge the world with righteousness, and the peoples with*
> *his truth.*

This is the faith that ultimately dispels and conquers all gloom and despair.

17

A FAITH IN LIFE ETERNAL

Easter

John 14:2-3

2 In my Father's house are many rooms; if it were not so,
would I have told you that I go to prepare a place for you?
3 And when I go and prepare a place for you, I will come again
and will take you to myself, that where I am you may be also.

S pecial days of the year confront us with special questions. On Thanksgiving Day, we ask, "Why give thanks? What have I to be grateful for?" At Christmas time, we ask, "Did God really enter into history in the form of a child?" At New Years a fair question is, "How can I make my life more meaningful during the coming year?" At Easter, however, the question confronts us with a more profound and perplexing query than any of the others. Perhaps, the writer of the book of Job, states the inquiry better than any we could formulate: *"If a man die, will he live again?"* This is indeed the question which confronts us on Easter Day.

Persons handle this question in many ways. Some are quick to answer that belief in an after-life is preposterous. They say such a belief cannot be proved and what cannot be proved cannot be believed. In other words, it is completely unscientific to hold to a medieval idea that man's life is eternal. For these persons, to believe in immortality is absurd.

Others feel that to believe in life eternal is contrary to the Christian concept of unselfishness. These persons maintain that Christ taught concern for others, not concern for self; therefore, one should not be interested in an afterlife, for such an interest is purely an expression of self-centeredness. The scientist Einstein called a desire for personal survival after death "ridiculously egotistical".

Still a third group of individuals, and their number is larger than we think, absolutely have no interest in immortality. Eternal life is not an intellectual, nor an ethical problem. Their position grows out of a mood or a feeling. Life has been unusually hard for them, and when it is finished, they want it to be over and done with. Swinburne expresses their mood in these words:

> From too much love of living,
> From hope and fear set free,
> We thank with brief thanksgiving
> Whatever gods may be
> That no life lives forever:
> That even the weariest river
> Winds somewhere safe to sea.

So go some of the common negative ideas of life eternal.

Against these intellectual and ethical arguments and feelings of despair against belief in personal survival is placed, however, Christian faith. Christianity makes no effort to prove or disprove personal immortality from rational argument or on the basis of ethical considerations. Neither does Christian faith attempt to offer personal life after death in order to make people feel good or comfortable. Christianity isn't interested in offering a philosophy that will assist people to whistle in the dark. The faith of Christians is merely a statement about the nature of the universe and that statement is said in no better way than we find expressed in the words of the writer of the Gospel of John. He quotes Jesus, *"In my father's house are many rooms."* The more familiar words are those in the King James translation, *"In my father's house are many mansions."* This word picture used by Jesus to express life eternal is another way of saying: "God has made a place for each one after death." Listen to the rest of the beautiful picture in words:

> *2 In my Father's house are many rooms; if it were not so, would I have told you that I go to prepare a place for you?*
> *3 And when I go and prepare a place for you, I will come again and will take you to myself, that where I am you may be also. (John 14:2-3)*

This is an expression of a faith in life eternal. Let us examine its implications.

First, this faith in life everlasting gives evidence of our deep affection for those we love. Far from being a self-centered, egotistical concept, faith in an afterlife tells us what we think of each other. Personally, I have met few people of mature stature who desired personal life after death for themselves. Such a thought was furthest from their minds but they believed in it because they devotedly loved their wives or their husbands, or their children, or their friends so much that they could not imagine that death would snuff out their existence.

Professor George Herbert Palmer of Harvard, as Dr. Harry Emerson Fosdick tells us, was a thrilling teacher of philosophy. He was acquainted with all of the ancient and modern arguments concerning immortality – both pro and con. But more than having an acquaintance with these arguments, he held a strong personal belief in immortality and loved to advance arguments in support of it. Perhaps, however, the most powerful argument he ever gave in favor of life after the grave was something he said following the death of his wife. He phrased his argument in a question which is worth repeating: Who would "not call the world irrational if out of deference to a few particles of disordered matter it excludes so fair a spirit?" This is not an egotistical voice speaking. This is the proclamation of love for another human being, a proclamation so profound and so penetrating that it discovers in God's world that things unseen are eternal.

The friends of Socrates did not hold to life eternal after his death because of any academic reasons he ever gave them. They believed in it because they loved Socrates: and out of that love for him, one of his staunchest disciples, Plato, wrote the *Phaedo,* the finest document of the ancient world containing an argument for immortality. The disciples of Jesus had no thought for themselves when they announced the glorious news of his resurrection. They issued the proclamation, *"He is risen,"* because their love for him had no other answer. Love is not blind. It sees what skepticism can never see, because as Thornton Wilder writes in the closing lines of his sensitive and deeply moving book, *The Bridge of San Luis Rey,*

"There is a land of the living and a land of the dead and the bridge is love, the only survival, the only meaning." Love, indeed spans the chasm between life and death and makes them one.

But there is another implication, too, growing out of a faith in life after death: It provides a climate in which persons can learn and grow to become decent and healthy men and women. The curse of materialism is not that it is poor philosophy. It does make sense and it has an uncanny way of appealing to bright and clear young minds because it seems to do away with so much unreality in religious and spiritual thought. The curse of materialism is that it is so brittle, hard, and impersonal. It seems to take the best there is out of human relationships and to leave us with a philosophy of the jungle, where the tooth and claw are supreme, devoid of human warmth and value.

Dr. Fosdick in his fine lecture on *Faith and Immortality*, from which many of my ideas this morning are taken, gives us this account. He writes that during World War II he talked with an American journalist who had covered news in Berlin up to our entrance into the war. Here is what the journalist said to him: "I came home from Berlin and went back to my old college campus, and I said to some of the professors there, 'You are teaching these students here the philosophy that has made Nazi Germany what she is. You tried to teach me that only a few years ago – a godless materialism that makes the physical the source and end of everything - that undermines the basis of moral principle and makes the whole universe a purposeless machine. And now in Nazidom I have seen what happens when that philosophy really gets going and comes to its logical conclusion, and I have come back to tell you that the stuff you are teaching here is about the most dangerous dynamite that is being scattered around the world.'"

This journalist had seen what happens, then, when the intellectual and cultural climate of a society devoids itself of personal values and human goals. Our democracy rests upon its dignity and its supreme worth. In order for personality to become humane, rich, and warm in its affection for others, it needs a climate to grow in that extols the dignity of the person, not delegates it to the dust and to the ground. Faith in immortality surrounds our lives with values we need, for it is the supreme assertion of the worth of every last human person.

Still, this faith we are witnessing to this Easter morning, saying that life does go on forever, also implies something significant about God. Think if you will, what belief or disbelief in life everlasting does to our ideas about God. To me this is really the crux of the matter. Belief or disbelief in immortality is important as we have tried to point out in reference to our concern for one another and regarding the climate in which we live, but most important of all, the decision we make here tells us what kind of God we really worship and serve.

What kind of God would it be who would bring human personality into the world and then would allow that most sacred of all treasures simply to die and perish? It is absolutely impossible for me to imagine a God who would allow so majestic a spirit as Jesus of Nazareth to walk this earth, to let loose a power so great, a love so deep, a courage so sublime, and then to assign that spirit to the earth. And imagine, if you will, a god who would give life to parents you have loved, to teachers you have admired, to leaders you have followed and then to cut off forever the expression of the best of their lives. If God does not permit eternal life, then he launches ships he does not sail. He makes bubbles of human life and then watches them explode. I simply cannot believe this of the God that

Jesus said was the Father of all mankind from the beginning even until now. I accept what Jesus said about God: *"In my father's house are many rooms... and where I am there you may be also."*

Well, if you still have a problem in comprehending how it is possible for God to love each one of us so much as individual persons that he has a place beyond for each one, then an illustration may help. Stand, if you will, sometime when you are at the beach, maybe Bethany Beach, if you go there this summer, and allow the waters of the great Atlantic Ocean to wash over your feet. Think as you are standing there with the ocean pouring over your feet that the waters of that same ocean at that same moment are washing the feet of other people who are standing on the ocean shore along the coast of France, or England, or Spain, or Africa. That vast ocean which seems so gigantic in size and depth possesses not only the properties to fill the vast expanses between the continents, but it also has the properties to wash upon the shore where you are standing and where others like you are also standing. Is God not like the Atlantic Ocean, only vaster in power and mightier in scope? He not only possesses the properties to create and to support the universe with its vast expanses and its millions of planets and solar systems, but this God also contains within himself the properties to be concerned about your personal life and mine. The Easter message tells us about this love of God for us all so simply, yet so beautifully and forcibly described by Jesus. *"In my Father's house are many rooms. I go to prepare a place for you... and where I am there you may be also."*

Sermon

18

A REQUIREMENT OF DISCIPLESHIP

John 21:17 Feed my sheep.

On this first Sunday after Easter, let us direct our attention to one of the truly dramatic scenes that one of the writers of the New Testament provides for us in connection with the resurrection appearances of Jesus.

The author of the Gospel of John, writing at the close of the first century some seventy years after the death of Jesus, draws upon an ancient traditional account prevalent in some parts of the church, that Jesus visited some of his close friends as they were fishing on the Lake of Tiberius or the Sea of Galilee. Peter is there and also Thomas, Nathana-el, James, John and two other disciples whose names are not given. There were seven in all.

Jesus appears on the beach as they are out in their boat but they do not know him. He inquires concerning their success in catching fish. They reply that they have not caught any fish, although they have been fishing most of the night. Jesus tells them to throw their nets on the right side of the boat. They follow his suggestion and amazingly enough they catch so many fish that they are unable to haul them all into the boat. Then, they recognize him and they all come ashore and join him on the beach for breakfast which evidently Jesus prepares for them.

As you read this almost exciting but almost sorrowful passage, you cannot avoid feeling the mystery that surrounds the event. There is no conversation recorded by John. All seem still and quiet. Even Peter does not speak and James and John are even reluctant to ask for favors. You feel you are almost invading a holy and sacred ceremony as you read John's description. Finally, the stillness of the moment is broken by a question that Jesus abruptly asks Peter. Here is the way John set down the conversations: *"Simon, son of John, do you love me more than these?"* He said to him, *"Yes, Lord; you know that I love you."* He said to him, *"Feed my lambs."* A second time he said to him, *"Simon, son of John, do you love me?"* He said to him, *"Yes, Lord; you know that I love you."* He said to him, *"Tend my sheep."* He said to him the third time, *"Simon, son of John, do you love me?"* Peter was grieved because he said to him the third time, *"Do you love me?"* And he said to him, *"Lord, you know everything; you know that I love you."* Jesus said to him, *"Feed my sheep."*

When I read that passage, I always feel sorry for Peter. True, he had denied his Lord after Jesus was captured by the Roman soldiers. Time and again he talked stupidly when he should have been listening. Peter, in many ways was dull and slow-witted and you do get angry with him at times for his lack of judgment. Yet, when he is put on the spot, as John describes the conversation between Peter and Jesus, you do feel embarrassed for him and you do wish that Jesus had not pressured him as though he were on the witness stand in a courtroom having his testimony questioned. Yet, that is exactly what Jesus does. He pushes him into a corner. He confronts Peter with the seriousness of this business of his discipleship. It is no laughing matter. "Do you, Peter, mean it when you say you want to be one of my disciples?" Jesus asks. "If you do, then your job is to assume responsibility for what I have been teaching and living and do for others what I have tried to do for you and for others." In other words, the significance of this encounter of Jesus with his disciples and specifically with Peter is not his surprise visit but his delineation and clarification concerning a requirement of discipleship – to be responsible for the mission of Jesus in the world.

Frequently, it is assumed that Christianity means coming to the church to receive what the church provides. People say, "I went to church yesterday and the choir sang beautifully and I liked what the preacher said." Or again you hear a statement similar to this, "I certainly do like that church. They are such nice people. They make me feel so good." Or another remark goes this way, "You ought to come to our church. We have a beautiful building and the finest group of people you ever met." Another attitude that gets around is expressed like this, "I really did something yesterday. I went to church for a change." This is sometimes heard on the morning after Easter Day.

Now, these are all fine remarks and they have something good to say about the church. They seem to imply that the church is providing something that is valuable and helpful to people. It gives something they need. We hope it is providing in part something of that which Jesus gave to mankind – faith in God, hope for the future, love toward one's self and others.

Yet, if the church only gave people something and did not demand something from them, it would not be faithful to the teachings and example of its Lord. Notice the condition of Peter. He had been with Jesus for approximately three years. They had good times together, Peter, Jesus, and the others. Jesus was their teacher. Constantly, he was giving out, teaching, preaching, healing, and being a source of encouragement, hope, and comfort to people he met and the disciples were on the receiving end. They were the recipients of the good life Jesus was proclaiming. But Jesus knew that the disciples could not continue in this dependent state. The time had to come when he withdrew and they assumed responsibility for the cause of Christian discipleship.

What we witness, then, in this resurrection account, early on a Palestinian morning on the beach of the Sea of Galilee after seven of the disciples had quietly eaten with Jesus, is the spiritual or psychological birth of Peter. Up until now, he is carefree and dependent upon Jesus for his spiritual resources. He could lean on Jesus for support and direction. But on the beach, Jesus cuts the psychological umbilical cord and tells Peter, as well as the others, "You are now on your own. You can no longer come to me and ask questions. You are in charge. You are the supervisors. You are the spiritual leaders. What happens from now on is your responsibility. So Peter, if you love me, *'Feed my sheep'*." It is indeed a frightening experience, as it must have been to Peter and to the other disciples, to be told that you are no longer children to be taken care of, and also that your mission is not only to take care of yourselves but you have an obligation for the welfare of others. The church by its very nature, not only then but now, has to give comfort and strength to those who come for worship, friendship, and counsel. Furthermore, it must place upon persons the demands of representing Christ in society. Persons only grow as they become involved actively in the life of the church, the home, and society. We only mature as we shoulder the obligations connected with justice, mercy and goodness. A sit down strike is not enough. What is required is an active participation in the affairs of faith, hope, and love. What Jesus said to Peter also applies to us. He also says to you and to me, *"Feed my sheep."*

Thus far, we have spoken in rather broad generalities. Now let us get down to specifics. Here are a few suggestions for feeding sheep.

Surely, first of all we have the responsibility to see to it that our children are properly cared for, have an opportunity to feel the love and affection of parents who are concerned, and are brought into contact with the teachings of the church. Thus feeding those for whom we have a responsibility. Our family is first. All else is secondary, for society either rises or falls with what is done or not done in the family. But concern for children is not to make them dependent on those of us who are parents but to train them and teach them gradually so that they are able to make their own decisions and to assume responsibilities for themselves, for a part of the family life, and for others. We do not do children any favors doing everything for them when they are able to do things for themselves. Jesus did not keep Peter a child. He put him on his own feet as soon as he realized he was able. Too soon is as bad as too late. It takes a wise person to know when.

Next, the Christian has a requirement to assume a share of the load for his church community – that is, to see that it has proper facilities, program, and resources to do its job. The church has a right to ask, "Do you love the Church?" just as Jesus asked Peter, *"Do you love me?"* If the answer is, "Yes, I believe in it and want to have a share in its program", then the reply is similar to the reply of Jesus, *"Then feed my sheep"* or to state the command more stringently, "Take care of it and do your part to support it in every way that you find possible to do so." The opportunities are unlimited.

Third, the Christian has a requirement to his community. Here too people live and here too there are demands to be met. By community, we mean our next door neighbor, our government at all its various levels, our educational system, our social and civic organizations, our hospitals, our aged, our sick, our orphans, our cultural and fine arts programs – there and in other worthwhile activities that promote, dignify and enrich life the Christian stands by to support and promote. His life begins in Christ, it expresses itself in humanity, and it terminates in the life beyond.

Therefore, you and I come here today not merely to drink the cup of salvation but we are here to gain strength and inspiration so we can go "out there" from where we have come to make ourselves available at those crucial junctures in ways we are able for the betterment of human life. In other words, our requirement as Christians is to serve.

Some years ago, I visited a beautiful military chapel that had in the foyer before you went into the sanctuary a picture of Christ praying in Gethsemane. When you went out of the sanctuary after services, however, you saw another picture - the same picture in many ways as the first, but also different. It was also a picture of Christ but he was on a cross. These pictures portray in terse symbolism the relation of each of us to the church. For those who are in the church and who love it, "We come each Lord's Day to worship but we also go out each Lord's Day to serve." That is your mission and mine if we are serious regarding our love for our Lord.

19

BELIEVING WITHOUT SEEING

John 20:29a Blessed are those who have not seen and yet believe.

In the resurrection account given to us by the writer of the Gospel of John when Jesus appears to some of his disciples to show Thomas the scars in his side and the prints of the nails in his hands, we come face to face with two ways by which we believe.

The first way we come to have a belief is by evidence that we see with our eyes, hear with our ears, smell with our noses, feel with our hands, or taste with our tongues. This is belief that is developed from information that is fed to our minds through the senses. Scientific persons call this approach empirical. Thomas, the disciple, was a first century empiricist. When told by the other disciples that they had seen the Lord, Thomas replied, *"Unless I see in his hands the print of the nails, and place my finger in the mark of the nails, and place my hand in his side, I will not believe."* He had to see and to feel before he would believe.

The second way of forming a belief is by a process we call impressionistic or intuition. We have a hunch or subjective interpretation. Sometimes we say regarding some decision we make: "Somehow I feel that this decision is right, although I cannot prove it, or I have no evidence to substantiate my belief. Yet, I feel it is the right thing to do." A hard-headed scientist frowns on this kind of an approach to a problem. It is fraught with many dangers, for feeling something is right or true may be only a reflection of our personal prejudices or bias without any objective evidence whatever. Still this way of arriving at a belief is widely and frequently used, perhaps more than the first.

Yet, Jesus seemed to place a high value on trusting one's personal feelings of subjective judgments. After Jesus finally did appear to the disciples with Thomas present and Thomas was convinced that he had indeed seen the Lord, the author of the gospel called John gives the impression that Jesus is somewhat irritated with Thomas' skepticism. After Thomas sees the scars and the wounds, he exclaims, *"My Lord and my God!"* The slight irritability of Jesus then comes through. *"Have you believed because you have seen me? Blessed are those who have not seen and yet believe."* This would lead us to conclude, then that Jesus, according to the gospel writer, places more importance or, at least, a higher value on sound subjective judgment than on belief that comes from objective evidence.

Let us not be led, however, into the trap that Jesus had no use for real, concrete evidence. Constantly, he pointed to nature and to the creatures as evidence to show proof of God's action in the world. *"Behold the fowls of the air... see the beauty of the lilies of the field... gaze upon the curiosity of the little child."* When showing evidences for the presence of the action of God in human life, we find him saying, *"The kingdom of God is like unto a mustard seed... or it is like a father who had two sons… or it is like a householder who went out early in the morning to hire laborers for his vineyard.*" Jesus did arrive at many of his beliefs through the media of the senses. On the other hand, he included feeling and intuition as another way of arriving at belief. Evidently, he felt that both are sound ways for arriving at answers. It is not a matter of using one or the other. It is a *both—and* proposition, but in the encounter in John, he stresses the importance of belief in the affirmations that are developed out of the inner spirit, out of the *Amens* that come from the depths of the human soul, the yearnings that emerge from the heart.

Surely, Jesus is stressing a dimension of personality to which we ought to give more attention. So much in our educational system today stresses getting something that someone else has done or someone else has said. A student reads history, learns to spell, hears a play, sees a movie, or becomes acquainted with formulas and theorems for solving problems in mathematics. I do not mean to underestimate these learnings. On the contrary, I place value on the facts, information, and knowledge we get from books, experiments, and lectures. Notice, however, that much of what we call education is material or information we *get from something out there.* Even in our religious experiences, we sometimes worship as a deity, the book we call the Bible, trying to make the Bible perform tasks which the writers never intended it to perform. Notice, however, how little attention we give to subjects that cause us to look inside and come up with something that is not put in but that comes out. How little we try to develop the creativity of our children, but I see signs of change – more and more I see attention being given to music, writing, painting, and the other fine arts. Also, in religious thought today, there is emerging an emphasis on the personal relationship between an individual and his God. In addition to children learning verses and books of the Bible, religious educators are attempting to create situations that permit children to express their feelings about religious matters in poems, in music, and in painting. I am also glad to see that we are encouraging persons in religious education classes not merely to listen but to express out of their personal experiences the meaning of religion in their lives. The testimonial meetings of the frontier days, I am sure, are not suitable for us today. Yet, the dynamic, I think, was valuable, for it gave persons an opportunity to give personal witness to their faith – not something poured in but something of importance that emerged from the depths of the human spirit of the individual. Sometime I would like to see us form a class on not what did Jesus say, but on how can we, out of our experiences discover for ourselves the lessons of life that Jesus discovered for his life. This then would be first-hand, not second-hand faith.

Here is an illustration that may help to emphasize what I mean. The other day in the Psychological Services Bureau at Georgetown University where I am counseling students and where I will be until the middle of June, one of the counselors came into my office to talk over a test he had given to a student. He was trying to assist the student in deciding on a vocation. He had given him a Strong Vocational Interest Test, one of the oldest and most reliable of all such instruments, and the test answers had been sent away to be scored. The test results came back indicating the student had a high interest in activities related to some vocation in the physical sciences or mathematics. The counselor said to me, "This somehow doesn't make sense. I don't know why but it doesn't feel right. It doesn't square somehow with this young man." We discussed it for a while and finally he told me he was going to send the results in again with a letter to the company that did the scoring and ask for a new scoring. He followed his hunch. In a few days, an answer came back with an apology. The test had been inaccurately scored and was scored properly now. This time it seemed to feel right. The student showed an interest not in the physical sciences but in journalism and in other vocations related to communicating with others in language. You see Jesus had a point and it is applicable in this situation. We need to test our beliefs, not only by what we see, but also by what we feel. *"Blessed are those who believe but do not see."*

Another area where believing without seeing is crucial is in our interpersonal relationships. Here outside proof is almost impossible. It is true that people tend to act the same tomorrow as they do today, but we cannot be sure. Human personality does contain elements of dependability but it also possesses characteristics of instability. There is perhaps nothing that we know of that is more unpredictable than human behavior.

We are forced, therefore, by the very nature of our existence as human beings to discover ways by which we can relate to each other so we can assist each other to achieve a high degree of consistency and stability in our behavior. Certainly, all research shows that persons are helped most in living consistent, unified lives by living with those they love in a relationship of trust. When we are trusted, we are strengthened. When someone has confidence in us, we want to be at our best. When someone is for us, we do not want to let them down. Nothing is so essential to decent behavior and reliable conduct than for someone to treat us as though we could be depended upon. To trust someone, then, means that we believe without seeing. Unfortunately, Thomas somehow could not trust his own judgment concerning the lordship of Christ. He had been with Jesus. He had heard his teachings. Somehow, though, he was insensitive to the feeling. He observed Jesus but he did not feel his strength and his power. He saw but did not feel. So he had to have proof. The impact of the personality of Jesus or his life was not enough. His relationship to Jesus, then, was based on outward signs, not on intuitive trust or faith. No wonder he had to see the nail prints and the scars. He only knew how to see. He could not trust.

But Jesus said, *"Blessed are those who believe but do not see."* Sometimes, I fear, though, we overlook the implication of this profound teaching in our relationships with others, even those who are nearest to us. Married couples sometimes demand proof of love from each other. They are separated sometimes and require that each write the other every day. There is certainly nothing wrong in persons who care deeply for each other to write every day, providing that daily letter writing is an expression of love but not an evidence of love. There is a world of difference, and the difference is significantly important in persons requiring proof of love and demonstrative acts of love. Persons kiss, I hope, not to prove love but to freely show love. Persons give gifts, not to give evidence of affection, but because they possess affection. Persons who deeply care for each either as lovers or friends do not require the other to prove their feelings. The concern and affection and love take place in a framework of trust. They trust because they love and no demonstration is required. Only the anxious, distrustful, uncertain person requires constant reminders of love. The trustful person knows the other cares as much as he cares and though notes, letters, and presents are appreciated, they are not required. Albert Sweitzer expresses this thought well in one of his writings. He states he always has had a tray full of letters to answer and he does the best he can to answer each one. He answers those he does not know first. He leaves the letters from his friends on the bottom of the tray, for he says they know I am busy. They accept me for what I am. They know I will answer when and if I can – or if never answered that is all right too, for they know I care for them. We trust each other. *"Blessed are those who believe but do not see."*

Do you see the point I am trying to make? Somehow, I feel, I have not expressed it quite well enough. Surely, if I haven't this will keep. Faith is grounded on a trustful relationship between God and man. We do not ask that he show his love for us even though He does. He does not ask that we show our love for Him, though the grateful Christian will do so. But if our relationship with Him is sure and steady, we trust Him to do what is best for us both in this world and the world to come. We demand no miracles, no supernatural feats, no signs. We only ask that we have the opportunity to live as productively as we can, to have the capacity to believe in ourselves and each other, and to be grateful that we have been fortunate enough to live in this life with others. That, it seems to me, is believing without having to see.

20

WHO IS TO BLAME?

Ephesians 1:4 Even as he chose us in him before the foundation of the world, that we should be holy and blameless before him.

There is something exciting about making a discovery, particularly when the fact that is discovered has been right in front of people's eyes all of the time, but has not been recognized. For centuries, people saw apples fall to the ground from trees but Newton, in the 17th century, saw something about an apple falling that people had never noticed previously. Newton saw a law of the universe, the law of gravity, operating in the falling apple. What an exciting day it must have been to have made a discovery of a law of the universe that had previously escaped the attention of others! Or consider the glow of satisfaction that must have been felt by Euclid when he discovered that the angles of a triangle equal the sum of two right angles!

Surely, Paul must have felt some of the same inner warmth that comes from discovery when he saw operating in the mind of Christ the spiritual processes that heal the broken relationships between people. He writes of this discovery in these words to the Christians at Ephesus, *"Even as He chose us in Him before the foundations of the world, that we should be holy and blameless before him."* These words are not evenly translated. A better arrangement is this: "In the order of things as created by God, we are made whole by approaching each other without blame or without fault finding." In other words, God and man can only become reconciled to each other as they relate to each other, not in suspicion or by finding fault with each other, but on a level of trust and confidence. They do not ask who is to blame for their separateness, or for the pain and misery in the world, or for the injustice and unfairness that is so prevalent on earth. They come only to unite and they unite on a plane of blamelessness. This was Paul's discovery regarding the role of Christ. – He was the one who had torn down the middle wall or partition between God and man. Because this was the ideal relationship between God and man, it was also the ideal relationship between man and man: A man can only relate in harmony with another man when the question "Who is to blame for our predicament?" is not raised.

At once, of course, we are faced with a dilemma for the natural impulse when things go sour among us is to ask, "Who is to blame?" Some feel so worthless that they take blame for everything, but no one has enough strength to bear such a burden. Naturally, some of us feel we are too perfect to be at fault; therefore, we look for the blame outside of ourselves. We put the blame for the wrong usually on the other fellow. Sometimes, of course, we say, well, I can't be held responsible for my failures, for my parents didn't raise me in the right way. Or a man drives his automobile into another car and hurts several people and he says, "Well, it wasn't my fault. I had too much to drink." Then again, another person will give this excuse, "I cannot be held responsible for my nasty mean disposition in the morning. I just don't feel right until noon." These and other similar words are heard and said by us every day. We have progressed hardly at all from the Biblical myth of Adam and Eve. God warned them not to eat the forbidden fruit. When they had eaten the fruit, however, and were questioned by God, Adam excused himself by saying that it wasn't his fault – Eve talked him into eating it. Eve, however, wouldn't take the bait. She said, "It wasn't my fault. The serpent told me to eat the fruit." So from that day until now, husbands have been putting the blame for their failures on their wives and wives have been placing the blame on husbands and each one has also been blaming children, in-laws, too much or too little money, too many outside interests, and a host of other reasons for their difficulties.. The common trait in all of us when things go wrong is to ask, "Who is to blame?"

The teaching of Christ, however, as Paul so carefully interprets for us, is that it is futile to ask "Who is to blame?" when life becomes snarled or when there is conflict and discord in our relationships with each other. There are several obvious reasons why such a question hardly gets us any place at all.

First of all, the question is futile because friction between persons is the result, not of what one person does or does not do, but develops out of the interaction of self-centered forces operating between them. One source of irritation is that each often brings a different set of expectations to the situation that brings them together. Man and wife marry and have different ideas of handling money. These different expectations are frequently in conflict and the result is sometimes disastrous. When labor and management gather around the bargaining table, we see at once what we mean when we say that parties develop conflicts because of different expectations. Representatives of labor want to get an increase in wages; representatives of management want to hold the line on wages. When each has a goal that is in conflict with that of the other, conflict is bound to occur. "Who is to blame?" The only possible answer from an objective viewpoint is that this is not the question to ask. Both are actually right. Blame is not the question to raise and to pursue the matter on a level of fault finding and name calling is a waste of time and a dissipation of valuable resources. The answer to the problem is not in finding who is at fault. The answer lies in an exploration of the forces that produce the conflict.

A second reason why blame-naming is a poor way to handle an error or a mistake is that it is dishonest and unfair. A golfer swings and misses his shot. Sometimes he complains about the poor club, the weather, or the terrible condition of the fairways. Seldom is the fault seen *within* the golfer. His excuses are simply untrue. A man sometimes gets into a business venture into which he invests his life savings and he fails. His wife, who was opposed to the idea, never lets him forget. As they struggle to make ends meet, she reminds him in front of the children that they wouldn't be so poor if their father had not been so stupid. You would think he meant to fail but a mistake in judgment is not a sin. To err is human and to call a man stupid for poor judgment is clearly dishonest and unfair. Such castigations do nothing to improve the situation. They only poison the streams of life and cause relationships to degenerate from bad to worse.

A third reason why fault finding is an inferior procedure for handling a bad situation in human relationships is that it avoids the issue. An attempt to blame sidesteps the main item of consideration and stalls the healing process. When a person is heard criticizing or attacking another person and blaming the other person for some irregularity that has developed between them, that person is actually, in most instances, using blame to avoid doing anything to improve the situation. It is much easier to find fault than it is to take action to improve a bad condition. It is much easier to remove a problem than it is to find a solution. One reason I grew weary of marches and *sign carriers* is that they are so negative in their approach to problems. If a man wants to improve a situation, let him offer a constructive solution and get down in the dirt and dig instead of carrying a sign for a day and then go back to his comfortable office. What we desperately need in our day are not fault finders – they come easy and cheap – but problem solvers. Dr. Fosdick preached a sermon once in which he asked, "Are you a part of the problem or a part of the answer?" That question ought to be put to every one of us.

I think what I am trying to say is that the way out of nearly every conflict in human relations lies, not in fault finding, or asking who is to blame, but in discovering a whole new set of attitudes, attitudes that have for their intention, not keeping the problem growing and fermenting, but healing the scar and promoting new tissues of healthy relationships.

One attitude that is inherent in the gospel is to forget who is to blame and to take positive steps to improve the situation. Notice in Jesus' parable of the Prodigal Son that the father did not seek to find fault when his son returned. He was not interested in blame. His only aim was healing the world of separation between him and the boy. So he said, *"Kill the fatted calf and let us have a party. My son who was dead is alive. He was lost and is found."* The relationship had been restored. Nothing else seemed to count.

A man once suffered a severe setback in business and also came down with a serious illness. As would most of us, his first reaction was to ask the question, *Why?* What had he done to deserve such ill luck? First, he blamed God and gave up his affiliation with the church. Then, he found fault with his wife. If she had helped him more, he might not have failed in business. Next, he blamed his business partner. If he had not invested their funds in worthless stocks, the business might not have gone under. He was irritated with the doctors and nurses; they didn't do anything right. Finally, the days passed, and in spite of himself, he became stronger. One day a wise friend visited him. The man poured out his story to this friend who had the patience to listen to his resentments and misfortunes. After Mr. Hard Luck had finished his story his friend said, "Yes, Tom, you have had it tough. You have told me what happened but I hardly think finding fault will do much good to improve your condition. Now, tell me what are you going to do about it?" The statement made the sick man angry and he asked his friend to leave the room. After his friend left, however, he began to think about what his friend had said to him. He saw how ridiculous he had been. He admitted he was asking the wrong question. "He came to himself", and from that day on, he began to plan how he would face and handle the future. He soon became well and today is back at the head of a thriving business. It makes a difference in life for all of us when we stop asking "Who is to blame?" and ask instead, "What can I do to make the most out of a bad situation?" This is the question asked by Christ who invites us, not to keep the fires of dissention and hatred alive, but to calm the troubled waters by finding a more excellent way to live, to love, and to work.

21

THE SERIOUSNESS OF SIN

Acts 5:1-11
1 But a man named Anani'as with his wife
Sapphi'ra sold a piece of property,
2 and with his wife's knowledge he kept back some of the proceeds, and
brought only a part and laid it at the apostles' feet.
3 But Peter said, "Anani'as, why has Satan filled your heart to lie to the
Holy Spirit and to keep back part of the proceeds of the land?
4 While it remained unsold, did it not remain your own? And after it was
sold, was it not at your disposal? How is it that you have contrived this
deed in your heart? You have not lied to men but to God."
5 When Anani'as heard these words, he fell down and died.
And great fear came upon all who heard of it.
6 The young men rose and wrapped him up
and carried him out and buried him.
7 After an interval of about three hours his wife
came in, not knowing what had happened.
8 And Peter said to her, "Tell me whether you sold the
land for so much." And she said, "Yes, for so much."

9 But Peter said to her, "How is it that you have agreed together to tempt the Spirit of the Lord? Hark, the feet of those that have buried your husband are at the door, and they will carry you out."
10 Immediately she fell down at his feet and died. When the young men came in they found her dead, and they carried her out and buried her beside her husband.
11 And great fear came upon the whole church, and upon all who heard of these things.

Sin is not particularly a popular word. When it is mentioned in sophisticated circles, people lift their eyes and respond with a kind of wise and jeering smile, as if to say, "Come off it! Who believes that stuff? Sin is such an old fashioned word. It belongs to another generation; surely, we are too intelligent in this modern age to talk about sin, much less believe in it." Even a noted theologian, Dr. Paul Tillich, once said, although understandably he later changed his mind, that he refused to use the word any longer.

Whether we agree with the smugness of the sophisticates or not, we do have to admit that the word sin does have a certain negative quality that isn't always beneficial. I think what has probably happened, as often occurs with so many perfectly good words, is that the word sin has become identified with the *don'ts* in religion that we are worn out with hearing. When we think of something that was once labeled *sin*, such as smoking, dancing, or playing an innocent game of cards, we naturally associate the word sin with the wrongness of these rather pleasant pastimes and in rejecting the idea that these pastimes are wrong, we also reject the word *sin*.

It is too bad that the word sin acquired such a bad name for itself. Sin is a perfectly proper word and it is necessary to understand this word if we are to have an understanding of our human predicament. Let us, therefore, this morning turn our attention to the seriousness of the concept of sin or the condition the word stands for in human life.

In getting at the real meaning of the term, we need to understand that the word sin, in the biblical sense, refers to a condition of the human spirit. It is related to but does not refer precisely to what a person should do or not do. Sin is not an act, it does not describe *do's* or *don'ts*. Sin means the moral flaw, the cleavage, or the split in the self. It means the state of separateness or apartness that exists in the heart of a man, or the estrangement between a man and his fellow man, or between an individual and God. Whenever we are separated from each other for any reason, whenever there is a division within ourselves, whenever we are not at peace with God – the highest and best that we know – then we may be said to be in a state of sin.

Now, Paul wrote to the Christians in Rome that "We have all sinned and fallen short of the glory of God." Anyone who is honest in his observations and conclusions concerning the life of others as well as of himself must admit that Paul was a shrewd and accurate observer of human behavior, for not one of us is ever completely *whole* in his life. Each of us lives constantly in the state or a condition of sin, for every moment of our day we are not a perfectly woven piece of cloth. These flaws of character are ever with us. At one moment, we mean to be honest but we tell lies. We mean to live in peace and charity with our neighbors but we have moments when we despise each other, often even those we love. We mean to love God with all of our heart and mind and strength but we love other things more. Since we do not possess perfect salvation, integration, wholeness, health or whatever you choose to call the opposite of sin, we do fall short of the glory of God.

Now because we live in a state of sin, we must not draw the inaccurate conclusion that we are all bad. We are not all bad, or else we would not have the conflict. There is goodness in each of us, and it is this goodness that keeps the bad from taking over. But at the same time, we are not all goodness, for the wrongness in us prevents the good from completely taking over. We live in a sense between the good and the bad. We are part devil and part angel – not all devil nor all angel – but both devil and angel – and this split or cleavage is what the Bible calls sin.

See how this is presented in the account in Acts of Ananias and Sapphira. Not long after the death of Jesus, the Christians banded together to await his early return and to be received into the coming Kingdom. They decided that they should practice communal living. They would put all of their property and earnings into a common account and each would share equally with every other person. For some strange reason, a man and his wife, Ananias and Sapphira, joined the Christian community at Jerusalem. They appear to be an unscrupulous couple, but at the same time, they were not all together bad. They sold a piece of property they owned jointly and placed a portion of the proceeds into the common bank account for the benefit of the other Christians, although they were supposed to put all they received into the joint account. Here we see at once in clear and sharp focus the moral split or sin in human character. They went part of the way in their commitment but not all of the way. They gave a part but not all. They represent the archetype or model of sin in all of us. Sin indeed is our human condition.

The second observation regarding sin is that it is not only our human condition but it is also our human perplexity, for this state in which we all live is baffling and confusing and raises questions which almost defy explanation.

One question that we find almost impossible to answer is, "Why bother with goodness?" Wouldn't it be easier to lie, cheat, deceive, pretend, offend, steal, or sleep every Sunday morning than to make an effort to do the opposite? Look at Ananias and Sapphira. They did not have to join the fellowship of Christians that were striving to live a life of moral and ethical excellence. They evidently were getting along perfectly all right. They seemed to have an adequate income and material wealth. They owned property and only persons of means in those days owned a piece of land. Yet, they joined up with those poor, and in many ways poverty stricken people called Christians. Why?

A second confusing question that comes to mind when we consider the implications of sin is this: Why does this condition cause persons to become deceptive, to pretend to be what they are not? We know how often we deceive ourselves. Someone will ask us, perhaps to help them collect contributions for the heart fund or the cancer fund. We say that we are not able because we are much too busy, yet we have plenty of time to spend several hours a day watching television programs. What is so sad is not that we spend time watching television instead of helping solicit funds for worthy causes but we actually trick ourselves into thinking that we *are* too busy to help out occasionally with a worthwhile project. We say one thing but we actually mean something else. Why this effort to fool ourselves?

Then, too, there is that awful temptation to make ourselves appear to be something that we are not in the eyes of others.

Someone told me recently of a family, not in Fairfax, not even in Virginia, who always enjoyed smoking and having drinks before dinner but who belonged to a church that theoretically opposed such practices. This family, I was told, has a false top to their dining room table so that if anyone comes to see them from the church, particularly the minister, when they are living it up, they can throw their *wrongness* into the false drawer and appear to be the picture of piety. This of course, is an exaggerated incident, but like the exaggerated incident of Ananias and Sapphira, why do we want to pretend to be what we are not? Ananias and Sapphira were not required to become a part of the Christian community. Even if they became members there did not appear to be any requirement to sell their property. But they chose to sell their property, and when they did, they lied about the amount of the sale and tried to deceive Peter and the other members of the community. A strange and perplexing situation!

A third question, and surely not the last one either but all we will have time to ask, is why can we not recognize our inconsistent behavior? But we are so frequently shocked, aren't we? Many times when we are reminded that we are pretending we say "That can't be me! I can hardly believe it." When David was told of a rich man who had stolen the property of a poor man, he wanted to arrest the man and put him to death. But when Nathan, the prophet, sternly confronted him with the rebuke, *"Thou art the man!"* David could hardly believe what he heard. And when Ananias and Sapphira were confronted with their deception, they were so shocked that they dropped over dead. What a shock it is when we are faced with a *moment of truth* about ourselves. The condition of sin in which we live *is* serious and is not something that we can deny and flippantly, in our blind sophistication, say that it doesn't exist.

The third observation that comes to mind, however, and perhaps more important than any of the others, is the matter of dealing with the split or flaw we find within ourselves. Is there any way out? There may not be any way out, just as there is no way to avoid the fact that we will one day die, but the Christian gospel does offer a way to live with the sin in our lives. There are three suggestions.

The first suggestion is to acknowledge that we are what we are. If we cannot accept the reality that we are capable of most any wrongness that there is in the book, then there is little hope of living with and handling our divided state. We are capable of anything any other person is capable of. Once we are aware that we can stoop to the lowest of temptations, we are on guard to avoid the worst that can happen. I believe Ananias and Sapphira were too brittle, too righteous in their behavior as well as in their deceit, and when confronted with their deception, they could not bear it, they could not face it, and death was the easiest way out. Better to die than to see themselves as deceitful. This is not just a story in the Bible, removed from the harsh facts of living. It is a story of life. Some years ago I knew a woman who appeared outwardly as righteous, honest and noble. It was discovered, however, she had embezzled a large sum of money from the company for whom she worked. When confronted with the misdemeanor, she became violently ill and could not see anyone for months. Not until a friend paid off her debt and she moved to a new location did she have the capacity to face life again. An honest acceptance of what we are capable of becoming can help us to avoid wrongdoing when it appears.

A second suggestion is to accept the forgiveness that is available to us when we do go too far. Ananias and Sapphira would not have been ostracized had they acknowledged their moral weakness. Peter, I am sure, was much too aware of how he had earlier denied his Lord when questioned about his relationship to Jesus not to allow Ananias and his wife to be restored to good standing in the fellowship. God knows our human predicament, for this is the way, in his divine wisdom that he made us. When evil gets the upper hand and lays us low, we do not have to wallow in the mud. We know that we can be forgiven and we can start all over again.

A third suggestion is to use every opportunity to participate in the goodness of life. It isn't enough to confess our sins and to avoid the temptation of wrong doing. There is also the possibility and the opportunity to practice the virtues and the graces given to us in our Christian faith. To practice telling the truth weakens the desire to tell a falsehood. To practice *openness* with others leads to a likeness for others. To be generous produces generosity. To forget one's self occasionally develops a fondness for selflessness. Paul summed it up rather well when he wrote:

> *8 Finally, brethren, whatever is true, whatever is honorable, whatever is just, whatever is pure, whatever is lovely, whatever is gracious, if there is any excellence, if there is anything worthy of praise, think about these things.*
> *9 What you have learned and received and heard and seen in me, do; and the God of peace will be with you. (Philippians 4:8-9)*

When we take these words seriously, we take sin seriously, for we know that what we need to heal our divided selves is God himself.

22

DISCERNING THE SIGNS OF THE TIMES

Matthew 16b You know how to interpret the appearance of the sky, but you cannot interpret the signs of the times.

Man seems to possess more skill in understanding the physical world than the realm in which he lives as a human being. We find it far easier to orbit the earth or to put a rocket on the moon than we do to live at peace with one another. Jesus also came to this conclusion as he observed the human scene in his generation. In one of his numerous pronouncements concerning the short-sightedness of the religious leaders of his people, he said, *"You know how to interpret the appearance of the sky, but you cannot interpret the signs of the times."* They had little difficulty, said Jesus, in forecasting rain or a storm, but they were unable to comprehend the qualities and structures of human relationships. They were wise concerning the structure and relationships of things but ignorant regarding matters of the human spirit. How amazing that mankind has progressed so little since the times of Jesus! We still are better in understanding the behavior of atoms than we are in living together as human beings.

Surely, not one of us wants to be ignorant concerning anything. We want to live at our best in our spiritual life. Let us, then, consider a few suggestions on how we can improve our skills to understand and to deal with that realm of life with which religion is most vitally concerned.

Obviously, the first suggestion is to develop the habit of asking *why?* concerning behavior that we ordinarily take for granted. A rabbit in a cartoon that I remember seeing at the movies some years ago, expressed the idea I have in mind. When this rabbit who talked came upon a strange situation, he would ask, "What's cookin', Doc?" The idea could hardly be expressed more succinctly.

Perhaps, one of the reasons the men of science have made such tremendous strides in interpreting and harnessing the forces of nature is that they have not been afraid to ask, *why?* For years, women died at childbirth more frequently than seemed necessary. Men began to ask *why?* This questioning continued. Dedicated men of research looked long and hard in microscopes, trying to find a cause, a reason. Then, one day, the answer came. Louis Pasteur, in the middle of the 19th century, discovered that living forms or organisms are in the air, settle on objects, spawn and grow, and are fatal to life if they are not controlled and killed. Pasteur's discovery caused the field of practicing medicine to clean and sterilize its instruments and other objects with which it worked and a new day for women and all mankind was ushered in because men dared to ask *why?*

Obviously, a value of religion is to preserve the best of tradition and religion does a fairly good job at this point. Yet, I also believe religion has an obligation to explore and discover better ways to assist man to live in harmony with himself and his society. Religion has not kept pace with the business of exploration. Religion has been slow to ask *why?* Instead religion in a sense has wanted to preserve and hold on to beliefs and ancient ways of doing things, and has discouraged questions and honest inquiry. Traditional beliefs and practices are indeed, valuable if they are maintained for good reasons; but if they are held onto merely because they are old and honorable, without meaning or purpose, then they are detrimental to life and creative expression. For religion to bring freshness and vitality to human life and to make an impression upon the problems of human life, the question *why?* seems essential. Questions should be encouraged, not discouraged, and no question should ever be too insignificant, too impertinent, too heretical for the man of religious faith to consider or ponder or discuss. My prayer for the church is that it can become a laboratory of spiritual inquiry in which the serious and perplexing problems of human life can be studied so that we can discern the signs of the times.

Moreover, we can draw help in interpreting the meaning of human events by making certain, where possible, that these events are meaningful to us. To my knowledge, there is no way of learning anything about any subject unless one immerses himself in the subject and becomes involved personally within it. No boy can ever learn to play baseball by reading a book of instructions or listening to a coach. Knowing the theory of the game is essential; let no one deny that. But that theory has to be translated into action on the ball diamond by the boy himself before he ever learns the game.

Every once in a while I hear someone say, "I don't believe in Christianity. It doesn't make sense." I suspect that the problem with such a statement is that Christianity for such a person is a theory or a set of intellectual beliefs about Christianity. But Christianity, although it makes certain theoretical assumptions concerning the world and the relationship of man to his world, is not basically a set of theoretical propositions at all. Christianity, at its deeper levels, is a way of life, and if a person is going to take Christianity seriously and make an effort to understand it, he must immerse himself in this way of life, become involved personally, and play the game. Knowing about Christianity is not enough for one to understand it. One discerns it, is able to comprehend the heights and depths of its proclamations, by becoming a part of it. Peter became the Rock, not by writing a theoretical formulation concerning his Lord, but by following Christ. We know Christ by participating in the life he taught and lived.

Perhaps it would do all of us good if we took time out to express in words what events in life have meant the most to us. Surely, we would write of those events or occasions in which we have been most deeply and intimately involved. It would not be something we have read or seen or heard, but it would be an experience we had actually lived. For example, there is the writer of the gospel of John. We do not actually know for certain who this man was, but we know what Christ meant to him, for his gospels are a testimony to the living presence of Christ in his life. Or read in the sixth chapter of Romans what baptism meant to Paul. He called it an experience of dying and being buried with Christ and being raised with him in newness of life. Baptism was a significant experience for Paul, for it symbolized exactly his own personal experience in relationship to Christ. It is no wonder Paul could say, *"I know in whom I believe."*

But once more we can capture the meaning of events not only by asking *why?* and by sharing personally in the occasions, but also by learning to evaluate each event not in terms of our reactions to similar events in the past but in light of present conditions and circumstances. We find it a real problem not to think of every experience as being like every other similar experience. A girl goes to a party and doesn't have a good time; so she refuses to go to any other party, for she fears the others will be like the first. Her vision of parties becomes distorted and she finds it difficult to make a wise judgment concerning parties because of the discomfort and unhappiness connected with the first party. How easy it is for our lives to become crippled and thwarted, impoverished and debilitated, because we insist on dragging the excess baggage of previous experiences into every other experience that is similar to the one where we acquired the baggage.

Sometimes, I hear people say, "I don't go to church because my father and mother made me go when I was young and I vowed when I could make my own decisions, I would never go to church." I used to hear this in a similar vein when I was in the Army from graduates of the United States Military Academy at West Point. Many officers who were close friends of mine and who would not attend chapel would often say to me, "Chaplain, I hope you understand why I do not attend your services. I was made to go every Sunday while I was a cadet at West Point and I decided that when I got out of the Academy, I would never go to church services again." Now, such an attitude is understandable. On the other hand, it seems unfortunate that persons must continually go through life determining their actions and feeling by something that happened years ago and which have no direct relationship to the present.

Are you wrestling with a problem that seems unreasonable and illogical, causing you unhappiness and mental pain that you wished you didn't have but somehow you can't throw it off? Perhaps this thing that you are stuck with and can't throw off manifests itself in disliking certain types of people, in disliking the preacher and the church, in not getting along with your wife or with your husband, in feeling uncomfortable with particular types of people, in disliking to go certain places, or eating certain kinds of food. It may be that these unreasonable feelings that haunt you and cause you to distort events and persons from what they actually are, are caused by reactions to unpleasant experiences that occurred long ago but are still with you to cause you and others who are close to you misery and discomfort. How much more we would get out of life and how much better our world of relationships would be if our views and reactions to events were free of impurities and imperfections that have their roots in the pains of yesterday.

Well when we consider the foibles and perplexities of human personality and the complications of human relationships, it is no wonder that progress in understanding and dealing with human behavior is so far behind the advances in the physical world. The situation is more acute because the problem lies not in some organic cell or in some material object but the problem lies within us; and until we come to grips with ourselves and recognize that it is us who need salvation, we shall wander hopelessly and aimlessly, seeking rest and peace but finding none. Christ still points the way here as in all ways and only when mankind recognizes his supremacy is there hope for any of us, for he is the way, the truth and the life. He is this truth because he places the problem where it properly belongs – within our hearts and spirits. Hear him say, *"Truly, truly, I say to you, unless one is born anew, he cannot see the kingdom of God."*

23

WHAT OUR GIVING THROUGH THE CHURCH MEANS

Matthew 5:15,16

15 Nor do men light a lamp and put it under a bushel,
but on a stand, and it gives light to all in the house.
16 Let your light so shine before men, that they may see your
good works and give glory to your Father who is in heaven.

Callers will be visiting today to obtain our financial commitment for the church year beginning July 1st. Such an occasion causes certain reactions.

Some may become resentful because they are asked to make a definite commitment for the support of the Church. They say they would rather give when the need arises or when they feel like it. Others feel it is much too commercial to establish a budget and ask people to support it systematically. That is the way a business firm goes about its affairs and the church ought not operate as a business. Others dislike to be asked because they feel uncomfortable. They feel they are unable to give as much as they would like to contribute. To be asked to make a pledge therefore makes them feel embarrassed. Others are irritated when callers come. They know they are spending more than they ought to spend for homes, cars, furniture, and various types of pleasure and there is none or little left over for the church. So they feel guilty and the guilt causes them to become angry at themselves. The anger at self is projected on the commitment system or commitment caller, so they are irritated. The spiritually healthy person, however, feels differently about his commitment. Instead of feeling resentment, uncomfortable, guilty, or irritated, he welcomes an opportunity to support the church and its program. Because he welcomes such an opportunity does not mean he is wealthy and can give any amount the church needs or that he doesn't have financial obligations, or that he is able to give all he would like to give.

He is receptive to making a commitment to the church because the church and its program are part of his life, such as purchasing a house, buying groceries, educating his children, buying clothes, and other necessary items. The spiritually healthy person includes the support of his church in his budget as he does other items because he believes in it and wants to share in its activities.

There is nothing mystical or unusual about such an approach. Nor is there a need to become overly pious or emotionally wrought over the matter, for to him the church is as important and essential to his way of life as all the other activities he believes in and he knows he cannot exist unless he supports it.

When a person has this approach to his church what does it mean to him to support the church? He has a sense that he is a light that gives light to the whole house. It is a way of expressing his concern for others.

Not one of us can do everything he or she would like to do to show interest in the lives of others. Most of us have other involvements, like a job to take care of - either in the home or outside the home. Most jobs today are demanding and require a considerable amount of our time if the job is to be done well. We have our children to raise. Mothers with small children have to take care of them. This is their first job – everything else is secondary. She might want to do more in the church than she does. She may want to help persons who are in need of help. But she cannot because she is needed by her children.

The father also is needed by his children – they need to be played with, taught things – given attention. He may want to help out more in civic and church activities but a wise father knows where his first responsibility lies.

There are people who have selected helping others in need as a way of life. There are social and welfare workers. There are directors and managers of homes for orphans and the elderly. There are doctors and nurses. There are teachers in churches, in schools and in colleges. There are missionaries who go to foreign countries to give education and spiritual enrichment to impoverished people. There are ministers who preach, teach and counsel for the welfare of others.

Although a church member who is serious about his faith perhaps would like to do all of these and many other welfare activities for others, he knows he is personally unable. He still knows these activities are important. He is concerned about them so he shows his interest and his concern by giving a part of his income to the church so that others who are trained and skilled can do the work for him.

Here are two examples: Recently I had a university professor call me about a serious problem between himself and one of his older children. He said, "May I come to talk to you?" We have met several times and things seem to be better. Again, two young people came, also from another part of the city, about a personal difficulty they are having and we have started talking, trying to work out life in a better way for them.

Now when I see these people, I see them in your name, for it is your support that makes it possible for this service to be performed. In a way, you are the ones who are helping them, for I as your minister, would be unable to see them if it were not for your gifts that make this church and counseling ministry possible.

The mature Christian understands the giving and sharing process and he welcomes the opportunity to share in it. He also contributes to the church because he realizes it keeps alive the Christian interpretation of life.

The Church performs acts of charity – helps orphans, older people, the impoverished, the hungry and the ill fed. The Church stands for social justice – it believes in equal opportunities for all people and strives to urge its people to be fair in their economic life.

The Church is interested in removing illiteracy. It sends missionaries to teach people in third world countries to read, write, and become informed about the world in which they live. It also believes in helping people to learn a trade, a skill, or a profession. It also comforts the lonely, the fearful, and the discouraged. It brings hope to the dying and strength to the bereaved.

But somehow the heart of the mission of the church is to bring to life and to people a way of believing about the world and a way of living in the world that has been given to us through Jesus Christ, who has told us what reality is all about.

Christ said man does not live without bread and bread is important but *"Man shall not live by bread alone, but by every word that proceeds from the mouth of God."*

The world is made by a God who cares and a God who can be called Father.

We are creatures with a spiritual heritage and a spiritual destiny and we are the children of God. Life consists in not what we get but by what we live. We grow not by sight but by faith. We discover the pearl of great price, true deep personal satisfaction not by trying to find prestige, popularity, power, friendship, but by losing ourselves, investing ourselves in causes that command our respect and our admiration.

These are salient and sound interpretations that cause life to become rich and buoyant. These are words of salvation. When we support the church in our budget we cause a hopeful light to shine in the world.

Then, let it be said, that the wise Christian who believes in the church supports its program to keep his own spiritual vitality alive. Christian faith can burn low and die out in a person's life as easily as a fire can go out if it is not given fuel to burn. The fuel of Christian faith is to become actively involved in what the church is attempting to do in the world.

Belief is not enough. It must be accompanied by personal action and involvement. No baseball player ever became proficient at the game by sitting on the sidelines and allowing another person to field the ball, go to bat, and do the running for him. He is only competent as he does these activities himself. The same is true for Christian faith. We don't talk *Christianity*, we don't watch faith, we don't study faith – we live faith.

It is not hard to understand why people give it up. It is usually because they have watched it but have not participated in it. We may grow tired and discouraged with all it sometimes asks of us but there is no way to get it but to live it. Deep involvement is the only way anything of any importance is ever accomplished. We may think there is a simpler, less demanding way, but it seems that there isn't. Our lives never receive the blessings of our faith unless we ourselves are there actively engaged and living out our faith. We can be there ourselves in whatever the church does by our support of its mission.

These are the reasons then that the wholesome man or woman actively supports the church:

1. It is a way of expressing concern for others.
2. It keeps alive the Christian interpretation of life.
3. It keeps alive one's own religious vitality and faith.

My prayer for you is that when you make your commitment to the church this coming year you may make it as the spiritually healthy person. Then will come to pass that ancient saying of Jesus,

"You are the light of the world. A city that is set on a hill cannot be hid. Nor do men light a candle and put it under a bushel, but on a stand, and it gives light to all the house. Let your light so shine before men, that they see your good works and give glory to your Father who is in heaven."

Sermon

24

ON REMEMBERING THE DEAD

Memorial Day

Matthew 8:22 But Jesus said to him,"Follow me,
and leave the dead to bury their own dead."

In 1945 when I was Post Chaplain on the small island of Attu in the Aleutian Islands, during those final months when World War II was drawing to a close, my Commanding General called me on the telephone in the middle of May to come to his office to discuss plans for Memorial Day which would arrive in a few weeks. Several members of the staff and I met with the general that afternoon and roughly sketched our plan. Among other events, we decided to decorate the graves of men who had been killed on the island during the battle that recaptured the island from the Japanese in 1943. We had two cemeteries on the island – one large cemetery near our main encampment and another on a distant, desolate part of the island that was almost impossible to reach and which contained only a dozen or so graves. I had suggested we not include the isolated cemetery in our program, but only the main one where most of our troops were billeted. I was overruled, however, by the Commanding General himself. After the main program was held at the large cemetery, the General, the Catholic Chaplain, the Jewish Chaplain, and I drove by jeeps to the small cemetery as far as we could drive. Then we walked about two miles over rough terrain and finally came to the tiny plot of white wooden crosses and two stars of David badly stained and marred by the terrible weather of the Bering Sea, and still covered partially by the winter snows. We attached a flag to each marker and then we bowed as each chaplain said appropriate prayers for the dead.

On the way back to headquarters, I remember confessing to the Commanding General. "I am glad you insisted we visit this cemetery today. I was wrong in thinking it was unnecessary." He was a stern but kind man and I remember his words. "I realize Chaplain, how you felt. It does seem unnecessary, but when you have lived as long as I have – I was only 29 then – you will realize how important it is to remember the dead." I've thought of these words many times since that May 30th in 1945, and have tried to capture in my mind their meaning; so this morning, I would like to share with you some of the thoughts that I have developed over the years concerning the significance of remembering the dead.

One thought that seems clear to me is that we should remember the dead with dignity and reverence. When death comes to a person who is close to us and is one we love there is very little anyone can say or do to assuage the grief and sorrow. It seems to me, however, that though we seem helpless and inadequate, we can do everything possible to surround the occasion with dignity and sacredness.

One quality it seems to me that is essential in dignifying any event is simplicity. Death is no time for gaudy ceremonies and parades. One of the underlying reasons, I feel, why I recall so vividly the scene I related to you on Attu Island at the remote cemetery was the simplicity of the occasion. No bands played, no gaudy display of formal dress and pageantry but only a few people, dressed in plain military work clothes, said simple prayers and quietly walked away.

Is it not true that the deepest and most lasting qualities of life are given to us in plain and simple dress? What hymn is best loved at Christmas – *Silent Night, Holy Night* – the words and music are uncomplicated, yet they catch the depth and meaning of the event. What psalm in the Bible is best known – the 23rd Psalm! Why have so many remarked that they enjoy this little chapel we come to each Sunday? - because, they say, it has an air of reverence yet it is not ornate. (This sermon was preached in the old house on the Fairfax Christian Church property.)

Surely, then, we remember our dead best and honor them most in the undertones of simplicity. But we are really up against it at this point, for there are those who insist that funeral services should be ostentatious and gaudy with expensive caskets, an over abundance of flowers, and an insistence on large and costly markers. If you dare to object, you are sometimes given the retort; don't you want to remember your loved one properly? You surely want only the best for one who is so important to you.

I am glad to see of late that there has been a change in public opinion concerning the ridiculous waste and expense connected with funerals. I think Jessica Mitford's book, *The American Way of Death* was somewhat overdrawn, but the book, I think had positive value. It has made us aware of what a funeral ought to be – a reverent expression of respect for the dead and an opportunity for persons to express grief and sorrow, done in simple taste and dignity.

Dr. Elton Trueblood makes this suggestion. He believes that when death occurs, only the family and a few close friends should accompany the dead as soon as possible to the place of burial, where an appropriate prayer from Holy Scripture is read such as the 23rd or 46th Psalm, then a brief prayer, reverent silence without intrusion of any words. There would be no curious onlookers. Then a few days afterwards notices would be made of the death and a memorial service held at the church or home of the deceased. Such a procedure he feels would dignify and honor the dead in reverence and sincerity and remove the stigma of gaudiness and pomp. Perhaps he has something here that ought to be carefully considered.

The second thought concerning remembering the dead that has occurred to me over the years is that the death should remain in the context of Christian faith.

I simply deplore the habit we have gotten ourselves into today of having funeral services in a funeral parlor or a funeral home. Death is preeminently an experience that is connected to the church and to Christian faith. Wouldn't it seem strange to have a baptismal service in some sort of a place that was reserved exclusively for baptizing people rather than the church? Wouldn't it seem odd to have a communion service in some building other than a church? You see, what I am saying, is that there are some events and experiences in life that are a part of our Christian faith and heritage and when these events are taken out of context they become unrelated to faith. Death and all events connected with it center in faith and we do ourselves harm when we sever the connection. What more suitable place for anyone of us to be remembered is there than in the place where people have worshipped and prayed through the years with their family and friends?

Have you ever noticed how gloomy a funeral parlor is? The whole affair is about as morbid as you can find anywhere. Yet, when you go to a a magnificent church such as Westminster Abbey in London or the Washington Cathedral, you may walk over a concrete marker in the floor telling you that a certain person is buried there – but you do not feel gloom. It seems natural and right. What is the difference? I think the difference is that in a funeral parlor you have a commercial institution whose business is embalming and burying people, detached, however, from the the church that surrounds death with hope and faith. In a church, however, where people are buried, you find children laughing and cheerful, you have the symbols that surround life with hope eternal, you have a sanctuary that gives stability and security to people, you have an edifice that places death in the proper context and it says to you in stirring words *the Lord is the strength of my life – of whom shall I be afraid? (Psalm 27:1)* "*They that wait upon the Lord shall renew their strength: they shall mount up with wings as eagles; they shall run and not be weary; and they shall walk and not faint.*"*(Isaiah 40:31)*

Surely one of the critical mistakes of the church has been to allow commercial enterprises to take over the cemetery. There is perhaps nothing that ought to be more associated with the church than the place where its people are buried. To see the graves and the markers as we come to church each Sunday reminds us, the present generation, of our connection with the past. Furthermore, it takes away the mystery of death, places it in the proper context, and keeps alive within us the idea that we are mortal, but that our hope and eternal destiny is with God.

But this brings me to say, then, that when we remember the dead, we remember them best, not by trying to capture the past, but by living in the present and for the future. Death is certainly inevitable for all of us. A hundred years from now not one of us is likely to be alive in this world and hardly anyone of us will be remembered by those then living. This is one of those stark realities life presents to us. Well, we may not be able to do anything about our death, but we can do something about the life we are now living. That is within our power - either to live it well or to live it feebly.

One way we can live it well is to keep faith with the hundreds of service men whose memory we honor today, Memorial Day, by trying to keep alive every opportunity for peace that is available.

That is accomplished in two ways. One way is to keep our defense forces modern and strong. At this point, we cannot be lax. Any letdown in superiority is fatal. It is costly and wasteful; but I see no other way by which to insure safety for ourselves and the other nations of the world who are depending on us.

But a steel ring is not enough. We must also seek ways to settle our disagreements by ways other than armed conflict. War is always an acknowledgement of an inability of a people to apply intelligence to an argument. Therefore, we must do everything possible to encourage our government, not only to maintain a strong and active military force, but to stay at the job of discovering peaceful means to our differences. Peace is a two-pronged attack – preparedness on the one hand and prevention on the other.

It seems futile, I know, at times to speak of seeking peaceful solutions to international problems but the criticality of a problem is no reason not to attack it and try to solve it. A Christian has no choice but to stay at the job. Hope of accomplishment is not the final concern of the Christian. His first and last concern is to be faithful and to do his duty. Whether the mission is ever attained is not his concern.

The spirit of Madame Curie at 84 and her husband seems the right note on which to end. They had worked for many months to separate radium from pitch. After the 387th experiment Monsieur Curie gives up and exclaims, "It can't be done. It can't be done. Maybe in a hundred years it can be done but it can never be done in our lifetime." His wife confronts him sternly, and replies, "If it takes a hundred years it will be a pity, but I can do no other than to work for it so long as I have life in my body."

Jesus listened to the young man who wanted to be his disciple but wanted first of all to go bury his father. But Jesus confronted him sternly — *"Leave the dead to bury their own dead, but you follow me."* What has happened is of small consequence in the grand scheme of things. We cannot change the past or alter it in any way. We are saddened by those who have died and are no longer with us, both our loved ones and our war dead. Yet, we cannot change or alter what has happened. What has occurred is over and done with. But we can honor our dead by making up our minds to do something positive and constructive about life now. What we can do, as he said to the young man, is for each one of us to strive faithfully and earnestly to make the way of Christ a living force in this life we now inhabit.

25

THE WISDOM OF CHILDREN

Matthew 18:3 Truly, I say to you, unless you turn and become like children, you will never enter the kingdom of heaven.

In our culture, we place great value on children. There is happiness when a child is born into our homes. We take extra care to see to it that our children have the best that we can provide for them. We want them to be exposed to religious and spiritual values so we go through all kinds of trouble to get them to church or Sunday school when it would really be much more comfortable and pleasant to stay in bed or loaf around the house on Sunday morning. Young couples have been known never to attend church; however, when children come into their houses, it isn't very long until you see these parents participating in the activities of the church with their children. These parents may not feel the need for church for themselves but they feel the need for their children. These and other concerns of parents for their children cause us to be aware of how very much parents want the best for their children.

All cultures in all ages have not given and do not give the same importance to children that we do. In Roman culture in the age when Jesus lived, children were tolerated but hardly valued. They were frequently sold into slavery by parents to pay off debts, misused by adults, perverted for sexual gratification, and were done away with if they did not suit the whims of parents. Ancient writings discovered by archeologists tell us that it was evidently a familiar practice for a husband when starting on a distant journey to leave instructions with a pregnant wife for her to kill the child if it were deformed or a girl.

The Jewish people, however, who lived in this kind of pagan world, held children in esteem. The rabbis praised kindness to orphans and waifs and Jewish parents welcomed the birth of children. We find, however, that Jesus elevated children to a level even beyond that of parents and the rabbis. Jesus, not only blessed, gave attention to children, and insisted that they should not be abused, but he went further. Jesus said that adults could learn from children those precepts that would make it possible for a person to gain entrance into the kingdom of heaven, or in that condition of life that enables a person to live at his best. Here is the way he said it, *"Truly, I say to you, unless you turn and become like children, you will never enter the kingdom of heaven."*

This is a strange saying. We believe that a child should listen to his elders, but here Jesus, the Lord of life, turns the situation the other way around. He tells those of us who are adults to look to children if we want to share in life what is blessed by God, the Reality which contains the best that life holds in store for us. But how can we emulate children? They are uninformed, helpless, forgetful, careless, selfish, and irresponsible. Is Jesus suggesting that the kingdom of heaven is for the childish person? Or did Jesus observe a deeper quality of the spirit in children that all persons need in order to find the higher life? What is the deeper wisdom that Jesus saw in children that caused him to say, *"Truly, I say to you, unless you turn and become like children, you will never enter the kingdom of heaven"*?

Surely, for one thing, Jesus was impressed with the curious, inquiring, questioning spirit of children. Anyone who has made even a casual observation of little children recognizes their almost insatiable thirst to look, to know, to discover, and to understand. They will take anything apart. They will wander far away from home. They will explore caves and sewers. They will ask endless questions without fear of being considered stupid. They will listen all day to a good story. How proud the child is when he learns to spell a word, to draw a picture, to have his first school book, to hear wonders explained to him. At least, this is the behavior of children if they are not made afraid by over-protective or over-controlling adults, not scolded or disciplined for expressing natural interest and instincts, not made to feel stupid because they do not know, not told to shut up because they are anxious to know, and are not made to learn before they want to learn. Learning seems to be the natural desire of children. If they do not have this quality, it is probably because they have been thwarted by adults who mean well but who are too demanding or too rigid in their treatment of the child or who do not provide properly for his physical and emotional needs. Also, children can be crippled by sickness or birth defects. Yet, even in spite of hardships, it is almost impossible to prevent this enquiring spirit of the child from expressing itself.

It is this thirst for adventure that keeps the person alive, alert, and radiant. We need food and drink to sustain the body. We need warmth and shelter to protect the body. We need human affections and emotional warmth to give the self a sense of safety and well-being. But these are not enough. *"Man does not live by bread alone."* He also requires a searching mind, an inquiring spirit, and a sense of adventure to keep a sparkle in his eye. These things give him the zest that enables him to greet each new day with the same enthusiasm at fifty that he enjoyed at five. Notice persons who are not engaged in adventurous living. They seem dull, lifeless, and listless. There is a certain heaviness or gloom about life. The body may be alive but the spirit is deadened. Someone has said that "millions now living will never die." This is true, for they are already dead, dead from a lack of interest in the wonder of life that is all about them.

Why is it we do not want to continue our interest or curiosity in what is going on about us and are sometimes more interested in giving up and sitting it out until death finally comes? Basically, the course lies in our refusal to give up ourselves and our concern in ourselves. We want today what we had yesterday — whether it is old friends, relatives, loved ones, wealth, a job, youth, or something else we cherished. Or we may want what we have never had or probably may never have — marriage, fame, admirers, or wealth. Although we know that these old memories or hoped for dreams may never come to pass, we still hold on and falsely believe they may come to pass. So we live in misery and self-pity, while life passes us by when there are so many other things that are available to us that can arouse us, and that give zest to living. It isn't always a matter of money. It is a matter of becoming as a little child in spirit and sometimes starting all over again to explore, to discover, to learn, to find new ways to make one's life rich and buoyant. I know one lady who graduated from college at 85, another woman who became an authority on Shakespeare at 75, and introduced others her own age to his plays, and there is the man with both legs off who became an expert on old coins. This is becoming as a little child. This is entering the kingdom of heaven.

Next, Jesus evidently saw in children their propensity to enjoy to the fullest what they were doing at the moment. Yesterday I noticed one of our neighbor children bouncing a tennis ball against the outside wall of her house. All by herself, she intensely threw the ball, caught it, and then threw it again. She was not concerned whether or not anyone was watching her. She was not interested in applause or approval. She had recently learned to catch a ball and now she was enjoying the thrill of doing a thing at the moment. She wasn't thinking now when I finish bouncing this ball, I will read a book, sew, play dolls, or do something else. Every ounce of her attention, energy, and concentration was centered on the activity in which she was engaged. Her satisfaction was in the thing she was doing at the moment. And such is the behavior of children at play.

It is wisdom to look ahead and plan for the future but it is also wisdom to realize that life provides us with some of its richest satisfactions when we can appreciate and enjoy the present moment. So many of us somehow along the way, forget to find joy in what we are doing now, because we are too anxious to get through the present thinking that somehow the better and more enjoyable life is somewhere out there in the future.

Parents often think that when their children are older life will be easier so they miss the joys of the present. Students trick themselves into believing that if they can get through school, then they can really live and they miss the present opportunities and fun of college days. Some men long for the day of retirement, and as a result, never get any real satisfaction out of the work they are doing now. I have seen men during an overseas assignment have their minds so set on getting the thing over and living only to get back home that they did their jobs properly, were miserable inside, and never gave themselves the chance to profit from the job they were doing or to appreciate the sights and the people of the country where they were living. How easy it is to miss so much now because we are too anxious about tomorrow. We somehow think that things will be better tomorrow; so, we miss finding satisfactions now, but we often wake up to the realization that whatever life has to offer, it is now, and unless we can find contentment now, there will be nothing better tomorrow. Much of the goodness of life can pass us by if we do not learn the contentment of the child in finding joy in what we are doing at the moment.

Then too, I think Jesus saw in the child the wisdom that is derived from using one's imagination. Let us play like we are soldiers. Let us play Batman. Let us play house. Let us play like we are riding horses. I'll never forget walking into the living room one day when my son was small. He had his toy soldiers, cowboys, and Indians scattered over the rug. He was sitting quietly over in one corner. I started to say something to him. He said, "Don't make any noise, Dad, they have had a hard day fighting. Now they are asleep. You might wake them up." Play is to the child what work is to the adult and the child finds in his imagination the resources to make his play colorful and always enjoyable.

It is that quality that makes possible the wonderful world of make-believe that adds enrichment to our lives as adults. We do not use imagination in the same way as children, for that would cause us to pretend. Nevertheless, it is imagination that lifts us from the world of numbers, formulas, and quantification and enables us to see beyond the ordinary, the obvious, and the commonplace. Imagination is the life of the discoverer, the inventor, the innovator, the creative mind; and business and scientific research are not so much interested in people who can add and subtract numbers - machines can do that — but they are interested in the person who has a new idea, a fresh approach, an active fertile imagination, for these are persons who can see what others do not see and who will dare what others are too timid even to think.

What kills the spirit is following the same old patterns, walking the same old tracks, doing the same old things, thinking the same old thoughts. Jesus had to break out of the strait jacket of faith which he inherited. He dared to imagine a faith that gave abundance to living, not gloom. Beethoven had to develop a new system of notes to play the music he heard in the depths of his imagination when he became deaf. Every new discovery has come about because someone dared to depart from old pathways and break the bonds of tradition.

One of the real dangers of our age is that we are apt to minimize the role that the human spirit plays in the great enterprise of life. We are in danger of shackling the spirit, dwarfing the imagination, minimizing the qualities of faith, hope and love. We need to recognize the wisdom of Jesus who reminded us of the wisdom of children, *"Truly, I say to you, unless you turn and become like little children you will never enter the kingdom of heaven"*.

26

A WAY TO THINK ABOUT THE HOLY SPIRIT

Pentecost

Acts 2:1-11
1 When the day of Pentecost had come,
they were all together in one place.
2 And suddenly a sound came from heaven like the rush of
a mighty wind, and it filled all the house where they were sitting.
3 And there appeared to them tongues as of fire, distributed
and resting on each one of them.
4 And they were all filled with the Holy Spirit and began to
speak in other tongues, as the Spirit gave them utterance.
5 Now there were dwelling in Jerusalem Jews, devout men
from every nation under heaven.
6 And at this sound the multitude came together, and they
were bewildered, because each one heard them
speaking in his own language.
7 And they were amazed and wondered, saying, "Are not
all these who are speaking Galileans?
8 And how is it that we hear, each of us in his own native language?

9 Par'thians and Medes and E'lamites and residents of
Mesopota'mia, Judea and Cappado'cia, Pontus and Asia,
10 Phryg'ia and Pamphyl'ia, Egypt and the parts of Libya belonging to
Cyre'ne, and visitors from Rome, both Jews and proselytes,
11 Cretans and Arabians, we hear them telling in
our own tongues the mighty works of God."

When we talk about divine properties, we are indeed treading on shaky ground, for we are mortals and what mortal is wise enough to comprehend the Mind or Spirit or Force that has made the universe and everything in it and holds the world in the palm of his hand? The writer of Job puts it well when he has God say to Job, who dared to question the judgment of God – *Job 38:1-7*

1 Then the LORD answered Job out of the whirlwind:
2 "Who is this that darkens counsel by words without knowledge?
3 Gird up your loins like a man,
I will question you, and you shall declare to me.
4 "Where were you when I laid the foundation of the earth?
Tell me, if you have understanding.
5 Who determined its measurements -- surely you know!
Or who stretched the line upon it?
6 On what were its bases sunk,
or who laid its cornerstone,
7 when the morning stars sang together,
and all the sons of God shouted for joy?

Indeed no man possesses the wisdom to deal adequately with these questions, for these are matters whose answers belong only to the Almighty.

Yet, throughout the long annals of history, mankind has made an earnest effort to understand the mysteries of the divine mind; and out of the constant searching, he has discovered some rather profound insights concerning what he believes the divine nature is like. The Christian, depending largely upon his knowledge of ancient Jewish history, has dared to say that God can be known in three ways. He is the Father or Creator of the universe and all creatures in the universe; He is the Son, his nature made known through Jesus the Christ; and He is Holy Spirit, that creative and vitalizing force of the world, which is observed in men and women of unusual ability, strength or wisdom. These three concepts of God we call the Trinity or the triune nature of God – one in three.

We must say at once that no one has ever actually seen with his eyes this God or looked inside of God and saw these three forces at work as one would look inside a room and see desks, chairs, tables, and rugs. What we do see are certain forces at work – we observe nature, we see the integrity and strength of the life of Jesus, we have felt love and power and strength. From these observations, we then infer that this is what God looks like.

This way of arriving at certain assumptions concerning God is exactly the way a scientist such as Sigmund Freud, for example, came to certain beliefs concerning the structure of human personality. In his clinical experience with patients suffering from emotional hysteria, he noticed three forces at work. He saw people driven by a desire for pleasure, by passions of anger, jealousy, and hate, by energies to destroy whatever got in the way of their own personal, self-centered interests and to these drives he gave the name *id*. Next, he saw that persons were able to control these drives because of the requirements of society and the realities of life and to this stability force of reality principle that controlled the id, he gave the name *ego*. The other component of personality, those moral demands that come from parents and other authority persons, he gave the name *superego*. Freud never opened a mind or a brain and saw these energy principles at work inside a person. He saw these forces or principles in behavior – on the outside so to speak – and so inferred that what he saw on the outside is what went on, on the inside; therefore, he gave the forces names – id, ego, and superego. It was by some such process that men of spiritual wisdom came to make inferences concerning the nature of God. Just as Freud observed that man by his behavior reveals himself and then certain assumptions can be made concerning his behavior, so men of unusual gifts, men of the Bible, whose names are familiar to us observed nature and history in all of its greatness and in all of its mystery and came to the amazing deduction that the unseen Force was revealing himself to them through his acts and they wrote down what they saw and what they felt. This in brief, then, is how we have come to the conclusion that God is known through his nature as Father, as Son, and as Holy Spirit.

Therefore, what we have, then, when we say God the Father, God the Son, God the Holy Spirit, is that we are calling attention to God as he is observed or as he is seen or as he is made manifest, or made known to the mind and imagination of mankind. This is a way of looking at the Trinity.

Perhaps, if we think this way concerning the three natures of God, we will have a clearer understanding of that unusual occurrence that took place after the resurrection of Jesus when the disciples were gathered at Jerusalem. Luke, the writer of the book of Acts, refers to the event as Pentecost which has come to mean fifty days after the resurrection of Jesus and the day the church received the gift of the Holy Spirit. The description is filled with so many unnatural happenings – a sound from heaven like the rush of a mighty wind, the appearance of tongues as of fire, and people speaking in unknown languages that were understood by all. So today we are incapable of understanding what really took place. The only safe conclusion we can draw is that something of unusual and dynamic power and inspiration came upon these few followers of Jesus and afterwards they were changed men. Whatever it was that changed them and gave them the drive to tell the people of the Greco-Roman world about a new life they had discovered, and a new Lord and Savior they had found; they called this power the Holy Spirit, and they believed it was God himself who was working in them, the same God and the same spirit that was so clearly discernible in the life and character of Jesus of Nazareth. It was a power outside and beyond them and this power compelled them, in a sense drove them, if we can believe the record, to share their experience with other people.

Now, the force which gives an individual extra power or unusual insight is attested to again and again by persons today. Not in the same vein, of course, but nevertheless real and powerful, is the extra power an athlete sometimes exhibits in a football game. A young man, for example, who has been playing on the second team, is put in the game during the last few minutes of play when his team is behind. He runs faster than he has ever run before. He weaves and shakes off tacklers nothing like he has ever done in another game, not even in practice. He scores a touchdown and wins the game. His coach says, "Son, you were terrific. What happened? I never saw you play that well before." And sometimes, an answer like this is heard, "I don't know, somewhere, I received a strength that wasn't my own. Something got a hold of me, picked me up, and caused me to run and weave like I had never done before." Is this something like what took place at Pentecost?

Another illustration may help. During the Korean conflict, I had a friend who was a Chief Petty Officer in the Navy who was captured by the North Koreans and Chinese Communists and held prisoner for over 19 months. He suffered as few men had to suffer. He was interrogated time and again but never once broke under the strain. He was made to stand in a narrow hole in the ground, unable to bend or sit, without seeing or talking to anyone, for days at a time, until he had no comprehension of night or day, but yet he came through it all without damage to his mental or emotional system. Somehow, he felt he had something to say about his experiences which he felt would benefit men who might have to undergo similar experiences as well as to the people of America who needed to be knowledgeable of the kind of enemy we face. He had no special training in writing but he wrote one of the most realistic and devotional books I have ever read. The Defense Department was so impressed with the book that it had thousands of copies printed and distributed them to troops around the world. It is not only a book of men under stress and manly strength. It is a book of faith and spiritual courage, the testament of a man who believed in God. When I asked Duane Thorin how he was able to write such a book, he replied quietly and humbly, "I don't know. I only knew I had to write it and something which I cannot fully explain came over me and wrote for me. It was like it was not me writing but some other thing or some other one." That was the way he explained here... Well, here is the book, *A Ride to Panmunjom*. Perhaps, you may want to read it. I don't mind loaning it if you will return it. *(The book is out of print, but is available on the web in its entirety. Search for* A Ride to Panmunjom *by Duane Thorin.)*

I give these illustrations to show, if I can, something of what may have happened at Pentecost. Duane Thorin had gone into the valley of death and he came out alive. He had confronted life in its most serious moments. He recognized that something sustained him that was beyond himself. He was willing to call it the power of God or the help of the Holy Spirit. The early Christians on Pentecost had had a traumatic experience. They had come in contact with the Lord of life, Jesus of Nazareth. The impact of Jesus upon their lives was not an experience they could forget. He had changed their whole way of thinking and living. When he left them, they could not feel he was dead and no longer with them. Such experiences and such a person do not die. They reasoned, then, that he was still with them in the abiding presence of his gracious spirit. That day at Pentecost they became dramatically aware of what had happened in their lives and they were caught up in an ecstatic and visionary experience.

They faced a moment of eternal truth – and something got hold of them, shook them, jarred them, and they became men with a message and a way of life to proclaim to the world. They believed they had come in contact with God himself and that He had given them a new spirit to guide and direct their lives. How is it in your life and mine? Do we believe that the Spirit of God is available to us, too? Are we receptive to learning from our unusual experiences – and we have many – and to see in them opportunities to make God's gracious spirit a living reality to those unaccustomed to thinking of the Holy Spirit as a positive and live force in the everyday adventure of life?

27

THE TRIUNE GOD

Trinity Sunday

Matthew 28:19 "Go therefore and make disciples of all nations, baptizing them in the name of the Father and of the Son and of the Holy Spirit,"

This is the day in the history of the Christian Church that is designated Trinity Sunday. We are not exactly sure when the day originated. In all probability, it began to be observed in the second, third and fourth centuries, those years when the great creeds and doctrines of the church were hammered out in the councils of the early churches. These were the years when Christian scholars as well as laymen argued about the nature of God as violently as people today argue the pros and cons of the civil rights issue.

Perhaps, no doctrine received as much attention in the discussions that went on among people as that which concerned the Trinity. Gregory of Nyssa, a theologian who lived near the end of the 4th Century and who was one of the most influential of all the theologians of that period in developing the doctrine of the Trinity, gives us this rather scathing caricature concerning the theoretical interest of that period of people regarding the Trinity:

> "Constantinople is full of mechanics and slaves who are all of them profound theologians, preaching in the shops and the streets. If you want to change a piece of silver, he informs you wherein the Son differs from the Father; if you ask the price of a loaf, you are told by way of reply that the Son is inferior to the Father; and, if you inquire whether the bath is ready, the answer is that the Son was made out of nothing."

Certainly, even the *New Yorker* magazine never had better satire than that. Well, we don't have this intense interest in the Trinity today and I hardly believe this is the way religious people ought to spend their time. Yet, I do believe it is helpful occasionally to consider the great doctrines of the church to see what they mean and to understand their relevance for Christian faith today.

First of all, it is rather interesting to trace the development of the doctrine of the Trinity. There was, of course, no Trinitarian formula concerning the nature of God in Judaism. In early Jewish history up until about the middle of the 8th century B.C., there is some evidence that the Hebrews believed in more than one God. One of the earliest names for God, Elohim, is a plural Hebrew word signifying that God was not necessarily one, but God was several. Furthermore, they believed in the gods of their enemies. Remember, the instance at Mt. Carmel when the people had to decide which god they would follow. Elijah showed that Yahweh was mightier than Baal but this did not mean that Baal did not exist. The exhibition only proved that Yahweh was more powerful than the god of the Cananites. After the 8th century, however, we find that the Hebrews began to be aware through revelation that their deity was not only mightier than the gods of other nations but he was the only God and they were his chosen people. So begins the development of the concept of monotheism or one god.

When Jesus came on the scene of history, however, and was accepted by the early Christians as the Son of God, he changed the ancient way of looking at God. His followers believed that God was revealing himself in some unusual way. Paul proclaimed that *"God was in Christ reconciling the world unto himself."* To the early church therefore, Jesus Christ was God himself in some special way, incarnate in the life of the world. The question arose "In what way was Jesus Christ related to God?" If he was God's Son, and they believed he was, then what did this belief have to do with the ancient belief in one God, monotheism? How could God and Jesus be related and still be separate?

There was also the issue of the Spirit of God, or Jesus Christ, being with them after Jesus was no longer with them in a physical body. They could not believe they were deserted and alone without a continuing comforter. At Pentecost they were struck with the realization that Jesus was with them through the Spirit or as they came to express it, God in the Spirit or Holy Spirit. So, now there were three concepts to wrestle with – God the Father, God in the Son, and God in the Spirit. The question then had to be dealt with: How are these three related – separate yet together? This question was faced perhaps in the last quarter of the first century and the formulation was developed – the Father, the Son, and the Holy Spirit. We see this expressed in the 19th verse of the 28th chapter of Matthew. The words are attributed to Jesus by the writer of the Gospel of Matthew. Scholars tell us they could hardly have been said by Jesus because the Trinitarian formula was not developed in his day. These words are an expression of faith by the early church perhaps 50 years after the death of Jesus. We are fairly positive that Matthew was written about the year 90 so in all probability he included them to express the faith that was in existence as he knew it in his generation.

So in Matthew's gospel we come into contact with one of the earliest statements that led to the doctrine of the Trinity, formulated finally in the Nicene Creed, accepted by the church as its official position on the godhead at the Council of Nicaea in the year 325 A.D. Let me read it. It is magnificent in expression as well as thought.

The Nicene Creed

I believe in one God, the Father Almighty, Maker of heaven and earth, and of all things visible and invisible.

And in one Lord Jesus Christ, the only begotten Son of God, begotten of the Father before all worlds; God of God, Light of Light, very God of very God; begotten, not made, being of one substance with the Father, by whom all things were made.

Who, for us men and for our salvation, came down from heaven, and was incarnate by the Holy Spirit of the virgin Mary, and was made man; and was crucified also for us under Pontius Pilate; He suffered and was buried; and the third day He rose again, according to the Scriptures; and ascended into heaven, and sits on the right hand of the Father; and He shall come again, with glory, to judge the quick and the dead; whose kingdom shall have no end.

And I believe in the Holy Ghost, the Lord and Giver of Life; who proceeds from the Father and the Son; who with the Father and the Son together is worshipped and glorified; who spoke by the prophets.

And I believe in one holy catholic and apostolic Church. I acknowledge one baptism for the remission of sins; and I look for the resurrection of the dead, and the life of the world to come. Amen.

We do not use such a creed to express our faith in our church today but it stands as a monument to the intellectual determination of the early Christians to present a theoretical explanation of the way they conceived the relationship of the Father, the Son, and the Holy Spirit to each other.

Now let us say at once that the doctrine of the Trinity as expressed by the Nicene Creed does not mean that the early church thought of three gods. Often times, this criticism has been leveled against Christians who subscribed to the Trinitarian formula to describe the godhead. Some critics have said that traditional Christianity has broken with Judaism and has done violence to the ancient concept of monotheism. Instead of one God, they claim, we Christians, at least the traditionalists have three gods – God the Father, God the Son, and God the Holy Spirit.

On first examination, it is not difficult to reach this conclusion. In fact, in my younger years as a theologian, I too, felt that the Trinity was a violation, even a contradiction, of the Unitarian concept of God, which the ancient Hebrews expressed in the Shema – *Hear, O Israel, the Lord Thy God is one God.* Every good Jew says this old statement at least once every day.

When we look closer, however, we discover that the Trinitarian formula does not establish three gods – it proclaims a triune god, or three in one. One way to think of it has been given to us by St Patrick who came to Ireland in the 5th century and evangelized the indigenous populations. Legend tells us that the natives of Ireland had a problem understanding the triune God so St. Patrick demonstrated the idea with a Shamrock. He helped these people to see that the Shamrock was one leaf yet it had three leaves, so he explained God as one but he is seen or known in three ways – as the Father creator, the redeeming Son and the innocent Spirit.

Perhaps, another illustration will help. Sometimes, we speak of the Godhead as three persons, although it is hardly correct to speak of the Trinity as persons at all but different manifestations of the same God. Nevertheless to say persons is beneficial in understanding the idea. The word *person* that we use today is from the Latin word *persona* which originally meant a mask or a false face, such as children wear at Halloween. When the Greeks gave their plays, an actor would sometimes play several different parts and he put a mask or persona over his face to represent the particular character he was portraying. Therefore, the early Church fathers at Nicea thought of Father, Son, and Spirit as masks or *impersonations* of one and the same God. Yet, they insisted that God always played all three roles at once but his mask or face or person or persona was seen as Father, Son, or Spirit.

If that isn't clear, let us try another analogy. Perhaps I will do. I am one person yet I am more than one person. I am many persons. I am a son to my mother and a little son at that. As long as my mother lived, I always was her boy and nothing ever changed to make me anything more and she did not hesitate to remind me. I am also a husband to Mrs. Cheatham and I can be nothing more and

I hope nothing less. I am also a father to my children, nothing more. When I am in the psychological services bureau at Georgetown University, I am a psychologist and am so perceived by students who come with their vocational, educational, or personal adjustment problems. To you I am your minister and I am so received and accepted. Although I am son, husband, father, psychologist, and minister, I am still the same person but not really the same person. I am many impersonations; I wear many masks or personae or am many persons. In a sense, just as you are, I am one but many. In a real sense, therefore, this is the way God is for the Christians. He is one yet he is three – father, son, and spirit. Not three gods but one god, but manifesting himself in several ways.

Do you see, then, what the early church fathers were getting at when they developed and formulated the doctrine of the Trinity? They were trying to give a systematic interpretation of the way they perceive their god. This does not mean that they changed the nature of God. God never changes. He has always been as He is. It only means that man's conceptions of him changes. It was not enough for God to reveal himself through laws and principles, values and ethical conduct. The early church had the insight to discover a newer revelation – that God can be known through the life and character of a person – they saw Him in the life and mission of Jesus Christ. Paul catches this idea and expresses it in beautiful symbolism: *"For God, who commanded the light to shine out of darkness, hath shined in our hearts to give the light of the knowledge of the glory of God in the face of Jesus Christ."* That is said about as well as it can be said, for this is our faith that we know God through Jesus Christ and through the indwelling of his gracious spirit among us.

Prayer: God we art mindful that thou art God and that we are more than creatures of earth. We are grateful for Sunday and for the church, for this reminds us that we do not live merely by bread alone. Working at our jobs, attending classes, keeping a house, and having good times with our neighbors and friends, we live to find out what life is all about and to discover a way to comprehend the way life can best be lived.

We give thanks that the church through its gospel provides us that way, the way that Christ provided for us. May we this day learn what he meant when he said that we must be willing to give of ourselves in order to find ourselves. This is a strange teaching and we are at once bold to confess that we do not understand the mystery of its depth. May our hearts be receptive, however, to learn and to know. Today, we ask that we may receive, we look that we may find, we knock that it may be opened unto us. So open unto us God the secret of life that our moments here together may be both pleasant and profitable. In the name of Christ we pray. Amen

28

GETTING OURSELVES TOGETHER IN ONE PIECE

Matthew 6:22b If your eye is single, your whole body shall be full of light.

Not one of us finds it always easy to do what we want to do. We say we are going to read that book everyone tells us we ought to read. We buy the book and have every intention of getting it read. We even begin reading, but frequently weeks pass by, and still we haven't finished it. We want to read it, we mean to read it, but distractions of one sort or another get in the way and the book never seems to get read.

Trying to read a book, however, is only one illustration of not getting done what we want to do, only one example of how we are pulled apart. Some of us find ourselves divided on more serious matters. Some have trouble keeping promises – they mean to keep their word but they allow their promises to go unkept. Others mean to give up excessive drinking but they go deeper and deeper into the pit. Still there are others who mean to be kinder, more understanding, and more considerate of their families or friends but somehow the mean, harsh judgments continue to have the upper hand. Well, the list is long of not getting done what we want to do, but somehow cannot do.

This predicament of being pulled in many directions at one time, and causing us to function at a lower level than we really want to function, is annoying. Life becomes unpleasant and miserable. Darkness enters the spirit, and we often become angry, dissatisfied, even depressed. The gloom that sets in because of disunity within our inner lives develops because we are beings who thrive best on getting done what we set out to do. We seem to be created to accomplish what we intend. To move toward a goal, to know we are progressing promotes inner worth and satisfaction. But not to move ahead, not to move forward, to do the opposite of what we intend, is indeed dismaying. It is no wonder Jesus made this observation: *"If your eye is single, your whole body is full of light."* We do feel right about ourselves when we take a cause and stay with it until it is completed. This is singleness of purpose and it floods the spirit and the mind with light, feelings of self worth and value. Well, how do we get ourselves together in one piece, so we are pulling together as one person, and not several?

First of all, there is the necessity of getting our various systems of the self in communication with each other. Carl Rogers reminds us that basically this self of ours is made up of three separate but related systems. There is feeling, that part of us that feels pain, anger and love. Our feeling system also includes our desire to be with others, to have a good time, to enjoy ourselves. Also, it includes the pleasurable satisfactions that come from eating, drinking, and sexual experiences. This is the emotional or feeling part of ourselves.

The second system is concerned with thinking, believing, making judgments, and decisions. Mind is another term for this system. It has the responsibility of keeping a check on our feelings and desires so they will not get out of control.

A third system, according to Rogers, is behavior. This has to do with our actions, and our conduct. Behavior is what others see us do.

Rogers believes that *the eye* or the self cannot be single and give the body light, self worth, or deep personal satisfaction until these three systems – feeling, thinking, and behaving – are in contact with each other and are working together as a team. When they are working against each other or in opposition to each other, they cause darkness in the spirit. The person becomes a divided self – anxious, upset, and miserable.

How is this possible? How can we be a divided self when we are one self? We do not know why, but we know that it happens. Here is an individual who has been taught from childhood that it is wrong to be angry. This lesson enters her belief system. She accepts this concept and firmly believes that to be angry is wrong. Yet, when this person becomes older, a friend offends her in some way. At once, her feeling system gets in the act and she feels a twinge of anger. But this is wrong her beliefs tell her, so at once she is divided – one part says, "you cannot be angry"; another part says "you feel anger". What is she to do? For one thing, she might put on a smile, act like she doesn't care, and say, "I don't mind what my friend says about me." Here we find three systems working at odds with one another – one says "no anger", another feels, "I am angry", and one is acting out a compromise, "I don't care." I suppose one can go through life behaving in this manner, but I am of the opinion that the person will become anxious, nervous, and an unsettled person. The eye is not single, therefore, the body cannot be full of light.

When the systems are in communication with each other, the situation is different. A far better way and one that gives light to the body is for a person to feel anger when anger is appropriate, for that is what the feeling system communicates. The thinking system can believe that anger is not wrong, but it must be properly expressed. Then feeling and thinking are together. The proper behavior is not to strike, but to say to the person who offended, "I am angry at what you said about me and I feel we ought to talk this thing over, for we cannot go on through life feeling this way about each other." Here is the light for the body; the eye is single, because feeling, thinking, and behaving are acting as separate, but related systems! *"If the eye is single, the whole body is full of light."*

Surely, then, another way for us to get together in one piece is to determine if there is any defect in any part of us, and, if so, make an effort to get it corrected. We have many parts, all are separate, but each can have a profound effect on every other part. An inferior part needs to be changed if it is a source of harm for it can hurt the whole self. Jesus put it this way: *"If your right eye causes you to sin, pluck it out and throw it away; it is better that you lose one of your members than your whole body be thrown into hell. And if your right hand causes you to sin, cut it off and throw it away; it is better that you lose one of your members than that your whole body go to hell."*

We need to say here that Jesus did not intend that persons go around dismembering their bodies. We need to be very careful that we do not take statements like these from the Bible literally. Jesus, as well as many Biblical teachers, spoke figuratively. We have to get behind the literal statement to see what principle of life the person, and in this case Jesus, was attempting to point out. I am sure what Jesus had in mind in these words we have just read, is that there are burdens, handicaps, misfortunes, imperfections of many types that persons carry around with them which are contributing to their downfall or failure. Because a poor performance in one area can contribute to poor performance in all areas, Jesus advises a person to correct the deficiencies, for it is better to lose one thing we enjoy than to destroy one's whole life.

There are so many satisfactions we enjoy that are seriously crippling to our total performance as persons, and only if somehow we could give them up, let them go, we would enjoy richer and more satisfying lives. One person may gain personal enjoyment from making insulting statements when around other people. He likes it but others are disgusted and wish he would keep his remarks to himself. Another person loves lying in bed too much. He gets up late regularly, is late for his appointments and for his work, and he is constantly in hot water for his tardiness. Some seem to delight in having their own way all of the time. They find themselves without friends and they wonder why no one seems to include them in their affairs.

Others find lying personally enjoyable, but when they are found out they become ostracized. Many have no sense of humor, others take everything literally, still others somehow find it impossible to bend and give themselves in friendly relationships with others. Then there are some who cannot stand life unless they are with others or are in a crowd or at a party. Others seem to enjoy putting everything off to the last minute. Many are always critical. Others appear to enjoy getting attention from others with a physical defect or handicap and they keep it before others all the time or they are ashamed of it and become shy, withdrawn, and timid. The ingenuity of persons to allow one negative behavior to ruin the total effectiveness is without limits and seems unbelievable!

If we seem to be always on the wrong side of life and never quite able to get as much out of life as we think we should, it may be there is one flaw we need to discover about ourselves and to correct it. We can get together and become a productive person rather than one who is always barely getting by. The suggestion of Jesus is: If your eye or your hand offends you, get rid of it, for it is better to throw away one thing that gives you pleasure than to enjoy it and have your whole life ruined.

A third suggestion in getting ourselves together in one piece is to have the capacity to find out what is important if life. We know how pulled we are in one direction and then in another. What is right, what is wrong? This is a question that many of us have to face every day in our lives, and blessed is the person who knows where he stands on issues involving morality. I suspect one of the reasons we find ourselves not in one piece is that we do not know where we stand. When we are unsure or undecided on problems of morality we often attempt to move in both directions and find ourselves split down the middle. Jesus has this to say: "*No man can serve two masters; for either he will hate the one and love the other, or he will be devoted to the one and despise the other. You cannot serve God and mammon.*"

Do you feel we are split down the middle in our society as I do at times? On the one hand our youth are exposed to every possible suggestion concerning the allurement and excitement of sexual pleasure. We see it in our TV, motion pictures, literature, and advertisements. An act that belongs only to persons who are married is made to seem all right for everyone. Yet, on the other hand, youth are told that this is not for you. If a young girl becomes pregnant out of wedlock, she becomes disgraced. Youth are encouraged on the one hand and denied on the other. Who is right they ask? Who are we to believe? No one can serve two masters.

At this point, those of us who are parents, teachers, and leaders in the churches have to present a firm and unequivocal stand. There can be no question of right or wrong at this point. Illicit sexual behavior is irresponsible behavior and irresponsible behavior is wrong behavior. Study after study, as well as the teaching of scripture is consistent and clear on this point. There are some things that are reserved for adults to which young people are not entitled. No one is allowed to drive an automobile at 12 years of age. No one can vote until he is 21. *(This was changed to 18 in 1971.)* Alcoholic beverages are not for youth. Sexual relationships are reserved for married persons who have the capacity and the maturity to assume the responsibilities of marriage. At this point, our beliefs must be clear and firm.

The play, *The Death of a Salesman*, speaks in no uncertain terms about what happens to a man who believes that nothing matters in life except to be liked. What counts to get ahead in life is who you know, the deals you can pull, the big impressions you can make. Willie Loman, the most tragic of people, doesn't care whether his sons cheat, steal, or lie so long as they are popular and make a big name for themselves in sports or something else. The boys, however, become failures and so does Willie. Willie can't understand, of course, what has happened, so in desperation, he takes his own life. As they stand over their father's grave at the funeral, one boy says, "Well Dad had a dream and that was to be Number One." But the other son knows his dad better and sadly but angrily remarks, "Yes, but Dad never knew who he was." Poor Willie, he was torn in a hundred pieces, because he never really knew what he believed or who he was. *"No man can serve two masters... you cannot serve God and mammon."*

The faith of Jesus Christ does not deny life nor take it from us. It offers us life, life at its best and life at its fullest. But it is not an idle, loose life as though it were a ship cut loose from its moorings. It is a disciplined and responsible life, one that has some semblance of unity and consistency. We discover that life as we learn to get ourselves together in one piece.

Sermon

29

MEN AND RELIGION

Ezekiel 2:2 And when he spoke to me, the Spirit entered into me and set me upon my feet; and I heard him speaking to me.

This month twenty-five years ago, June 8th, 1941, I was ordained to the Christian Ministry. One of the questions that has interested me during these twenty-five years is: why are so few men interested in the church and religion? During the twenty years I spent in the Army as a chaplain, I thought about this question frequently for I noticed that the vast majority of soldiers seldom attended chapel. Many times I conducted services for a mere handful of men when the unit had hundreds assigned. The best attendance I ever saw was when 25 to 30 percent of the division came to church services each month rather regularly. Those of us who were chaplains in that division were delighted with these figures but still we had to admit that the other 70 to 75 percent did not participate. This Father's Day seems a good time to think about this question:

Why are men not overwhelmingly attracted to religion as it is represented by the church?

One way to answer this question is to compare the interest of men in religion with that of women. It is fairly well assumed, I think, that women generally are more attracted to religion than men. I suspect many husbands would not be here today were it not for the insistence of women. Some say that the reason that women are more attracted to the church than men is because the minister is a man. The reason lies in the age-old attraction between men and women. The better looking the minister, the more women are drawn to him. Some have even gone so far as to say that the reason Billy Graham draws such large crowds is his good looks. Men, of course, go to his meetings too, but they attend; say those who hold to this Freudian position, because they are urged to go by the women. The only way, I suppose, you could ever prove this theory would be to turn all ministers into women and then to see what would happen. If the figures then reversed themselves – more men went to church than women – then I suppose you would have fairly good proof for this position. But, if this did happen in a particular situation, knowing men as I do, this lady minister would have to be really good looking. A priest friend of mine said to me only last Sunday afternoon at a reception Mrs. Cheatham and I attended when we were discussing this very subject that a woman priest or minister would have a hard time of it. She would probably be picked to pieces by women in the congregation if she didn't wear the proper dress, hair-do, or make-up. Persons who hold this view, point to Jesus and stress the number of women who were attracted to him. They say it was more than merely religious reasons that prompted them to seek him out. Well, what do you think? Are more women than men interested in religion because the minister is a man? Or is this reason simply another indication of the male conceit? It may not be the reason, but it is rather interesting to consider.

Another explanation advanced is that many men reject religion because it detracts from their manliness. Those who hold to this position may have something, for frequently I hear a young man say, "Who wants to go to Sunday School? That is sissy stuff and is only for babies and little kids!"

In many parts of culture, there is an insistence that to be a man, a person has to know how to swear, be tough, know how to fight, smoke cigarettes, and drink liquor. In this kind of subculture, such things as courtesy, thoughtfulness, kindness, decent language, the kind of qualities that the church has been known to stand for, are frowned upon and ridiculed. Well, if a boy grows up with this kind of thinking, you can imagine how quickly he wants nothing to do with the church. Some military commanders with whom I served represented this tough, aggressive, profane approach to their troops. These same commanders often downgraded church attendance. They believed that religion and soldiering belonged in separate camps and they let it be known in no uncertain terms that they didn't want the religious camp contaminating their troops. Such commanders, and many are excellent military men, too, are the men who enjoy referring to chaplains in such derogatory terms, as *Holy Joes*, for so far as they are concerned, religion degrades a real man.

There is another facet to this belief that religion detracts from manliness. Men are supposed to be self-sufficient, aggressive, and independent, to possess the stuff to stand on their own feet, whereas religion comes along, and tells a man that he is not self-sufficient, but that he is dependent upon God. Perhaps you have read the life of Ernest Hemingway that was recently published, written by his friend of many years, A. E. Hotchner. One cannot but admire the carefree, devil-may-care life that Hemingway so fully lived. He was an excellent writer, one of the greatest of our generation, and he was also a robust, hard-drinking, free-loving, fast-living individual, one who was the life of the party. Yet, you also get the impression as you read his biography that he could not stand what he thought religion stood for. Religion would have reminded him that he was a man, creative yes, but also limited by the conditions of being a human person. Religion would have him admit that he had to make peace with his limitations and to accept one's years and the infirmities that accompany old age. These precepts, however, Hemingway never accepted. When he was ill during his last years, despondent because he could not live the fast life which he loved, he made several attempts to take his life. When his friend Hotchner tried to intercede to dissuade him form suicide, Hemingway said, "Hotch, if I can't exist on my own terms, then existence is impossible. Do you understand? That is how I've lived, and that is how I must live – or not live." These were admirable words and they inspire us, but religion would call them foolish because they do not recognize that a man cannot have life altogether on his own terms. Life has to be lived on God's terms, says religion. It is for this reason that many men reject religion: Religion seems to cut the ground out from under a man's desire for self-reliance. It detracts from his manliness.

There is a third observation that may explain the seeming lack of interest in religion by men that I believe is more important than any I have mentioned. This explanation says that men have been repelled by religion because Christianity has been grossly and falsely represented and interpreted by a large segment of the church. Somehow or other, many churches have presented Christian faith as a sweet, soft, soothing, comforting debilitating affair. Sometimes it is called *Sweet Jesus* religion, a kind of religion that nauseates any young person who wants to be a real man, and not a soft, sobbing sentimentalist. When a person is introduced to this type of religious faith, he naturally assumes that this is what Christianity is; so, not wanting to be identified with weakness and softness, he rejects the church and religion.

What has always been amazing to me is how this interpretation of Christianity ever got started, for if the religion of Jesus is anything at all, it is certainly not sweet, soft, or weak. If the church has made Christianity this way, the church is at fault and not Jesus. From the beginning of Christian faith, it has always been a faith that demands a person stand up to life. Consider the account of Ezekiel's call by God. Ezekiel beholds the majesty and holiness of God in various visions. The prophet is overcome by what he sees and by what he feels. He falls to the ground in subjection and self-effacement but out of the void comes the stern demand. *"Ezekiel get up!"* Here is the way it is said by the Biblical writer: *"And when he spoke to me, the Spirit entered into me and set me upon my feet; and I heard him speaking to me."*

This is what God does to a man. He doesn't coddle or caress. He doesn't hide him from life's temptations and demands. He doesn't make of him a sniveling, subservient, obsequious dandy. He sets a man on his feet and dares him to be a man of courage, responsibility, and backbone. When God got hold of Jesus, he set him on his feet. He did not excuse him from the cross nor make it easy. Jesus had to endure the worst of pain and suffering. This is what happens when the Spirit of God enters into a person. The person has to get up off the ground, stand on his feet, and meet head-on whatever confronts him in the way of duty and danger.

These qualities, then, seem to be in a man when the Spirit of God gets hold of him. He becomes courageous. I do not mean he has to fly a jet plane or become a sky diver. These are feats of adventure but they are not necessarily courageous. Courage thrives when it is not absorbed by people telling you what you should think and be. It means not to lose one's inner freedom to think, to work, and to live as one feels is right and best for him. The greatest curse of all to courage is to perform for others and to seek their praise and adoration. The person who requires others to say they are nice, or beautiful, or intelligent, or good, has sold out his powers to adoration. The man of courage, and Jesus was such a person, is one who has the capacity to stand on his feet and act on his own convictions because they are simply what he believes.

The second quality is responsibility. Perhaps I have gotten the whole matter backwards. I have advanced the claim that many men reject religion because it is not manly enough. It may be many men will have nothing to do with the church and religious faith because it demands too much, for it does insist in its best sense that a person stand up and be counted. For example, in our current financial commitment program, a man who is a member of this church cannot really be a Christian man and not assume his rightful share of the financial program of the church, for Christianity requires each one to carry his load for the advancement of the cause of Christ and his church. "*If anyone will be my disciple, let him deny himself and take up his cross and follow after me.*" Could any statement be clearer?

The third ingredient of Christian manhood is to stand up and take what comes. We are not measured always by what we can do or by what we know. We are also evaluated on the basis of what we can stand. Last Sunday, Mrs. Marion and Mrs. Vore sang selections from Handel's *Messiah*. We marvel at such inspiring music but did we know that this superb musical production once hung delicately in the balance? Handel's biographer writes: "His health and his fortune had reached the lowest ebb. His right side had become paralyzed and his money was all gone. His creditors seized him and threatened him with imprisonment. For a brief time he was tempted to give up the fight – but then he rebounded again to compose the greatest of his inspirations, the epic *Messiah*." So the *Hallelujah Chorus* was written not only because Handel could compose thrilling music, but because he could stand up on his feet and take it!

What I want to emphasize today is that Christianity cannot be rejected because of claims by uninformed persons that it is unmanly. If persons are to cancel out Christian faith, they must do so on other grounds than that it lacks masculine qualities. Let us free our faith from some of its caricatures, particularly those that associate it with weakness, softness, and cheap sentimentality. We can underwrite our faith with courage, responsible living, and backbone by seeking to develop those attributes in our own living, for only when those of us who wear the badge of Christian faith learn to be what we claim to be, can Christian faith be a challenge and an adventure both to women and men. There is no such thing as our faith belonging exclusively to men or to women. It belongs to all of us because Christ lived and died that all of us might have life and have it more abundantly.

30

THE FATHER OF THE PRODIGAL SON

Luke 15:11-24

11 And he said, "There was a man who had two sons;
12 and the younger of them said to his father, 'Father, give me the share
of property that falls to me.' And he divided his living between them.
13 Not many days later, the younger son gathered all he
had and took his journey into a far country, and there
he squandered his property in loose living.
14 And when he had spent everything, a great famine arose
in that country, and he began to be in want.
15 So he went and joined himself to one of the citizens of
that country, who sent him into his fields to feed swine.
16 And he would gladly have fed on the pods that the swine
ate; and no one gave him anything.
17 But when he came to himself he said, 'How many of my father's hired
servants have bread enough and to spare, but I perish here with hunger!
18 I will arise and go to my father, and I will say to him, "Father, I have
sinned against heaven and before you;
19 I am no longer worthy to be called your son; treat
me as one of your hired servants."'

20 And he arose and came to his father. But while he was
yet at a distance, his father saw him and had compassion,
and ran and embraced him and kissed him.
21 And the son said to him, 'Father, I have sinned against
heaven and before you; I am no longer worthy to be called your son.'
22 But the father said to his servants, 'Bring quickly the best robe, and put
it on him; and put a ring on his hand, and shoes on his feet;
23 and bring the fatted calf and kill it, and let us eat and make merry;
24 for this my son was dead, and is alive again; he was lost,
and is found.' And they began to make merry.

An often repeated saying is, *Don't get stuck in a rut*. For one thing, avoid doing a thing in the same old way; else you will become stale and lethargic. It also means watch out from doing something just because it has always been done. The reason why the act started may not be present any longer and to continue the act any longer is purely ridiculous. It may also mean to take a new look occasionally at an old familiar story. You may find something in the story you never saw there before that may be beneficial for life.

This morning I am going to take seriously the advice, *Don't get stuck in a rut,* with regards to the ancient parable of Jesus we call the parable of the prodigal son. I am going to ask you to engage with me for a few moments in the task of looking at the parable with a new approach. We say it is a parable about a son who left his father's home, ended up in reckless living, found himself in an uncomfortable condition, realized the stupidity of his behavior, and returned to his father's home to get a new start. Instead of looking at the parable, however, with our concentration on the son, let us look at the parable another way. Let us look at it by focusing our attention and imagination on the father. And what better day to consider the parable in the light of the father than on a day our nation has set aside to remember fathers. What does the parable have to say about the father of the prodigal son?

One thought that comes to mind as I read this parable is that this father gave his son something that he was entitled to – the chance to take responsibility for his own life. This concept hits us almost at once when we read the parable. Jesus offers no introduction to the parable such as, "Now I am going to tell you about a father who gave his son responsibility to lead his own life." At the end of the parable, neither is there any conclusion concerning what one should do after reading or hearing the account. This is a pure parable, the kind Jesus seemed to enjoy telling. He takes a slice out of life that has serious moment, serves it to his hearers without garnishes or embellishments, drops the curtain without comment, and allows the audience to draw their own conclusion; therefore, if we are going to get anything out of this *pithy little episode of a throbbing life situation*, we have to allow the parable to fit life as we know and like it and allow it to do its own work of enlightenment and edification.

At once, then, the parable introduces us to a father who had two sons and the younger said to his father, *"Father, give me the share of property that falls to me."* The boy had become of age to receive his inheritance. Since he was the younger boy, he was entitled to one third of the inheritance according to Jewish law. If you are interested, you can consult Deuteronomy 21:17 for the details of the law. The first born son would have been entitled to twice this amount. Notice the father does not argue with his son. Immediately, the story continues with the reply of the father, *"And he divided his living between them."*

Giving this boy money is not merely giving him something to live on and get him started in life. Rather the act represents a whole set of personal relationships. It acknowledges the fact that the father accepts his son now as a person who has to learn to manage his own life. The father cannot always be with him, holding his hand, keeping him from harm and danger. The father may have wanted to shield him from the hardships which life presents to young men and women. Yet, the parable implies that the father knew this was impossible if the boy was ever to be a man and to take his place in the world as an adult.

Perhaps, this father also suspected this boy was really not yet capable of managing life for himself. Yet, he had reached the age, chronologically, when he was entitled to make his own decisions. The father knew, however, that the boy felt he was ready to go out on his own and the father believed he had to respect his judgment and his position and give him the chance to find out if he was really capable of managing for himself. Evidently, the father knew he and his son would never know the boy's capability until he had a chance to be his own boss. Experience does teach us that you can never really know how well a person can do any job until he is put in the job and allowed to do it. Furthermore, the father was well aware that the boy would make mistakes, just as he had made them when he was a young man. Still, the father was also aware that a young person must be allowed the privilege of making mistakes, or of experiencing failure; otherwise he will never become a responsible person. So for better or for worse, the father of the prodigal son gave his son the chance that every person needs as he moves along through life – a chance to take responsibility for himself. This time comes at all ages — from the earliest years to later adolescence. The one year old must be allowed to fall before he learns to walk and a young person must be allowed the privilege to make his own mistakes in order to develop into a responsible person. The basic question always is: Is he ready? Is he old enough to do what he asks? The determining factor in answering that question is this: He is old enough if he can handle the consequences of failure. The father of the prodigal felt his son could take the consequences of failure if he gave him his inheritance. He didn't have to give him the inheritance at that time. Perhaps it would have been better to wait until a later date. The father, however, thought he was ready, so he divided the inheritance with him.

Another human factor we see developing in this story is that the father was deeply concerned about his son and how he was faring in the cold and heartless world. He did not merely hand over the money to the boy and say "Now, be gone. You don't want to stay here any longer. You think we are not good enough for you, your brother, the family, the servants, and me. So get going and don't ever come back." We find none of this sourness and sarcasm that is so often expressed when a person is told by someone he is very close to that he wants to think for himself.

This attitude is not evidenced at all in the father of the prodigal son. He is really a big man, a father who understands human behavior, particularly the desire of a young man to reach out and to find out for himself what the world is all about. The father seems to realize that because his son wants to leave home, it doesn't mean at all that his son doesn't love him any more or has no regard for him as a father. None of these feelings of being rejected by his son seem to enter the mind of the father at all. Instead, the opposite seems to be the case. The father seems to be aware that because his son does love him, he can ask to leave. If the son had not loved his father, he would not have asked his permission to leave. He probably would have stayed on hoping the old man would die so he could get his inheritance or he would have simply left without even asking. Real love between two persons always carries with it the right or the freedom for the other person to disagree, even to accept the renouncement of love from the other. There are no strings attached to love, no contracts, no legal binders, and no covenants. The only concern that one who loves another is that the other person may have the opportunity to grow and mature and to become a person in his own right!

31

WHY PRAY, ANYWAY?

Job 21:15 What is the Almighty, that we should serve him?
And what profit do we get if we pray to him?

A friend who is active in community affairs told me of a conversation she had recently with a public official that sets the stage for our thought this morning. My friend was in charge of a committee to arrange a program for a gathering which was to be attended by physicians, nurses, and other professional people in the field of medical care. She had included on the program an invocation. The public official who had to approve the program my friend had prepared told her he thought the program she had worked out was excellent except he wondered why she had included a prayer. He phrased his remarks with the question, "You don't really believe we ought to have a prayer, do you? What good will that do?"

This question is almost precisely the question raised by Job in conversation with his friends concerning the meaning of his suffering. Job was a good man and he could not understand why he was ill, for the accepted theology of that day was that illness and misfortune were retribution for wrong doing and good health and good fortune were the rewards of right doing. The question, then, faced by Job, if the accepted belief was true was, *Why had he lost all his wealth, his family, and his health when he had so faithfully served God and obeyed all of his commandments?* He is very angry and bitter regarding the whole affair. He is also angry with God; therefore, he poses the question, "What profit do we get if we pray to God?" The questions of the public official and that of Job, although they develop out of different contexts, are, in a sense, the same, "What is the good of praying?" or "Why pray, anyway?" Let us, then, consider this question.

First of all, for the sake of clarification, let us say that a person prays because it seems the decent thing to do. One of the earliest lessons taught us when we were small children was to say "thank you", when someone gave us something, did some kind deed in our behalf, or said something nice about us. Times haven't changed either since you and I were children, for today I find that mothers and fathers are very conscious to teach their children as our mothers and fathers taught us to say "thank you." Perhaps there is no act that embarrasses a parent more than for their child to accept a gift from an adult and not to say "thank you." If the child accepts the gift and says nothing, very shortly the parent sharply reminds the child, "Say thank you", and gives the child a hard stare. How pleased the parent becomes when the child, sometimes out of fear, replies "thank you." Well, this custom of expressing thankfulness seems to be a part of every culture. To my knowledge, there is no language that does not have a word or a gesture for expressing gratitude. The sentiment seems to be a part of the human enterprise. To be grateful appears to be a part of our lives as human beings. To be grateful is the decent thing to do.

What does gratitude then have to do with praying? Primarily, they are related because there are so many favors and blessings in life that come to us which appear far beyond our abilities to comprehend. We do so little to earn them – life, friends, family, opportunities, and good fortune – that we feel in a way that we do not deserve them, so we naturally feel that to give thanks is the most decent gesture we can possibly make. Some have said that faith in God began because man realized that the life he lived and the earth which gave him his food and his clothing and his shelter was not something he had earned. It was given to him for reasons which he was unable to understand. He realized these benefits came from somewhere so he turned to heaven, the source of rain and light, and gave thanks to the Supreme Being whom he believed was out there making it possible for him, his family, and his friends to exist. How natural prayer is when we think of it in terms of expressing gratefulness for all the good things with which our lives are so bountifully blessed.

Perhaps the problem of the public official who questioned prayer was that he did not really understand prayer at all. Perhaps he conceived of the act as something that was magic and belonged to the realm of the superstitious. Perhaps he failed to comprehend that prayer at its highest and deepest level is the most mature of all acts for it is a means by which we say thanks to that great unknown but beneficent being who provides for our basic necessities. Just as it is a decent act to say thank you to some person who has favored us, so it is a decent, respectable, polite, and cultured custom to give thanks to the God who made us and who has provided so plentifully for our lives.

This leads us to say then that prayer also is a means by which we acknowledge our insufficiency as mortals and our dependency upon a being that is beyond ourselves. John Bennett, the President of Union Theological Seminary in New York City and who some years ago was one of my teachers, commented on this topic one day in our Contemporary Theological Trends class. He said that at the end of the century there was an opinion prevalent among intellectuals that man had make such profound gains in the technological and scientific fields and that he was making such rapid strides in making a heaven on earth, that God was no longer necessary. In every way man was getting better and better. But, observed Dr. Bennett, with the onslaught of World War I, then the horrors of World War II, and the anxieties and terrors created by the atomic bomb and with the insidious schemes of Communistic Russia, the climate has changed. Now, intellectuals no longer ask why have a God? The question is asked somewhat differently by the existential philosophy that is having such a revolutionary effect on philosophy, literature, education, psychology, and even science - but in a sense it means the same thing. Leaders in this school of thought are asking, "What is the meaning of existence?" and "How can we find meaning for life within existence?" These questions have as their underlying motive that man is insufficient within himself to make any sense out of life. He must turn to a philosophical principle or a theoretical framework to explain what life is and especially what his own individual life means. TV's, automatic machines, high-powered sleek automobiles, automatic data processing and other cybernetic machines, jet airlines, wall-to-wall carpeting, air-conditioning, good looks, gray-flannel suits, prestige, sophistication, cocktail parties and a hundred other possessions we think we need to get along are not enough. Even those who profess no god say these things are not enough. Man must still find meaning for his existence outside of these possessions, as important as they may seem. Job thought, too, that wealth, position, influence, good health, a sound body, and a long life were sufficient to give substance to his life. Did they not prove, he believed, that God was for him and on his side and no harm could come to him? God existed to make these possessions possible for his life. If he did not exist for this purpose, then, why pray? In other words, the early Job conceived of God as a kind of cosmic Santa Claus that brought *sugar and spice, and all things nice* to all good men and women. But Job was shaken to his very boot straps. Everything he had, everything in which he so frantically believed was taken away and he woke up one day to find himself in sackcloth and ashes. What then was he to believe? The Book of Job is a play, the finest of existential dramas, that reveals Job evaluating and wrestling with this problem of his existence without possessions. The result, of course, is a complete transformation of his former juvenile beliefs. He discovers that faith in God has absolutely nothing to do with gadgets and wealth, good health or poor health. The only ground for belief is faith and prayer is a reaction to that faith. Where is meaning for existence? Where is there a philosophical framework that will sustain us? Job emerges with this declaration, *"Though he slay me, yet will I trust in Him."* This is the final word of faith. It affirms our insufficiency. It proclaims our dependency. This is prayer and it carries within the reason why prayer is given and why prayer is practiced. The disciples of Jesus were aware that within him was the answer to the most serious of all life's imponderable questions and finally they summed up their conclusions in these words, *"To whom shall we go?"* or "Where do we find a philosophical principle to sustain our life?" They answer their own question. *"Thou hast the words of eternal life!"* Why pray? What else is there to do?

32

PERSONAL INTEREST AND SOCIAL RESPONSIBILITY

Numbers 32:6b Shall your brothers go to war while you sit here?

f I understand correctly, one of the jobs of the minister of the church is to hold up before the congregation the message of the Bible and allow that message to speak to the people, confronting them with the demands which Biblical faith places upon their lives. In other words the mission of the preacher is to allow the Bible to speak to us concerning the predicaments of life which each one of us has to face. My intention, therefore, this morning is to confront each of us with the message of the Bible concerning what seems appropriate in handling the predicament between one's own personal interest and his social responsibility. Each one of us, if he has any conscience at all, is confronted with this question almost every day of his life. How much of my resources, how much of my time, how much of my leisure shall I devote to my own personal development or enjoyment and how much shall be given to worthwhile causes that are akin but are not necessarily my own responsibility?

This morning I want to hold before our eyes an instance where this question is dealt with in the Bible. My hope is that we may discover for ourselves how we might handle the question when it is presented to us.

In the book of Numbers we read the account of Moses' leadership given by the writer known as P, or the Priestly author, who wrote some 600 to 700 years after the events. The Hebrew people had traveled for some forty years on their trek from Egypt to the land east of the Jordan River. And so they stopped for several years to establish and organize their forces. Their goal was to take the land west of the Jordan from the Canaanites who occupied the territory.

While they were getting ready for this venture, some of the people grew to enjoy the area where they were staying. The land was bountiful and their cattle prospered. The people of the tribe of Gad and the tribe of Reuben decided they wanted to stay in the Trans-Jordan and not to go across the Jordan River. The leaders of these two tribes, therefore, came to Moses their field commander and requested permission to stay. Here is the way the writer of Numbers has the leaders of Gad and Reuben make the request of Moses, *So the sons of Gad and the sons of Reuben came and said to Moses and to Eleazar the priest and to the leaders of the congregation, "Ataroth, Dibon, Jazer, Nimrah, Heshbon, Elealeh, Sebam, Nebo, and Beon, the land which the Lord smote before the congregation of Israel, is a land for cattle; and your servants have cattle." And they said, "If we have found favor in your sight, let this land be given to your servants for a possession; do not take us across the Jordan."*

The request does not seem unreasonable. They liked it where they were. They were thoroughly enjoying life. They had found a home. The only difficulty, however, with their request was that they were a part of a larger community to whom they had pledged themselves. They were to enter Canaan and insure the land for their generation and for generations to follow. At least, that was the way the Priestly writer perceived the situation writing hundreds of years after the event. The leaders of Gad and Reuben wanted to violate their contract of allegiance to the community so that they could live in comfort and ease.

Moses was angry at their request. They, the sons of Gad and Reuben, had faced the problem of personal benefit versus social responsibility and had decided for personal interest. Moses saw the matter differently. He felt the sons of Gad and Reuben were slackers and drones; so, he confronts them with their obligation to the larger group. He becomes their super-ego and hits them hard with this question, *"Shall your brethren go to the war while you sit here?" "Why will you discourage the heart of the people of Israel from going over into the land which the Lord has given you?"*

So there is the predicament that you and I face, as clear and as crisp as one could possibly state the case: Gad and Reuben want to take their ease, enjoy the fruits they had grown and learned to love and to let their brothers go to war and fight the battles for the community to which they belonged and to which they had given their allegiance. Moses sees it differently. His reply is that they have no moral right to make such a request. They have an obligation first to their community; and Moses phrases that obligation in clear-cut language. *"Shall your brethren go the war while you sit here?"* How do you feel about the question that is posed by this Biblical event? Who is right, the sons of Gad and Reuben, or Moses? Let us consider each side of the coin, for surely each side had something to say in its favor.

The people who adhere to the position of the leaders of Gad and Reuben claim that individuals should only look after their own interests and those of their immediate family. They have their jobs to perform, their children to educate, their friends to enjoy, their houses to build, their lawns to cultivate, their golf games or their tennis matches to play, their sleep to get in, their parties to attend, their trips to take, their hobbies to develop, and a hundred other activities that enrich life and provide living that is zestful and pleasant. This is life they say, and they are quite honest and frank to admit that they do not have time for anything that is not in some way connected with their own personal pleasure, enjoyment, or satisfaction.

Persons who hold to this position usually loathe persons who they say are *do-gooders*. They ridicule, poke fun at, and look down on individuals who spend time collecting funds for the Community Chest, helping out on a voluntary basis in hospitals, schools, or day nurseries. They also think the idea ridiculous that persons will give up part of their time assisting in political activities, participating actively in the life of a church or helping out when a neighbor is in need. They laugh at the Peace Corps and call the program a sop for a lot of crock pots. They also find every excuse imaginable to save their sons from serving in the armed forces when their sons' turns come around. I have met these persons often in my life. I recall vividly a mother calling me frantically one day when I was on duty in the Pentagon asking me could I not do something to keep her son from going to Korea. I thought there was illness or an emergency in the family. "No," she said, "there is no emergency but he is my only son and I cannot stand his being away from me for so long. He might get killed. There are so many others who can go," she said, "and why can't another boy go in my son's place?" What would have been your reaction to that plea? This is exactly the type of request that was presented to Moses by the Gadites and the Reubenites. This cry epitomizes precisely the philosophy of those who accent personal interest. *"Do not take us across the Jordan."*

The opposite of complete personal interest is total involvement in social concerns. There are persons who sacrifice everything, even themselves, for the common good. They refuse even to marry and have a family because family life would interfere with complete devotion to the cause in which they believe and to which they have given their lives. Colonel David Lawrence, known as Lawrence of Arabia, gave his life almost completely to the task of uniting the Arabs against the Turks during World War I and insuring national independence for the Arab states. Lawrence felt that some divine command had been placed on his shoulders to carry out his mission. We know also that many leaders of the American Revolution gave up their lives and fortunes to insure political and social freedom for the cause of American independence. Here is what they said in part, in the Declaration of Independence:

> And for the support of this declaration, with a firm reliance
> on the protection of Divine Providence, we mutually pledge
> to each other our lives, our fortunes and our sacred honor.

Surely, the person who stands above all persons in shouldering responsibility for the community is our Lord, Jesus Christ. *"No one takes my life from me, but I give it of myself."* Here is complete abandonment of personal interest. The only concern is *"to do the will of my Father who sent me."*

Moses represents a modified form of complete abandonment of all personal concerns for the social community. He believed that a person had no right to expect personal favors when there was a crisis at hand and the life of the common good was at stake. At the particular moment when the Gadites and Reubenites came to him a campaign was developing to cross the Jordan and every man was needed to wage that campaign. No wonder he was angry when these men came wanting to beg off and stay behind because they had never had it so good. A national effort was needed to cross the Jordan and wage war against the Canaanites. It was not that Moses was against their living in the Trans-Jordan where their families were enjoying life, their crops prospering, and their cattle thriving. Moses said, "You can come back but right now there is a job to do and you have no moral right to beg off. Your job is to do your best for your community, and then you may return to live here after your obligation to your nation is completed." The men realized the stupidity of their request. They agreed with Moses that they would first serve the larger community then they would return. Here are their words after they have seen the light, *We will not return to our homes until the people have inherited each his inheritance.*

Is this not the position that seems reasonable and fair to all of us? The Biblical message, as I understand it, teaches balance and flexibility in all matters of serious issue. There is a place for a person to enjoy his family, his friends, his hobbies, and his personal interests. There is a time also for one to give up these individual concerns when a crisis is imminent and the life of the common good is at stake. There is a time for a man to say as did Nathan Hale, "I regret I have only one life to give for my country." These are the extremes but life is not always lived at the extremes of the continuum. Most of the time we live not in the face of emergencies, but partly facing social demands and partly facing personal pleasures. If the Biblical record has any validity at all, it holds that both horns of the dilemma have to be included in our repertoire of activities. Make time for personal pleasures and interests, but also time for the welfare of the society of which we are all a part. There is time enough and time to spare for all that we want to do if only we can be wise enough to budget our time as carefully as we ought to budget our money.

As we face this new year in the church (fiscal year of July to July), there are many jobs for you and me to do. It can be a happy and satisfying year for each one of us if each one will do what he is able to do for the advancement of the program of Christ and his church. All that anyone is asked to do is to be sure that he allows some time each week for what he or she is asked to do. Don't get overburdened but don't get underburdened either. We have a real challenge and task before us. I am sure each one will do his best.

Sermon

33

EXPLORING OUR RESENTMENT TOWARD THE GOOD FORTUNE OF OTHERS

Jonah 4:1 But it displeased Jonah exceedingly, and he was angry.

The book of Jonah has traditionally been one of the most intriguing writings of the Bible. Persons have been amazed because the story tells of a man who lived for three days and three nights in the stomach of a whale. Some have been fascinated because some interpreters, seeking to see in the story an allegorical reference to Jesus Christ, have claimed it foretold that there would be three days between the death and resurrection of Christ. Still the book has been a source of mystery to others because the historical situation in which the story is couched as related by the author does not equate with other data of the period uncovered by historians who study ancient documents and civilizations.

These and other mysterious findings and interpretations concerning Jonah, however, are not the reasons for the importance of Jonah. If these elements had been in any way related to the importance of the book, Jonah would not have been selected by early Jewish scholars for a place in the Old Testament canon. The intriguing element of Jonah and the cause of its significance is that it is a parable concerning some of the most baffling foibles of human existence. One of these foibles and the one which will concern us this morning – is the resentment or anger a person often feels when good fortune comes to another person. That was not only a flaw in the character of Jonah but it is also a spiritual disorder in our own lives. This flaw interferes with our ability to develop wholesome relationships with other persons, not only those we do not know, but even our friends and persons in our families.

Let us look at this problem, first of all, as it was lived and experienced by Jonah. We do not know all of the background of the book. It seems, however, it was written not too long after the Jews had suffered exile in Babylon. They were sent into exile by Nebuchadnezzar the Chaldean in the year 586 B.C. They were permitted to return in 538 B.C. – almost 50 years later by Cyrus the Persian, after he had defeated the Assyrians. Naturally, the Jews rejoiced because they were free to leave Babylon and return to Jerusalem but they were also bitter because they had been driven into exile. They felt, at many did, that they were better than the Babylonians and the Babylonians had no right to humiliate them by forcing them to live in a foreign country. They believed - many did - that God was only for them and was against the hated Babylonians. Jonah was one, according this story, who held to this exclusive position – hatred for the enemy and pride in his snobbish religious views.

Some great teacher, however, whose name we do not know refused to be contaminated by this kind of spiritual sickness. The way he saw the matter, God was the God of all peoples and he was as much interested in the Babylonians as the Jews. He wrote this book, therefore, to lift the vision of the people so that they could see how ridiculous their exclusiveness was in the sight of God.

He developed the parable something like this: Jonah was a prophet of God – some say he symbolized the Jewish nation – who was righteous, correct, and pious in all his ways. He believed God was all for him because he was all for God. He was safe, secure, and snug in the little plan of salvation he had worked out for himself. But one day God, the God Jonah thought he knew so well, upset his comfortable, self-contained, and neurotic existence by telling him to preach to the people of Nineveh. "The people are in trouble," God told Jonah, and they need the word of the Lord. But Jonah refused, ran away, and ended up in the stomach of a whale – a perfect symbol for a man who is lonely because he has isolated himself from God and man. Finally, he was thrown up on dry land. Again, Jonah is hounded by God and told to go to Nineveh. Then, Jonah goes and preaches to the Ninevites and they repent and they are spared the sorrows and pain of spiritual disorder. But these are the hated Ninevites and Jonah is angry because they repented. You would have thought he would have been glad and that he would have rejoiced at their good fortune - but not so! Jonah was angry because God wanted him to help the Ninevites - those he thought of as inferior people. He was bitter, resentful, and angry. He says so to God and shows his real colors - and here is the way the writer describes his spiritual sickness.

Jonah 4:1-4 But it displeased Jonah exceedingly, and he was angry. And he prayed to the Lord and said, "I pray thee, Lord, is not this what I said when I was yet in my country? That is why I made haste to flee to Tarshish; for I knew that thou art a gracious God and merciful, slow to anger, and abounding in steadfast love, and repentest of evil. Therefore now, O Lord, take my life from me, I beseech thee, for it is better for me to die than to live." And the Lord said, "Do you do well to be angry?"

You can certainly compliment Jonah for his honesty. He let God have it. He told God in a sense, "I told you so. Now you see what has happened. These foreigners and heathens are now as good as you and me. Now you know why I ran away and hid. But God, you weren't satisfied. You had to show this kindness and mercy and consideration. Now they are no longer wicked men, but they are well people. I cannot stand it for anyone to be as well off as I am. So God please let me die and escape the pain of seeing anyone else finding good fortune."

There is the problem the book of Jonah deals with – the predicament of feeling resentment when another gets a break. Let us explore this problem briefly to see if we can get to its roots. It may help us to handle such a predicament in our own lives.

First, I feel sure people are annoyed by this problem because they have been taught to have an exaggerated opinion of themselves. Jonah and the people of his nation who he represented had been impressed since childhood with the idea that they were the chosen people of God and that persons of every other nation were inferior and spiritually illiterate. Naturally, having this belief constantly pounded into their heads, they would grow up thinking of themselves as living on a pedestal, surveying the unfortunate people of other nationalities as uncouth, ill-mannered, and ill-bred. They would also believe that God had no use for other people and that God favored only his chosen people. No wonder Jonah was angry and resentful. His smug self-contained belief system was shattered when he found that God was interested in the Ninevites and that the Ninevites were also as decent and morally upright as he was. If I had been Jonah, I think I would probably have felt as angry as he was.

Have you heard the story that I did? It is the same story that we find in Jonah only it happened only a few years ago. The Negro scientist, George Washington Carver, who was born of slave parents, exhibited on one occasion many articles he had produced from sweet potatoes and peanuts. After Carver had lectured and displayed his inventions, two men who had not been blessed with many cultural and educational advantages, walked up to Carver, obviously impressed with what they saw. They could not believe that a Negro, whom they had been taught were stupid and ignorant people, could have such good fortune come to him. It was more than they could stand. They looked down on Negroes, but here they had to look up. Naturally, they were confused, frustrated, and uncomfortable. They felt angry because good fortune had come to someone they basically despised. Finally, in desperation they blurted out, "Well boy, you certainly have done good making all these here gadgets. But don't forget you are still a nigger." The spiritual sickness of Jonah is as contagious and active today as it was almost 2300 years ago.

Next, consider if you will, that a person can become resentful at the success of another because of an overworked spirit of competitiveness. This is not quite the cause of Jonah's sickness but it is the same illness. Just as a fever in the body or a headache is caused by any number of organisms or psychic malfunctions so resentment of another's good fortune can result from any number of unbalances and disorders in our interpersonal relationships. An over emphasis on getting ahead of the other fellow, striving to be number one, the necessity of having to outdo the other fellow can certainly result in feelings of intense bitterness when the other person comes out on top and one has been outdone.

Bob and Tom were good friends all through grade school and high school. Bob was popular, smart, and a leader in his class. He had to be on top or he was unhappy. Tom was quiet, made only fair grades, and was content to hunt and fish and not interested in school politics or being the best liked, the best dressed, or the best anything. The boys, though different, were friends. They seemed to need each other. But about mid-way in college, something happened. Suddenly Tom came out of his shell and walked off with top academic honors. Bob became resentful toward Tom because he found himself in a situation which was strange and unfamiliar. He did not know how to handle a situation in which Tom was on top. Like Jonah, like the men who spoke unkindly to Dr. Carver, Bob was frustrated and confused so he lashed out at Tom and broke off their friendship. One can easily go sour when all he knows is being on top of the heap and finds someone else there instead. Teaching our children to outdo others and to be the best has its merits, I suppose, but it can lead to serious emotional disturbance. Certainly, we want our children to do well but it is far healthier to encourage them to develop their own resources rather than to demand that they race ahead just to outdo the other fellow.

Now, the last cause of the kind of resentment we have been discussing that I want to mention is repressed anger toward a person that has become generalized. You are aware that a child can be taught to shake hands with his uncle when the uncle comes to visit in the child's home. At first, the child only shakes hands with his uncle but soon after coaching and practice he begins to learn it is polite to shake hands with all adults he sees after a long time. He learns to shake hands with one adult person but he soon learns to shake hands with all adult persons. This is what we call generalized learning from a specific event.

A similar phenomenon occurs also in our spiritual development. We can learn negative feelings just as easily as positive feelings, probably much more easily. For example, a person may have an unpleasant, miserable childhood. Perhaps his parents died when he was young and he was taken in by relatives who did not want him but there was no one else. Perhaps the relatives grew tired of him and placed him with foster parents who took him only for the money. So the child grows up unwanted, feeling no one cares for or believes in him. Not always, but sometimes such a person allows his unfortunate childhood to warp and distort his perspective toward life in general, so he becomes suspicious, fearful, angry toward life and people in general. Is it any wonder that such a person will become resentful toward the success of another person? He may find it impossible to ever break the chains of anger in which he finds himself enclosed. Understandably, such a person is deeply sick and is in need of help from someone who cares and understands and is competent to provide assistance.

What I think we learn from this parable of Jonah is that spirituality is not altogether a matter of attending a service of worship each Sunday, taking communion regularly, saying our prayers regularly, or bringing our tithes and offerings. All of these Jonah did and perhaps he engaged in many other acts of piety and devotion. We learn instead, that spirituality has to do with what is occurring at the depths of our personalities. We can pray and still be spiteful. We can tithe and still be hateful. We can know theology and still be resentful. We can be righteous and pious and still harbor bitterness. In other words, we can serve God but still violate the basic spiritual laws of life, for we only discover spiritual health as we face ourselves honestly and seek to establish relationships with others that are as free as possible of resentment, bitterness, and ill-will, and attitudes that divide but do not reconcile. The writer of the first epistle of John put it succinctly when he wrote, *"He that says he loves God and hates his brother is a liar, for he who does not love his brother whom he has seen cannot love God whom he has not seen."* That is about as clear as one can possibly state the matter! It seems that our relationship to God finally depends on healthy relationships with each other.

34

UNDERSTANDING AND FULFILLING OUR ROLES

Mark 8:29 Who do you say that I am?

Life is a series of roles which each of us performs. In one day, one man may be a father, a husband, a grandfather, an office worker, a committee member, a friend, a neighbor, a church member, and any other number of roles.

We have the same person, but he expresses himself in a different way, depending on his relationship to the person or persons with whom he communicates and the demands or expectations of the situation.

Life is lived at its best when persons understand the various roles they perform and properly fulfill the expectations of these roles as they move from one role to another.

A man was a foreman in a large industrial plant. His job was to fabricate automobile bodies and to move them within a certain time frame through his shop from the time he received them until he turned them over to the department that was responsible for the next task on the bodies. This job required a foreman who was firm and demanding of those under him. He was a man known for his toughness and hardness. One day the wife of this foreman and the wife of one of the men who worked in the plant under the foreman met at the supermarket. The wife of the man who worked under the foreman finally allowed her curiosity to get the best part of her, and she said to the foreman's wife. "My husband tells me your husband is one of the hardest, most demanding men he ever worked under. Tell me, how can you live with such a person?"

The other lady replied, "My husband is the most gentle man I have ever known. He isn't as you say, tough or hard. I have never known a kinder man. A woman could not have a better husband."

Were they talking about the same man? This was a healthy man, he knew his job at the plant and did it – he also knew his role as a husband and he carried it out in an admirable manner. This is what we mean when we say a person has many roles. The wise man understands the roles he has to play in life and fulfills these roles according to the demands and expectations of the various roles he plays.

When a person, however, tries to carry out every role in the same way he is injurious to himself and destructive in his relationships with others. A sergeant I knew ran his family like a military outfit. The children were treated like junior officers. The story goes that the little boy said he wanted to know how to apply for a transfer! We cannot run a family like a military unit. We need to be pliable.

If one does not measure up to the requirements of the role or mission he is supposed to perform he confuses people and causes people to become frustrated and angry and the situation becomes sick. A bad situation can develop in a business operation when the supervisor of a department fails to give firm and clear directions and guidance to those working under him. If persons come in late to work, take long breaks, overstay their lunch hour, or are allowed to be sloppy in their work, the whole operation breaks down, people become unhappy and dissatisfied and you find a large employee turnover. If a person is a supervisor, he is expected to supervise, and problems develop if he allows poor performance to continue without correction.

Sometimes when persons move from one culture to another culture they produce confusion among people because they are unaccustomed to carrying out the role expected in the new situation. Role understanding and role fulfillment are musts for harmonious human relationships.

What has all this to do with religion? A great deal – religion is concerned with healthy attitudes, satisfying human relationships, and persons performing their roles in an effective way – this is applicable in the home, the office, in our play, and in all of life's relationships, as well as in the church.

Jesus asked, "Who do people say that I am?" He was concerned about himself and the nature of his mission. He tested what he believed about himself with what others had to say about him.

Another question that came to his mind was - if I am going to fulfill a Messianic role, what kind of role will it be? Will it be what I think it will be, or what others think it should be? These were crucial questions for Jesus and he had to have significant answers. Here with Peter and his disciples we find him searching, inquiring, testing, and trying to arrive at understanding how to fulfill his role in keeping with what he believes to be the expectations of God. Role knowledge and role fulfillment were crucial for Jesus.

Now one of the roles that confront you and me is the role we perform as Christians and members of the church. Evidently we are concerned about this role in our lives or we would not be here this morning. The degree of our participation in this task determines the value we place on this role.

Some believe in this role for their lives. They are committed to the church and know and fulfill this role in their lives. They come to the church and bring their children. They share in the life of the church and generously support the church and its programs. This church is fortunate in having so many people of this category in its membership. The chairman of the board was telling me the other evening of the excellent support he receives from the church members. Seldom, he said, do I call on anyone for a job who doesn't respond in a fine and cooperative way.

Perhaps, other persons here this morning are in the church as members in one way or another but are not quite sure of this role in their lives. They still wonder whether they belong or not. They attend some, participate some, support some, but are not really convinced of the importance of this part of their lives. They may understand but do not fulfill the role. Others perhaps are not members in any form but go once in a while but are not sure why.

There seems to be some attraction or perhaps feeling of guilt inherent from childhood that somehow urges them to check in occasionally to find out if things are getting along all right.

I can fully appreciate the person in the decision making process concerning any venture, whether it is church affiliation or something else. If this is where you are, I hope you will allow me to help you meet this problem and deal with it by attending the classes that will soon be starting. I hope these classes are not merely means *to get* people in the church but to provide persons a chance to come to grips with and find a more satisfying position regarding their role as a church member and their relationship to the church. For surely our relationship to the church is related to our total philosophy of life and until a person has found a satisfying position in this area of life he is an incomplete, detached and alienated person, for indecision, uncertainty, confusion, as valuable as they are in the scheme of decision making, can never be ultimately relied upon to help us understand and fulfill the significant roles that life thrusts upon us to perform. What is required for wholesome, well-rounded and productive being is knowledge, a sense of conviction and commitment concerning one's relationship to the world in which we live and the God who made us.

35

THE DANGER OF CARING TOO MUCH

Genesis 27:13 His mother said to him, "Upon me be your curse, my son; only obey my word, and go, fetch them to me." (Rebekah helps Jacob to steal the blessing of Isaac from his brother Esau.)

Christians are fond of saying that Christianity is not a religion of law but a religion of the spirit. Paul conveyed this concept in these words, *"The law killeth but the spirit giveth life."* I take this to mean that the application of Christian faith to human behavior is dependent upon one's spiritual capacity to estimate what is appropriate and proper at a particular moment and in a particular situation. Rules and codes are not set down for us to govern behavior. Instead, we are forced to utilize our best judgment in making decisions in every new situation. Our only guide, our only control, is the spirit of love. Paul expressed it this way, *"It is the spirit of Christ that constrains us."*

For example, we are admonished to care for the sick and the poor; to be concerned about the discouraged and the lonely; to be interested in noble and righteous causes; to love our children, members of our families, our friends, and even our enemies; and to give ourselves in devotion to the cause of Christ. Yet, we are never told how much or how little we should love or be concerned. The degree is a matter of spiritual discernment – what appears to be the best at the moment and in the particular situation.

We are often admonished to care abundantly but seldom are we advised that it is possible to care too much. And when we carefully consider the matter, we do find that there are dangers in caring too much. We should recognize these pitfalls, for in our caring too much we may do more harm than good, that is, in some situations and under some circumstances. Let us see how this matter of caring too much is possible by allowing the Biblical account of Rebekah and her ambitions for her son, Jacob, to speak to us.

Rebekah's over-concern, her compulsiveness, to have her son, Jacob, receive top honors caused her to break one of the basic laws of her society. She wanted so much for him to be number one that nothing else mattered, even if it meant violating one of the sacred and honored moral codes of Judaism.

We know the story. Rebekah and Isaac had two sons, Esau and Jacob. Esau was the older, Jacob the younger. Esau was a hairy man, red in color, crude in his manner, coarse in his speech, slow witted in his mental functioning. What Esau was not, however, Jacob was – handsome, brilliant conversationalist, pleasant in disposition, shrewd, crafty, a man who knew what to do in polite society. Rebekah probably would say she loved both boys the same, but she didn't like them the same. She seemed only to tolerate poor Esau, but she was devoted to Jacob. Well, who can blame Rebekah? What parent wouldn't enjoy the company of Jacob more than Esau, though both were sons? We know in our relationships to our children that it is more pleasant to be around some than others.

But Esau had the edge on Jacob in only one respect: Esau was the older. He was the elder son, the highest privilege any child could have in a middle-eastern family and the same is still true in parts of the middle-east today. One of his privileges was to receive the greater part of the family inheritance when the father died. Another privilege was that when the father died, the eldest son could be the head of the family, even of greater authority than the mother. This was an ancient and sacred rule of family life among the Hebrews. It gave order and stability to the family and helped people to know who they were in the family and where they belonged.

Rebekah, however, could not accept this custom for her family. She wanted her favorite son, Jacob, to have this honored position, not the rightful heir, Esau. She connived, therefore, with Jacob to deceive her husband, Isaac, who was on his death-bed. She dressed Jacob in sheepskin, had him go in to Isaac who was almost blind and had him pretend he was Esau. Isaac blessed Jacob, thinking he was Esau, and bequeathed to him all to which the first-born was entitled. Later, Isaac discovered he had been deceived, but the blessing could not be changed; once invoked it was irrevocable. So Rebekah cared too much for Jacob's welfare. It caused her to violate the law of the first-born, one of the most sacred of all the ancient laws of the Jewish people.

Now, this is an old story, but the dynamic quality is contemporary. Modern parents will often go to any extreme to get what they want their children to have, even if it means breaking rules, violating regulations, or subjecting themselves to any compromise. Officials in some of our top-ranking universities report that one of the gravest and most delicate problems they frequently have to handle is that of wealthy and influential parents who want their son or daughter to attend a certain prestigious university but the son or daughter does not possess the academic qualifications for admittance. Sometimes bribes are offered, jobs threatened, pull from higher officials tried – any scheme is attempted because of caring too much. Seldom do students do well who are admitted under such pressure. Academic performance is a matter of scholastic ability, student interest, and hard work, not who one knows or how much pull one has.

Wherever you put your finger, however, you find the compulsiveness of Rebekah at work – persons driven by need, caring too much, using devious means to achieve their purposes. No wonder we have anti-trust laws to curb the overly developed desire of business men to gain the control of a commodity market, and checks on labor union officials who must have power over their union members even at the expense of those they seek to serve. It is indeed a terrible sickness when people must break all the laws of common decency and fair play to get what they want. We can care too much about success.

Next, we find that because Rebekah was overly anxious for her son Jacob, she even corrupted him. Her love was an unhealthy love. She wanted so much for him to be the recipient of Isaac's blessing that she was willing to destroy him. One wonders whether she was actually interested in Jacob. The evidence seems to show she was really more concerned about her own ambitions, which she was seeking to realize in Jacob, than in Jacob as a person. It is difficult to accept the proposition that she truly loved Jacob, for surely one does not corrupt the one who is loved. Yet, that is what happened! Her love, or what is often called love, for her son corrupted his life.

See how she corrupted him! Rebekah taught him to use deceit to attain his ends. She had him dress as Esau, to say he was Esau, to imitate Esau. At first Jacob objected, *But Jacob said to Rebekah his mother, "Behold, my brother Esau is a hairy man, and I am a smooth man. Perhaps my father will feel me, and I shall seem to be mocking him, and bring a curse upon myself and not a blessing!"* We certainly cannot praise Jacob for his high level of morality. The idea that he did not approve of his mother's scheme because it was dishonest and a lie does not come through. His only concern was not to get caught. Yet, in a way, he does object but his mother presses him further. She replies to Jacob's warning and says, *"Upon me be your curse, my son; only obey my word, and go, fetch them to me."* If we learn from our parents at all, then Rebekah must stand in judgment before the Lord, for in these words, she teaches her son the fine art of shrewdness, dishonesty, and deceit.

One of the tragedies of this story is that Rebekah deceives herself into thinking that she can bear the blame or curse for the treacherous act Jacob is about to commit. She thinks she can bear the curse, and why not? She loves him so much she believes he cannot be blamed for wrongdoing. But Rebekah is mistaken! No one can assume the curse of misconduct for another, not even a mother who cares too much about her son's attainments. Later on, we read of the treachery of Jacob in other ways, but no one blames Rebekah. The irony of it all is that poor Jacob, who was taught so well by a possessive, over-ambitious mother to be crooked, is held accountable for his crookedness. And this is the curse of Jacob — he cannot blame anyone for his underhandedness. He has to stand responsible for himself. And that is what you and I have to do, too. There comes a time in the life of every last one of us when we cannot place the blame on Mom or Dad, a school teacher, God, or anyone else for what we do or fail to do, but we must shoulder the glory or the shame for ourselves. The tragedy is that so many parents think they can bear life for their children but they cannot. Always, what we do for our children, either for good or for bad, they must eventually assume for themselves.

Now, the curse on Jacob, which Rebekah thought she could take on herself, was not only learning deceit, but also being driven to perform an act which was not really in his interest. Yet, as a dutiful son, he went through with it anyway. How easy to demand from our children what they do not want themselves. Surely, encouragement is vital and essential. But undue pressure on children can be harmful, even when they do what parents want them to do. A child may even want what the parent wants, but rejects what both want because the parents want it, so fed up do they become with the constant pressures on them. As one young freshman told me, "I'm here in college because my parents want me here. Now that I'm here, I like it, but I would never give them the satisfaction of knowing I like it and I don't know how I can stay and pretend I don't like it when I do." That is a modern example of a girl living with a curse bestowed by parents who have cared too much!

But let us look at another danger of caring too much. Rebekah was so anxious about Jacob's receiving the blessing of the elder son that she crippled her total effectiveness as a person. One factor in her life was so everlastingly important to her that it drastically interfered with her functioning as a complete person. The accounts of Rebekah's early life with Isaac reveal a woman of rare beauty, grace, and charm. She and Isaac seemed to love each other deeply, but after the birth of the boys, Esau and Jacob, their relationship seemed to change. The writer of this fine narrative seems to indicate that there was an unhealthy favoritism on the part of the parents toward the children. The writer tells us that *"Isaac loved Esau, but Rebekah loved Jacob"*. Evidently, competitiveness developed between the parents concerning their sons. One gave his all to one and neglected the other. The other gave her attention to the other and slighted the first. This often happens. As a result, we discover that Rebekah became so wrapped up in Jacob that she became a different person. Isaac also changed and became wrapped up in Esau. As a result, the love that should have continued between Rebekah and Isaac was transferred to the respective children. So we see Rebekah became overly concerned and anxious about Jacob and crippled her ability to function as a healthy mature woman.

How easy it is for each of us to care for something or someone so very much that it becomes the organizing center of our lives, making it impossible for us to live complete, well-rounded lives. Too much concern about anyone or anything is always unwholesome. Too much religion is as bad as too little. Too much concern with keeping a house straight and in order is as bad as too little concern. Too much attention to appearance is as unproductive as too little interest in appearance. Too much caring about what children are doing is sometimes as bad as too little caring. Too much caring about one's pet projects can make life miserable for others as well as one's self. Too much interest in other people's problems incapacitates one's ability to help other people with their problems.

I don't look at TV often but I saw a program recently called *Life with Father*. It was corny in spots but I like something the father said. His family had been after him to go on a vacation but he said he had too much work to do. He couldn't go. A few days later he came home and announced that he was ready to go on a vacation. "What caused the change?" his wife asked, "What about your work?"

"Well," he said, "I began to think about what I had said about being too busy to go on a vacation. I decided I was wrong in my evaluation of my work. I considered work my reason for living whereas I should have thought of it as a reason or a means for making possible my home, my family, and my friends. Work is important," he said, "but it cannot be the only reason for living." Right or wrong, he discovered that no one activity is so essential that it cannot be put aside for awhile for other activities which are also important for the abundant life.

How pertinent the gospel is to life! It lays down no rules and regulations. Rather it fills life with zest and adventure. It doesn't demand we live by a clock or by a regulator. Rather it presents us with a complement (something that completes or makes perfect). It holds that we can be governed by the gospel of love and that we can discover the spiritual resources to know how much to care. We need to care for all good things very much and very deeply, but we need to understand that no thing or person can be cared for too much or else it becomes an idol to worship. Worship is not reserved for a man or a woman or a child or a job or a church or a religion. Worship belongs only to God, only He deserves our final and ultimate loyalty, for did not Jesus our Lord teach us that the first Commandment is this, *"That thou shalt love the Lord thy God with all of thy heart, and with all of thy strength and with all of thy mind."* When God is first, we do not have to be worried about the dangers of caring too much.

SEEING THE GOSPEL AT WORK

Luke 19:1-10

1 He entered Jericho and was passing through.
2 And there was a man named Zacchae'us; he was a
chief tax collector, and rich.
3 And he sought to see who Jesus was, but could not, on
account of the crowd, because he was small of stature.
4 So he ran on ahead and climbed up into a sycamore
tree to see him, for he was to pass that way.
5 And when Jesus came to the place, he looked up and said to him,
"Zacchae'us, make haste and come down; for
I must stay at your house today."
6 So he made haste and came down, and received him joyfully.
7 And when they saw it they all murmured, "He has
gone in to be the guest of a man who is a sinner."
8 And Zacchae'us stood and said to the Lord, "Behold,
Lord, the half of my goods I give to the poor; and if I have
defrauded any one of anything, I restore it fourfold."
9 And Jesus said to him, "Today salvation has come to
this house, since he also is a son of Abraham.
10 For the Son of man came to seek and to save the lost."

An interesting incident reported in the *Readers Digest* some years ago, which perhaps many of us remember, described a large cargo trailer that was stopped on the road, unable to go under an overhead trestle, because the top of the trailer was about two inches too high. Traffic was held up and men were gathered around trying to figure out some simple solution to the predicament. The answer came from an unexpected source. A small boy came along on his bicycle, sized up the situation, and said to the confused men, "Perhaps, the trailer will go through if someone lets some of the air out of the tires." And it worked!

When a new dimension is brought to a perplexing situation that changes the snarled condition into a smooth flowing operation, such as the insight the small boy brought to the truck stuck under the overhead bridge, you have an illustration that helps to understand what occurs when the gospel is at work.

Zacchaeus, for example, was snarled up in his relationships with the people of his village. He was a Jew but he was also a collector of taxes for the Romans who occupied the towns of Palestine. Whatever he got from the people over and above the regular tax, he was allowed to keep for himself. Naturally, he was despised by his countrymen, for they figured that no job could be lower than for one of their own citizens to collect taxes for the hated Romans. Evidently, Zacchaeus was getting rich at the expense of his people and he was socially ostracized. What caused a man to become a quisling? The reasons are hard to fathom. Any number of underlying causes are possible. It may be that in Zacchaeus' case, he was using his position to get back at people in his village who perhaps had ridiculed him because of his small stature. People can often be cruel in their remarks and attitudes toward persons who are deformed or handicapped in some way. Again, he may not have been ridiculed at all but he was just bitter because nature or God had played such a dirty trick on him to make him smaller than other men; therefore, he struck back at society because of dissatisfaction with the condition of his life. These are, of course, only guesses about Zacchaeus and the inner drives that held his life in chains and caused him to be less than he was capable of becoming; but, we do know he was not a healthy person. He was spiritually sick and needed salvation.

Then, Jesus came into his life. What transpired between Jesus and Zacchaeus we do not know. But one fact is certain: Zacchaeus was unloosed from the chains of frustration, fear, and corruptions that had surrounded his life, and he became a new person. Luke gives us this brief account of what happened, *"And Zacchaeus stood, and said unto the Lord; Behold, Lord, the half of my goods I give to the poor; and if I have taken any thing from any man by false accusation, I restore him fourfold."*

Such a change in a person's life occurs when *something* allows him to stop struggling against what is blocking his development and growth and permits him to emerge into a new self. While once he was cramped, tied up inside, cranky, irritable, spiteful, and all at once or gradually, he lets go of his defenses and becomes a new person. The old theology called this something that blocked or interfered with growth, sin, or estrangement from the source of being.

This something that trips the lever or ignites the spark is what Christian tradition calls the *gospel*. Jesus brought the gospel to Zacchaeus or better, Jesus established the conditions that allowed the gospel to ignite and it caught fire in the soul of Zacchaeus. When Jesus heard Zacchaeus proclaim the release of his soul from sin and declare his intention to express healthy attitudes and behavior toward his countrymen, Jesus quietly summarized the situation by saying, *"Today salvation has come to this house."* The fruit of the gospel is indeed the salvation.

This *something* that ignites a change in a person is not easy to define. In fact, I seriously doubt if it can be defined. About all that can be done is to point to it. The little boy brought *something* to a confused situation that was desperately needed and it allowed a traffic jam, heated tempers, and a perplexed driver to straighten out. Jesus also brought *something* to Zacchaeus that released him from confusion and allowed the best of Zacchaeus to shine through. Now it is certain that the little boy and Jesus did not bring the same *something* to conditions that were mixed up and we must be careful not to confuse one *something* with another *something*, although they probably do have some characteristics that are similar. The boy brought what we might call rational judgment – the ability to solve a problem by a gestalt or a configuration of many things seen in balanced relation to each other. Jesus, on the other hand, brought the spirit of love, the Holy Spirit, that quality of spirit that is seen when one human being brings concern, understanding, and hope to another human being. This spirit I take it, is what we call the gospel, that power or force that causes a person to let go of the chains that cramp his life and to permit the deep resources of the human spirit to shine through.

I hope you have noticed that I have said that the gospel is that power or spirit that makes it possible to drop or let go of something that is clogging life. Let us emphasize that *holding on* to something prevents us from becoming productive persons. The conviction has grown on me within the past few years as I have listened to persons talk about their personal lives, that most of us are dwarfed in our spiritual lives because we are actually holding on by defending something that we consider important to us. But unfortunately, this *thing*, whatever it may be, is like a chain or rope around our spirits that is holding us back and interfering with our becoming real, live, active, buoyant people. It is as deadening to human life as a malignancy is to an organ of the body. Somehow if we can get at that thing through the spirit and allow its barnacles to drop from our shoulders, we can become what the New Testament calls *new persons in Christ*.

Here are some things I have found people hold on to:

1. Defiance against authority – no one is going to tell me what to do.
2. To be cared for – I insist others have to take care of me.
3. Feelings of wrong doing or guilt – I *must* feel unworthy.
4. Staying to one's self or fear – I don't want to be with others.
5. I must have things my own way – This is selfishness.

Well, when these and other drives control us, we are hooked and they produce some frightful behavior. They can cause laziness, poor performance on the job or at school, carelessness in dress, habitual lateness and irresponsibility, lying, stealing, being over-weight, headaches, back pain, addiction, alcoholism, and a hundred other illnesses and behavior problems.

For example, a young college woman came to my office several months ago, as she said, to get some help on study habits. After we had talked a while, I began to have a hunch that her difficulty was not study helps but something much more serious. I learned that she had a brilliant mind but she was failing most of her courses. Finally, she came out with it, after a few talks together. "It's my father! He drives me until I am crazy. I'll never study until he gets off of my back."

This fine, bright, but over-driven girl wanted to do well in school but she was *holding on* to a deep resentment against her father. She didn't study because it was the only way she had of striking back against her father's continuous pressure on her to make good grades. But notice this defiance of her parent – the *thing* that she had to hold on to was also the chain that was making her a prisoner, restraining her from doing what she really wanted to. But defiance was more important than school success. That had to be released, let go, before she could have salvation come to her life. Luckily she responded to the atmosphere of understanding, trust, and respect that was provided during our conversations. She saw finally what she was doing and how badly she was hurting her life. She gradually gave up her defiance and started the long hard road of academic pursuit, not to please or displease her parent, but because she wanted to learn and grow herself. The gospel still works just as sure and certain now as it did when Jesus brought it to Zacchaeus.

This brings us to conclude then, that the action of the gospel is not confined to any particular situation or institution. It works wherever the Holy Spirit is allowed to work and when persons are able to respond to its grace and power. The church is its main channel of grace but the church as an institution cannot hold it, contain it, or make it its only and sole property. Often, it happens that those persons who believe in its power have been forced to leave the institution in order for the Spirit to live and breathe in the lives of people and society. Jesus found that he was unable to bring the Spirit within the ecclesiastical institution of his day; so, he carried the Spirit through him to the roadside and the villages wherever he found persons who needed the grace and blessings of the gospel. To the Jewish community, he brought freshness and a gospel of love, hope, and faith, not laws, customs, rituals, and observances. To the Gentile community, he brought through the gospel decency of life, dignity of the individual, and the love of God for all humanity. Luther had to break also from an institution gone mad with power and privilege in order to allow the gospel to live in the lives of the humble people. William Booth also had to break with the institutions of his day to bring the gospel to the dispossessed in the slums and alleys of London.

The gospel today works not in the same form that it has always worked but still its work goes on. The fields of medicine and the behavioral sciences also have devoted men and women who are changing the lives of the spiritually ill. Notice also the government has instituted a new program called *Headstart* to make it possible for young children who have been denied cultural opportunities to receive instruction in an atmosphere of warmth and concern so they will be prepared to have a better chance of learning when they begin school with other children in the community whose backgrounds have been more favorable. These and other educational programs are vital to permit children to move from darkness into light and to prepare them to handle the social demands of our culture.

This is certainly no time for the church to establish itself as the only organization that carries the fruits of the gospel. We give witness to it and we welcome all others who bear the same witness. Dr. Paul Tournier reminds us that the gospel is really often all a highly personalized experience between two or three persons who deeply feel for each other and are genuinely concerned as to what happens to one another. It is not the property of anyone or any agency. The Spirit is where it lives. Your mission and mine is not to berate those who are not in the church, acting as though there were two camps, the saved and the unsaved, and crying come to us, for we possess the truth. Rather we must say to them as well as to ourselves - Let us sit together, repent together of our self-righteousness, and turn to Christ, for He only possesses the truth that we all require for salvation to come to our lives He is the gospel at work.

37

LAW AND SPIRIT

*Galatians 5:1 For freedom Christ has set us free; stand fast
therefore, and do not submit again to a yoke of slavery.*

No one who seriously studies the condition of Christendom can
deny that the church, in many respects, is in conflict with itself.
The conflict takes various forms. There is difference concerning the way the church should be organized – shall the form be
episcopacy, presbytery, or congregational? There is also divided
opinion regarding the position of the ministry, the nature and effi-
cacy of the sacraments, the degree of importance that should be
attached to the Bible and tradition, and a host of other differences,
some of major importance and others of a minor nature.

Many of these differences, however, are actually symptomatic
of conflicts that run much deeper and are of far greater consequence than some of the differences already mentioned. One of
the conflicts that is deep seated and is responsible for many others
is concerned with the fundamental nature of one's inner life, with

the very dynamics of motivation, that which causes our lives to take a particular direction or as Adler called it, to develop a particular *style or way of living*. Religion refers to this motivational activation as law or spirit. One segment of the church insists that religion is law. Another segment insists that religion is spirit. The lines cannot be drawn denominationally or even theologically. The difference between religion of law and spirit is basically an individual matter but it is important that we know the difference, for the approach a person takes largely determines the kind of a person he is.

Let us consider, first of all, what is meant by a religion of law and a religion of spirit. A religion of law places emphasis upon requirements. An act is performed because it is demanded by an authority outside of the person's life or an action is not done because it is forbidden by the authority. For example, in Roman Catholicism there is a law that a person must go to confession and Holy Communion, at least once a year. Also, a Catholic is required by the laws of the church to be married by a priest of the Roman Catholic Church. To be married otherwise is unacceptable. Also, in ancient Judaism, a faithful Jew was forbidden by law to eat pork, and among Seventh Day Adventists, there are laws which forbid eating meat, and require tithing. Then too, if you belong to certain Protestant groups, the Church of the Savior, for instance, in Washington, D.C., one of the most productive of all churches that I personally know anything about, there is a law requiring persons who belong to the church to attend a certain number of instructional classes each year and to give a certain proportion of their income to the church. These are churches or religious groups who insist that persons live by certain rules and regulations if they are going to be a part of the congregation.

A religion of the spirit, however, operates somewhat differently. There are no rules, regulations, requirements, or codes that one follows because they are imposed from the outside, for spirit is a disposition of the inner life which guides one to behave in a particular way because one desires or wants to engage in or refrain from a particular type of behavior, because he wants to, out of an inclination of the human heart. Such a person is directed from the inside of his life rather than by a requirement or law from the outside. He goes to church, not because it is demanded but because he wants to go. He gives to the church a certain amount each week, month or year because he feels this is what he wants to do. A religion of the spirit may observe laws of eating or giving but he does so, not because of the law, but because he believes such observance is best for his life and that of his society,

The difference between a religion of law and spirit is vividly portrayed in the conflict between Paul and Judaizers. Primitive Christianity – that period in the life of the church immediately following the death of Jesus – comprised Jewish men and women who accepted Jesus as Messiah. They continued to observe all of the ancient laws of Judaism – circumcision, holy days, fasting, and all the rest. The only difference between the Jews who were Christians and the Jews who were not Christians was that Christian Jews accepted Jesus as Messiah and the other Jews did not. Paul, however, disagreed with this position of the Jewish Christians and opposed them with all of the arguments he could muster. He believed that Jesus did away with the laws of Judaism and brought a religion of the spirit. The Jewish Christians, however, who opposed Paul, insisted that Gentiles who became Christians should be circumcised and made to subscribe to the Jewish laws. These Judaizers, as they were called, often visited the churches Paul established and told the new Gentile Christians that Paul was a nice fellow but there was a lot he did not know. These Judaizers told these new

Gentile converts if they were going to be acceptable to God in their new faith, they would have to begin by accepting circumcision. The people of Galatia when presented with this problem wrote to Paul to find out what he thought. Do we have to be circumcised? Paul is angry with the Judaizers and his reply is a firm "No!" His position is abbreviated in this verse of the 5th chapter of Galatians, *"For freedom Christ has set us free; stand fast therefore and do not submit again to a yoke of slavery."* In other words, Paul is saying, divorce yourselves from a religion of law and accept in freedom the grace of the Holy Spirit who will direct you in all the ways of your life. What is so strange in Christianity today is that we have not heeded the wisdom of Paul, for even today there is in Christendom the conflict that existed in the early church between those who insist on requirements and those who stress the inner life of the spirit.

Let us not be misled, however, in thinking that a religion of rules, codes, and regulations is unprofitable. There is much to be said for a religion that imposes obligations and demands upon people, and expresses its faith in a code or a book of regulations. For one thing, a religion of law is clear cut. A person knows what is required of him, for the book tells him what to do and what not to do. A man who is a Catholic once said that he liked Catholicism because the rules, the dogma, and the interpretations of Scripture were clear and unequivocal. He didn't have to be anxious about his faith so long as he followed the prescribed regulations.

In the next place, a religion of law is beneficial because it makes a person feel safe and certain. He knows if he follows the directions he *has it made*, so to speak. There is indeed a great deal of satisfaction in knowing that one is in good standing when he has carried out the requirements that are imposed on him.

Is there, then, no place for law in a religion of the spirit? Paul also seems to answer this question. The law of Judaism, he holds, was imposed, according to his interpretation, because of the sinfulness of the people. Once he said the Jewish people did live by faith or by spirit but their childish and sinful ways made the law necessary. In other words, the law of Judaism became necessary when people failed to respond to the openness and the freedom available under the spirit. This seems to say to us, then, that law is required when the spiritual life is not developed. This is certainly true of children. They must live under law at early ages else teeth would never be brushed, hair combed, baths taken, studying done, and a hundred other acts children are required to do to be healthy. Once they attain growth and begin to apply reason to life, they gradually throw off parental rules and perform the acts of life necessary for health and good living because they want to, not because they are told to.

But childishness is not reserved merely for children. Childishness is a mark of every age and when persons fail to respond to the life of the spirit - the life of the truly adult person - then laws must be imposed. Is it not true that if all of us followed the guidance of the Holy Spirit as we know it in Christ laws would be practically unheard of? But because of our inability to live by the Spirit we are frequently made to live by the law. Look what has happened only recently in our national life that makes this observation vivid and real. Because certain persons in certain states refuse to recognize the rights of all people under the Constitution to vote without intimidation or limitation, a law has been passed by Congress requiring what is already a natural condition given them under the Constitution. When the spirit fails, the law seems to be necessary.

As Dr. Fosdick has said so well, "If man will not control himself from within, he will be controlled from without."

Now, certainly you and I who bear the name of Christ know that we are children of the spirit and not of the law. I am glad and I hope you are that we are privileged to be a part of a section of the church that has tried to follow the example of Christ in regard to the Spirit. We claim no corner on truth. We do not place any requirements on anyone except what persons care to place on themselves. No one is told to come to religious services by the dictates of a law or creed. No one tells us how much we should do for the church or how little. No one dares to say how we should vote or not vote. No codes are set down as to what persons must do or not do in their private lives or in their social activities with others. Certainly problems are discussed, considered, and the best answers available are sought. But, in the end, each person must come out with the answer that he finds best for him and his family in the light of spirit that we know in Jesus Christ. We may differ in the final outcome but differences are unimportant so long as we are motivated, surrounded, and directed by the graciousness of God's Holy Spirit. My prayer is that we continue to witness and to pray that our religious life together may live in the life of the Spirit.

38

THE IMPORTANCE OF KNOWING HOW

Matthew 6:16-23

16 "And when you fast, do not look dismal, like the hypocrites, for they disfigure their faces that their fasting may be seen by men. Truly, I say to you, they have received their reward.

17 But when you fast, anoint your head and wash your face,

18 that your fasting may not be seen by men but by your Father who is in secret; and your Father who sees in secret will reward you.

19 "Do not lay up for yourselves treasures on earth, where moth and rust consume and where thieves break in and steal,

20 but lay up for yourselves treasures in heaven, where neither moth nor rust consumes and where thieves do not break in and steal.

21 For where your treasure is, there will your heart be also.

22 "The eye is the lamp of the body. So, if your eye is sound, your whole body will be full of light;

23 but if your eye is not sound, your whole body will be full of darkness. If then the light in you is darkness, how great is the darkness!

o you become disgusted as I sometimes do with the constant pressure we are subjected to by persons who want us to try something so that something miraculous will happen to us? We are told that if we *know how* we can do almost anything. We can learn to play a piano, we are told, in 10 easy lessons. All we have to do is buy these lessons and we will have the *know how* to be an accomplished pianist, at least, that is the implication. Then young people are told that if they use the right deodorant, toothpaste, or mouthwash, they will have what it takes to get that right boy or girl. Then, the most ridiculous suggestion of all is that all a boy needs in life to make him attractive to girls, charming to his friends, and *the hottest thing in town* is use the right hair dressing, not the greasy kind but the kind that girls love to touch. I thought girls were meant to be pretty and to have soft, lovely hair but now it seems the men are stealing their feminine charms. Here is what I heard an attractive woman say recently, "What is happening to our image of a man? Is a man to become a cute darling instead of a robust, masculine person? Personally, I prefer the cave-man image for a man rather than one who is a powdered, perfumed, deodorized, curly haired, dimpled, dandy!"

But I have gotten off my subject this morning before I have even begun. What I meant to say is that *know-how* is important but more essential still is *to be* something. The *what* is basic to any life worth living. Yet, I want to stress this morning, that although we become disgusted with our modern emphasis on *know how*, we still do need to *know how* in order for the *what* to become alive and real.

As you may know I have a keen interest in psychology and I suspect that sometimes you may in good *jest* make a little fun of this preacher's dabbling in psychologizing and I sometimes laugh at myself and think how stupid I am to spend so much time reading, studying, and practicing in the field. Yet, I know that psychology is a significant and important science because it gets at the how of behavior. How do we learn? How do we develop? How do we best raise our children? How do we relate properly to people? How do people react under certain social conditions and pressures? These are important questions and the answers that psychology provides, although they do not always agree, are extremely essential for better living.

Psychology, however, never provides the *what*. That belongs to religion and philosophy. What shall we teach our children? What shall we do with our lives? To what shall we give ourselves? What will be our stand on the great social issues of our day? These are questions that are within the province of religion and faith. But *what* is not enough. And *how* is not enough. A how and a what are required to get the job done. I believe, therefore, that religion needs psychology to learn the how so that the what becomes translated into healthy language and life. In a sense, the insights and contributions of psychology provide the vehicle on which the values and truths of religion may be transported into the life of persons and society.

What we are saying, then, or rather implying is that religion cannot be presented in just any way. Persons often say that it really doesn't make any difference what church people go to so long as they go to church. Although, I think I know what persons mean when they make such a statement, I find it difficult to subscribe to this point of view. It does make a difference and the difference lies not in the content of religion as much as it does in the way it is presented. Would we say it doesn't make any difference what book a person reads so long as he reads? Would we say it doesn't make any difference what school a person goes to so long as he goes? Would we say it doesn't make any difference how a person spends his time as long as he spends it somewhere? How easy it is for us to take liberties with religion we dare not take with any other function. Let me illustrate.

Some years ago I was visiting a Sunday school of a particular denomination and I happened to pass a room where small children were singing a song called *Love Lifted Me*. The verse they were singing when I passed the door went like this, "I was sinking deep in sin, far from the peaceful shore." I can imagine some derelict singing that tune, or someone fighting a battle with corruption, but I cannot possibly accept an innocent little child 5 or 6 singing "I was sinking deep in sin, far from the peaceful shore."

This is not only bad music but it is bad religion. It is bad religion because some children are extremely sensitive to any connotations that indicate they are bad little children. If the church through its music reinforces these feelings, the church causes the child to grow up making him feel unworthy and guilt ridden when he has no reason to feel that way at all. No wonder so many persons have a constant feeling that they are no good, unworthy, or incompetent that plagues them throughout life and cripples them from becoming alive and buoyant persons. They are carrying around feelings of deep guilt that were put there in childhood, perhaps even by the church. These feelings of guilt are there because someone made the mistake of telling them they were *sinful* or no good.

I remember so well a young girl coming to see me in the first church I had after graduating from seminary. The young girl, about 18 or 19, was in tears. She told me how sinful she had been and she guessed she was no good. When I asked her why she felt that way, she said that the leader of the young people's group in the church had told her she was sinful because she had gone to a party with a young man and she had danced with him.

"What about the sin," I asked, "What was that?"

"Why dancing," she said, "that was the sin and I don't know what to do about it."

This became a real problem to this girl, and although she went to other dances after our talk, I don't think she ever really enjoyed herself. All because someone, in the name of religion, failed to grasp the centrality of religion and unintentionally passed along to a sensitive young woman in the name of religion her own frustrations and guilt. Of course, it matters what church we go to. It is important how religion is communicated.

Jesus frequently advanced his views regarding the right and wrong way of practicing one's religion. He believed devoutly in prayer but he also insisted it be done in the right way. *"And when you pray, you must not be like the hypocrites; for they love to stand and pray in the synagogues and at the street corners, that they may be seen of men. Truly I say to you, they have their reward. But when you pray, go into your room and shut the door and pray to your Father who is in secret; and your Father who sees in secret will reward you."* Notice Jesus is stressing *know how* — pray quietly, not to be seen, but to be ready to receive the grace of God's love in the stillness of one's own inner citadel.

Jesus believed in fasting. At least he didn't condemn it but he did say that when you fast do so properly, not to gain anything, not to appear as a devout, holy, and pious person, but to express in personal sacrifice, not a dismal and dowdy complexion, but a clean and joyful countenance. Here again are his words, *"And when you fast, do not look dismal, like the hypocrites, for they disfigure their faces that their fasting may be seen by men. Truly, I say to you, they have their reward. But when you fast, anoint your head and wash your face that your fasting may not be seen by men but by your Father who is in secret; and your Father who sees in secret will reward you.*" Our Lord did believe in getting the things of religion accomplished in ways that are positive, growth producing, and joyful.

Notice also in this statement of Jesus the absence of compulsiveness or demand. He says *when you pray*, not *you must* for Jesus teaches us that the effectiveness of prayer depends on a disposition of heart, a desire to learn, a congeniality of spirit for growth, a naturalness with others of like mind and attitude.

But how easy it is for prayer to become a meaningless routine. Some years ago I was in a home where there were several children. They had a custom in the home that after dinner each person said prayers to himself. After the evening meal, everyone started his prayers but one little girl about 8 or 9 slipped away from the table to play. Her mother promptly called her back and said, "Annie, you sit yourself down there and you had better be sure you say your prayers." Poor Annie, I hope she accepted it all with kindness and with an understanding of the harassment that her mother was confronted with in trying to run a large family. I hope that these episodes did not destroy the girl's interest in matters of faith. Such an adult tantrum if consistently experienced can have several negative effects. It can cause a person to give up and never return to prayer again; or cause a person to pray because she felt guilty if she didn't, yet hating it because she was forced to do something she didn't want to do.

Then I remember visiting another home not so long ago where there was also a large family. When I left everyone stood around, joined hands, and each said a prayer. There was no pressure or coercion. Instead there was an air of naturalness and warmth and everyone joined in gladly and gratefully. Children here will grow up without negativism or resentment toward matters pertaining to religion because wise parents are acquainted with the know how of introducing children to prayer.

What I deeply yearn for in this congregation that is so new and enthusiastic is that each of us will strive to become acquainted with the wisest and best educational methods available to introduce our children to the rich insights of our religious faith. We desire an approach to faith that is in keeping with the best in educational methods and materials and child development. We want a faith that does not make a child or a person afraid or upset or resentful. We want a faith that is intelligent and that uses, not denies, the best knowledge that is available in the sciences and in the humanities. We want a faith that builds and supports the mental health of the person. We want a faith that is open to new discoveries wherever they may be found in all areas of knowledge and one that conserves the best of tradition. We want a faith that is fully informed concerning the world in which we live and that is anxious to have the gospel correct social injustices and abuses wherever they may be found. In brief, we want to find the best ways to help each of us "… *grow in wisdom and in stature and in favor with God and man."(Luke 2:52)*

39

ARE WE HELPING OR HINDERING?

Mark 8:27-33

27 And Jesus went on with his disciples, to the villages of Caesare'a Philip'pi; and on the way he asked his disciples, "Who do men say that I am?"
28 And they told him, "John the Baptist; and others say,
Eli'jah; and others one of the prophets."
29 And he asked them, "But who do you say that I am?"
Peter answered him, "You are the Christ."
30 And he charged them to tell no one about him.
31 And he began to teach them that the Son of man must suffer many things, and be rejected by the elders and the chief priests and the scribes, and be killed, and after three days rise again.
32 And he said this plainly. And Peter took him, and began to rebuke him.
33 But turning and seeing his disciples, he rebuked Peter, and said, "Get behind me, Satan! For you are not on the side of God, but of men."

L et us pray. "Draw near to us, and bless us, O God, and cause Thy face to shine on us, that Thy ways may be known upon the earth, Thy saving help to this generation." Amen

What is the distinguishing characteristic of a Christian? A friend of mine who served as a chaplain in the Army during World War II told me that during his military service he was unable to distinguish Christians from non-Christians. At the other extreme, another friend of mine who was also a chaplain during the same engagement told me that he observed during his military service that he had never seen such an unusual display of Christian character as he observed during his service.

Now, these conflicting reports coming from sincere and competent leaders of religion, remind us, perhaps, that there is no one distinguishing characteristic of a Christian. In all probability, there are many factors that cause a person to be judged a Christian or not a Christian. It is my task, therefore, to offer for your consideration not the dimension, but a dimension that may be helpful to us in understanding one characteristic of Christian witness. This dimension is concerned with HELPFULNESS.

A person who hinders is not manifesting the spirit of Christ in his life. The person who is helping is manifesting the spirit of Christ in his life, for Christian faith is not concerned with death, but with life; not with hopelessness, but with hopefulness; not with darkness, but with light; not with hindrance but with helpfulness. Now it seems rather simple, doesn't it, to say that a Christian is one who is helpful in all of his experiences wherever he may find himself? Perhaps the interpretation, however, is not so simple or clear as it may appear on the surface.

Consider, for instance, that each one of us is asked frequently to support or to participate in various causes and movements. And surely the serious Christian asks himself the question "Is this particular cause or movement consistent with Christian faith?" This places the requirement on us, of course, first of all, to be informed. It seems, therefore, that to help, we must know what we are going to help. It certainly seems foolish to waste our time on causes or movements which are inconsistent with our Christian witness.

We must be informed regarding the nature of our Christian faith in order to measure adequately the Christian consistency of the movements or causes that request our interest or support. Surely, a Christian cannot properly provide an effective witness to his faith unless he has knowledge of what it is all about! Consider, if you will, Peter, that man who was so faithful to his Lord. He wanted to be a faithful follower of Christ, but he did not adequately understand the nature of the mission of his Master. Jesus had to remind him that he was interfering with the accomplishment of His mission. When Jesus announced that he was going to Jerusalem and would die, Peter rebuked him. He took Jesus aside to counsel with him, but Jesus rebelled against Peter and informed him that he did not really know what the mission was all about. Mark records Jesus' reprimand of Peter in these words, *"Get behind me Satan, for you are not on the side of God, but of men."*

Now I seriously question Christians who participate in a hate movement such as the Klu Klux Klan. I do not doubt that these are sincere Christians, but I do doubt their understanding of Christian faith. For, such an organization as the Klu Klux Klan is inconsistent with the very heart and core of Christian faith. It is also true that many times we find individuals, leaders of the Christian movement, who want to identify the Christian gospel with a particular movement, or a particular cause, but Christianity cannot be identified with any human institution or any cause, no matter how significant it may appear. We do not have to look back through history very far to recognize the same thing. Persons who were interested in passing the prohibition amendment wanted to identify it with Christianity. Persons who were interested in the labor movement wanted to identify it with the Christian gospel. And today we find people who insist that certain movements concerned with minorities, or with other kinds of causes, are *The* expression of Christian faith. Now, surely, Christianity is interested in improving the social condition of mankind. Christian faith is very much concerned about social injustice. But we must be very careful not to identify Christianity with a particular movement, a movement created by the imagination and the interest of man. We must also be very careful not to call the church and the gospel the same. The revelation of God in Christ stands above history, to judge and evaluate all movements and causes. Now, your job and my job is to understand the nature of our faith so that we will be informed. We need to be knowledgeable so that we will have an understanding of whether we want to be a part of movements or causes that vie for our attention, our support, and our money. The reason that we have religious instruction in the church is to make it possible for those of us who bear the name of Jesus Christ to be informed concerning our faith. Then, we will be able to relate it intelligently to the various movements and causes and organizations of our day.

This leads us to say, then, that before we can lend our help to those who ask for it, we must also be informed concerning the nature of the particular cause or organization. A Christian is not one who lives in an ivory tower, who shuts himself behind monastic walls. Rather, the Christian is one who knows about the world in which he lives. He is very much familiar with and informed concerning all of the activities and institutions *out there*, that we designate *the world*.

Some years ago there were many Christians who felt that Communism was the answer to the economic and social evils of our age. Many Christians became involved in the Communist movement, but later they awoke to discover that they had been deceived, not really deceived, but they had not been fair to themselves because they did not take the time to understand the evil core and nature of Communism.

Well, it really isn't so simple to be helpful, is it? We have to have a great deal of knowledge and understanding in order to be helpful to those interests who ask for our helpfulness. Having said this, let us also consider that to be helpful, we must know *how* to help. Many of us make mistakes in life because we are absolutely ignorant of what it takes to get along in life and to avoid mistakes. There are persons who do not understand that in order to have friends they must be friendly. Some do not understand that in order to have people smile at them and be pleasant that they have to smile and be pleasant. It is basically a matter of knowledge.

Now, the same thing applies in this business of being helpful, a characteristic of a Christian. We need to know how to be helpful. Poor Peter, he wanted so much to be a sincere follower of Jesus Christ but he didn't know exactly how to go about it, and Jesus had to tell him, "Peter, you really don't know what you are talking about. I appreciate your conscientiousness. I am grateful for your support. I am deeply honored that you are a part of my movement, but Peter, you do not yet know how to be helpful to me." Perhaps, Jesus went on to tell Peter, "You want me to play it safe. You want me to stay in the countryside and to teach and to enjoy our friendship together, and for me to become an elderly person. But Peter, this is not my interest. My concern is to be faithful to my mission as the Son of God as I understand it. You help me when you encourage me to accept the fullness of my responsibility as the son of my Father who is in Heaven!"

When we do become a part of different social groups and organizations, sometimes we hinder them by being critical. I cannot imagine any attitude or behavior that is more detrimental to any organization than for persons to be critical of it, in a sour, malignant way. Sometimes I hear persons criticize the church and I accept the criticisms. I realize that the church is far from being a perfect institution. I know, also, most of the deficiencies of the church. I sometimes have the feeling, however, that persons who are so critical of the church are using it as an excuse for not being a part of the church themselves. You see, it is so much easier to criticize, to sit back and be a *Monday Morning Quarterback* than it is to become a part of the church, to give one's loyalty and support to it, and to assist the church in becoming the kind of institution that is a worthy representative of Jesus Christ. We hinder when we find fault! We help when we get in and become a part of it!

Quite often, when we are in groups, we are called upon to state our views or to cast our vote concerning a particular action that is being considered by the organization. We hinder, we hurt, and we destroy, when we attempt to inflict our own particular viewpoint on the group. How often we cast a vote, not because we want the organization to grow and prosper, but just because we want to have our own way. We all grow up with certain presuppositions and prejudices, don't we? How often we want to inflict them on the group of which we are a part so that we will have our own way. But we help when we listen to what the other person has to say, when we evaluate the pros and cons, and then cast our vote, not on the basis of our own individual prejudices, but on the basis of good honest reasons.

More and more, I am convinced that we hurt ourselves, destroy ourselves as groups, because individuals within the group insist on their own way rather than thinking of the good of the organization as a whole. It isn't really so simple, is it, after all, this matter of being helpful?

But let us pass on, if we may, to the most sensitive relationship that there is in life in which you and I are involved, the family. Here is the laboratory of the most critical and serious type that either makes or breaks persons. Some young people that I have talked to entering marriage have the most bizarre and destructive attitudes toward marriage. Sometimes, the young woman has the idea that the sole purpose of the husband is to support her and to care for her all the rest of her days. This is the reason for the husband! And then, sometimes, a young man will think of his wife as the one who is a kind of a servant, who must wait on him, and serve him all the rest of his life. It used to hurt me deeply when I was in the Orient, when some of our servicemen who wanted to marry Asian women would say, "I like Asian women because they know how to be a servant to their husbands."

The question, then poses itself, "Does a man want a servant or a companion?" These are two entirely different kinds of people and I am not sure a wife can be a servant or a servant a wife. The helping relationship that counts in the family is each trying to serve the needs of others. Certainly, the wife wants to help the husband in developing his resources so that he will be more competent in his profession and in his role as the husband in the home and to give him all the support and encouragement that every man so desperately needs. And surely the husband wants to give his support and his encouragement to help the wife to be a better mother and wife in the home, and at the same time, to assist her in fulfilling her vocational ambitions if this is her desire. We can never say how this should be done, for so much depends on the interest and the capabilities of the individual persons. As I see persons who come to the end of life, who have been happily married all the days of their life, however, I think the clue is that each has tried to serve the needs of the other - to offer encouragement, to give affection, to build up the other person as much as is possible, and do nothing that will destroy or hurt or harm. It isn't easy to be a helping person, but when we are, let it be said that then we are discovering what it means to be a follower of Jesus Christ.

In the name of the Father, and of the Son, and of the Holy Spirit. Amen.

40

THE GREATNESS OF ALBERT SCHWEITZER

Mark 8:35 For whoever would save his life will lose it; and whoever loses his life for my sake and the gospel's will save it.

A week ago today (September 4, 1965), the life of Dr. Albert Schweitzer came to a close, a period that spanned over 90 years, from 1875 to 1965. Dr. Schweitzer was one of those unusual persons who appear on the human scene perhaps once every 100 years. We know his story. He grew up in Alsace, that part of Germany that later was ceded to France. He became a French citizen, and was educated at the University of Strasbourg. Before he attained age 30, he was a noted philosopher and had written a definitive book on Immanuel Kant. He was also a first rate theologian, upsetting the field of New Testament scholarship by his radical interpretation of the life and teachings of Jesus with his book, *The Quest for the Historical Jesus*. Furthermore, he was a parish clergyman as his father and grandfather had been before him and was also a university professor. He had won acclaim as a musician. He was considered a leading authority on the music of Johann Sebastian Bach and had a wide reputation as a builder of pipe organs. Still he was dissatisfied; so, he entered medical school at the age of 30, and graduated at age 37 to become a medical missionary in the Belgian Congo, at a place called Lamberine in the province of Gabon. There he stayed until his death, providing medical care for Africans under the most primitive conditions and, at the same time, observing and interpreting the human drama through his writings. He came out occasionally to accept the gifts the world wanted to bestow on him. In 1953 he was given the Nobel Peace Prize. The qualities that illuminate Schweitzer's greatness are too numerous to evaluate; but to concentrate even on a few, should inspire each of us to be more than we are.

Albert Schweitzer was great because he lived as well as talked about his religious faith. In his autobiography, which he called *Out of My Life and Thought*, which to me is one of the most inspiring devotional books I have ever read – you can buy a copy for 50 cents in paperback – he describes how he decided to become a doer rather than merely a talker or a writer. On October 13, 1905, he resigned his position on the theological faculty at the Theological College at St. Thomas in Strasbourg and made the announcement that he would soon enter medical college to prepare himself to become a doctor in the jungles of Africa. Let me read from his autobiography so we may get the feel of the way he made his decision:

"The plan which I mean now to put into execution has been in my mind for a long time having been conceived so long ago in my student days. It struck me as incomprehensible that I should be allowed to lead such a happy life when I saw so many people around me wrestling with care and suffering. Even at school I had felt stirred whenever I got a glimpse of the miserable home surroundings of some of my school fellows and compared them with the absolutely ideal conditions in which we children of the parsonage at Goonsbach lived."

"While at the University and enjoying the happiness of being able to study and even to produce some results in science and art, I could not help thinking continually of others who were denied that happiness by their material circumstances or their health. Then one brilliant summer morning at Goonsbach during the Whitsuntide Holidays, it was in 1896, there came to me as I awoke the thought that I must not accept this happiness as a matter of course but must give something in return for it. Proceeding to think the matter out at once, with calm deliberation, while the birds were singing outside, I settled with myself before I got up that I would consider myself justified in living till I was 30 for Science and Art in order to devote myself from that time forward to the direct service of humanity. Many a time, already, I had tried to settle what meaning lay hidden for me in the saying of Jesus, *'Whoever would save his life shall lose it, and whoever shall lose his life for my sake and the gospels shall save it.'* Now the answer was found, in addition to the outward, I now had an inward happiness."

We see at once from these words that Albert Schweitzer took the words of Jesus seriously. He did not use them in judging the behavior or thinking of other people. He applied them directly to himself. He asked the question, "What do the works of Jesus have to say to me?" In this moment of truth or encounter with himself, he made his decision to give himself in direct service to humanity.

Now Schweitzer has been criticized by many leading Christians because he did not accept the traditional interpretations concerning the life and teachings of Jesus. At the same time, although Schweitzer did differ with the traditional interpretations of Jesus, he did not differ with Jesus! There is a world of difference between an interpretation of Jesus and Jesus himself. Schweitzer understood Jesus about as accurately as one can possibly understand him. Schweitzer saw as Jesus saw that truth is mediated not through a spoken or a written work. He discovered that the truth of God which is most real in life, is revealed in a life of committed action, in the living deeds of persons. This is what is meant when it is written *"and the word became flesh and dwelt among us."* When the truth of the living God is caught up in a human act, then you have greatness, and that is the basic reason why we call Schweitzer a great man.

The greatness of Dr. Schweitzer is also seen in that the motivation for his life was in contribution rather than acquisition. This, perhaps, is another way of stating the words of Jesus that so thoroughly captivated his life, *"Whosoever would save his life shall lose it, and whosoever shall lose his life for my sake and the Gospel's shall save it."* The secret of life, therefore, as seen in the life of Jesus, as well as in the life of Schweitzer, is to live in terms of what we can give rather than in what we can get.

If we want to contrast the difference between a life of contribution and a life of acquisition, let us look at the lives of two men: William Randolph Hearst and Albert Schweitzer. Last Monday (Labor Day), I hope you were able to rest as I was able to. During the afternoon I happened to turn on the television for a little while and I watched the end of the picture, *Citizen Kane*. I am told that this picture is a parody of the life of William Randolph Hearst. As I watched that picture, I could not help but compare the life of Hearst with the life of Albert Schweitzer. Here it seems to me, you have in bald relief the difference between a life which is interested in acquisition and accumulation and a life of contribution. William Randolph Hearst was a tremendous person. No one can deny that the newspaper publisher was in many ways a great man, but the end product toward which he seemed to be striving was power, wealth, and success. He gained it all – certainly he was one of the most dynamic and powerful men in the newspaper business that our nation has known. He accumulated a vast fortune that included a 230,000 acre ranch, a home as large as any medieval castle, and art treasures of untold monetary value. He seemed to have it all, but if the picture *Citizen Kane* is any criterion for his life, he died miserable, angry and hated. Hold up, then, if we may, the life of Schweitzer and see what it contains for us to examine. Schweitzer, too, was richly endowed – a driving restlessness, keen mind, ambitions, an ability to attain success and to be the best in his field, a capacity to have power over others. Yet, he died contented and quietly, was buried in a simple wooden box without ceremony and left behind him no material fortune, for his motivation was to use what he had for the benefit of his fellowman, not in acquiring or accumulating anything that he did not need.

Some say Schweitzer was a stupid old man whose approach to medicine and hospital care was an anachronism, suitable perhaps to the 19th but not to the 20th century. True, his hospital was a series of huts and improvised buildings. The patients lived as they lived in their natural surroundings in the jungle. He was little interested in disease prevention. His only concern seemed to be treatment.

His methods were primitive and unsystematic. Yet, if we look only at his procedures and facilities, we miss the greatness of the man. To see Schweitzer we must focus on the person of Schweitzer — what made him tick? One of the finest evaluations of Schweitzer I have read was made by Norman Cousins, editor of *Saturday Review*. Cousin's statement was quoted in an article appearing in the latest issue of *Newsweek*. He said,

> "Schweitzer's aim was not to dazzle an age but to awaken it, to make it comprehend that moral splendor is part of the gift of life. He has proved that although a man may have no jurisdiction over the fact of his existence, he can hold supreme command over the meaning of existence for him. Thus, no man need fear death; he need fear only that he may die without having known his greatest power — the power of his free will to give his life to others."

The greatness of Schweitzer's life was, then, that he found the meaning of existence, as did Jesus, in using his freedom, not to accumulate clothes, trinkets, prestige, or success, but to contribute what he had to offer to the welfare of other human beings.

Let us finally say that the jungle doctor was also great because his religious outlook in providing assistance to others was based on moral earnestness rather than bland sentimentality. He went to Africa, not because he liked African people and wanted to make them his brothers. He was wise enough to understand that to love a person does not mean you have to like him and to have him as a part of your family. He knew that love means to feel responsible for a person whoever he is, if he needs your help. Schweitzer went to Africa because there were people there who needed medical attention and he felt he had a responsibility to do what he could to alleviate their suffering and misery. He wasn't interested either in converting them to his faith, for that would mean he would use medical care to manipulate them to accept his particular religious outlook. He went because of the need of persons. His fondness or nonfondness for them was completely beside the point.

He helped people as he saw they needed help and he was not hoodwinked by people's folly and irresponsible behavior. He could be as stern with an African as a policeman with an offender. Once he had Africans working on a roof and after they worked for a few hours, they wanted to quit and come down. Schweitzer knew their lack of tenacity so he took the ladder away and told them they could come down when they finished putting on the roof. He also believed people had to accept responsibility before they could enjoy freedom. He once said, "I love these stupid, senseless, dishonest people; I give my life for them; but pray don't ask me to give them rights." We may not agree with his harshness but we must respect the element of realism he represented in Christian ethics.

We need some of his realism in our programs of Christian action. I can remember when I was a boy hearing ministers urging young people to become missionaries and arousing their emotions to the point of tears. Some of these disgusting displays of sentiment almost turned me against the entire missionary enterprise, for they were so incompatible with the stern demands that Jesus placed on life. How can anyone urge anyone to do anything unless one knows whether or not the person is intellectually, emotionally and spiritually equipped to do the job? But one fact we notice about Schweitzer - he became a jungle doctor missionary not only because he wanted to give direct service to mankind, but he also knew he had the qualifications to do the job. He counted the cost

– 7 more years in medical school and turning his back on fame as a leader in 4 fields of knowledge. He appraised his ability – his past performance told him he had the mental ability. He understood his emotional stamina – he had no trouble working long hours without applause and in solitude. He understood God's will in terms of facts about himself and circumstances that were offered to him, not nice little feelings about one's impractical desires. He did not insist that any man follow his way, for his way was only for him, not for you or for me. But one factor he would insist on for any man or any woman: Discover who you are and what you are and give it your best, but always find time to give of yourself in service to another human being whose pain, suffering, or misery you can help alleviate, for therein lies greatness. Did not our Lord remind us, *"Let him who is greatest among you, first of all, be your servant."*

41

THE UNIVERSALITY OF CHRIST

Philippians 2:9 God has highly exalted him and
bestowed on him the name which is above every name.

When Abraham Lincoln died, someone standing at the head of his bed is reported to have remarked, "He no longer belongs to us. Now, he belongs to the ages." This person expressed in these words one of the astute observations man is capable of making - to see in the life of a human being qualities so everlastingly real and enduring that the one who possesses them belongs, not to a particular time or set of circumstances in history, but to all mankind.

In a deeper sense, what was said concerning Lincoln is written in Philippians regarding Jesus Christ. Paul, the author of Philippians wrote, *"God has highly exalted him and bestowed on him the name which is above every name."* Here Paul proclaims the universality of Jesus Christ. Perhaps universality is an attribute that is necessary for one to possess qualities of deity. Surely, we need to know what it is that caused a man such as Paul to make a universal claim regarding Jesus. Let us see why Jesus Christ is universal, why he can be referred to as divine.

First of all, Jesus Christ is universal because he is available to all people. If he were not available to all people, he could not be called *Lord of Life*. Anything less than total availability cannot be universal and anything that is not universal cannot possess qualities of deity. Paul says that because Jesus comes equally and equitably to all men, then every knee can bow before him and proclaim him Lord of all.

When the claim is made that Jesus is available to all peoples, this means that he cannot be owned by any group or anyone. Just as the math equation $5 + 5 = 10$ cannot be the property of any one individual or any group of individuals. It belongs to all and is applicable to all. No race or nationality can make the proclamation that Jesus is its property and no one else can approach him. No denomination can make the claim that it possesses the full truth concerning Jesus and he can only be found as one becomes a part of that denomination and believes exclusively as that denomination states its case. Sometimes, denominations try to build a wall around Christ and make the ridiculous claim that Christ is theirs to interpret and he can only be found as one enters their little fortress of doctrine.

At this very moment, the Roman Catholic Church is facing the precise problem we are discussing this morning. One of the so-called *hot issues* the princes of the church are discussing at the present session of their Third Ecumenical Council is whether or not freedom of interpretation of religious faith is allowable under canon law. For centuries, the Roman Church has insisted officially that freedom of conscience could not be permitted in countries that are traditionally Roman Catholic because truth cannot give sanction to falsehood. In recent years, however, some of the best minds in Roman Catholic circles have questioned such claims and finally, they have attained sufficient influence to have their beliefs seriously considered by the high officials of the Church. At last, the Roman Church, at the decision level, is coming to grips with the question we are considering: How can a Christian institution claim absolute truth for itself, and, at the same time, hold to the universality of Christ? One position has to go, for you cannot have both. Either Christ is available only for those who accept Roman Catholic doctrine and no one else or he is available to all men who see in him other than what Roman Catholicism sees. This is not to say Roman Catholic teaching contains no truth. It means that they do not have the whole truth just as no one or no institution has the whole truth. Not even all of Christendom has the whole truth concerning Christ. All we Christians can do, whatever we believe, is to witness to the truth in Christ and proclaim his universality - that he is for all mankind and not only for us.

Jesus Christ is also universal because his life and words are timeless. It would indeed be strange for his words to apply only to the first century but not to the twentieth. If this were the case, he could not be called a universal Christ, nor could he be identified with divinity. Divine means eternal, everlasting, always, and forever. *Jesus Christ*, said the writer of Hebrews, *is the same yesterday, today and forever.* The case cannot be stated more succinctly.

If we consider a key concept of Jesus, we discover that it is appropriate to any age. Jesus taught that the first consideration in any person's life should be the subject of loyalty, or as Tillich expresses the matter, ultimate concern. In other words, Jesus maintains that a person needs to face what it is that is supreme for him over all other considerations. Is it good looks, stylish dress, being the best liked, being the center of attention, having control of others, honesty, fairness, consideration for others, obedience? Jesus holds that the matter of loyalties is one of the crucial items of human existence.

Loyalty, in a sense, is what determines the way a person goes about life. If his loyalty is supremely to his nation, then, no matter what his nation does, he is for it. Many Germans violated all principles of human decency during the Nazi regime because the nation was for them their supreme loyalty. See what havoc the Nazis, however, brought to the world because extreme ideas of race and clan were put first. One of the critical issues that our generation is also facing is nationalism. Many nations are so intent on their particular interests that it makes no difference what the other nations want so long as they get what they want. The same is true of the conflicts between management and labor. Right now, the newspaper industry in New York City is practically idle because of the unsettled issue between management and labor regarding the use of automation in newspaper publishing. Furthermore, family members are in conflict with each other because each insists that he must have his own way. Let us not be led astray in thinking that nations, labor unions, management, or any side in a particular argument should not stand up for its position and be heard. What I am saying is that each side in an argument can go too far in insisting upon its point of view and can destroy any possibility of settlement, and bring harmful results, not only to themselves, but even to a whole society, even to an entire world. This is as certain in our generation as it was in the times of Jesus and even centuries before his age.

Jesus established a new loyalty for human relationships. He called it the Kingdom of God. His admonition is *"But seek first his kingdom and his righteousness, and all these things shall be yours as well."* In other words, says Jesus, instead of seeking and demanding only self interest, try to seek truth, fair mindedness, and openness to what the other person is trying to get across, a real desire to achieve a state of righteousness for all concerned. Jesus pled for a higher level of human association, a universality of concern rather that for a narrow exclusiveness and provincialism. His approach is wisdom for any age, for Jesus Christ is timeless.

Still, Jesus Christ is a universal truth because he speaks to the deepest needs and longings of the human heart. He touches human life, every human life, not only the life of the White or Negro American, the Englishman, the Hindu, or the Chinese, the poor or the rich, but he comes down to every person and meets him where life is most real. He meets us at that point that is deepest for all of us.

The place that is deepest in life for all of us is at that point where we come into personal contact and involvement with another person. It is no accident that so many of our songs, plays, stories, movie productions, and TV shows deal with the joys and pains of love between human persons. There are the satisfactions and conflicts between parents and children, the sorrow and happiness between friends, the excitement and the heartache of life and love between a man and a woman. When we add it all up and make a serious effort to understand why there is such a fuss over our relationships with each other, we come out with the answer that human affection is the deepest quality in human life, no matter where that life is or what it is. Dr. Blanton wrote an interesting book a few years ago and he used the intriguing title *Love or Perish*; and that about sums up the choices of a human life. We either learn to live together in love or we perish. That holds firm and sure for any kind of human relationship, whether between persons, groups of persons, institutions, or what have you.

Nothing is so important to a person as his friends or his family. People hunger for human encounter, participation, involvement with others in close, harmonious relationships. When they do not experience these close ties of human affection, they become aggressive, belligerent, and obnoxious, and bring destruction to themselves and to others. If a person is not loved, therefore, he will demand it. If love is taken away, he will become hostile and angry. If he loses love, he becomes sad and sorrowful. Usually, we find that when there is any friction, malfunctioning, conflict between persons who are important to each other, the cause is usually a fracture in the love between the persons or love that is improperly or unwisely expressed.

It is here, I think, that Jesus shows us the way. He is a universal figure because he emphasizes what is essential in order for life to be rewarding and satisfying and also because he tells us how to love. *"Love your neighbor as yourself"* - treat others as you would like them to treat you.

Do not love each person the same way, but look at each person as an individual and relate to him and help him in terms of his own needs. Do not wrap up your love in one person but make it available to all who need it. Do not hold on to and control those you care for but allow them as they are able to become persons who do not even need you. Do not sap the energies of persons you love by always tying yourself around their necks, by prying into their lives and keeping check on their behavior, but make an effort to allow them to grow up to be themselves in an atmosphere of encouragement, trust, and deep respect for them as persons. We have a long way to go to live as Jesus tells us but what he reminds us to do, whether we are able to do it or not, we know it is right and is the most help for any and every person.

The verses we read in Philippians that lift Jesus to the level of universality probably are not original with Paul. It appears possible that they are words from a hymn that was composed and sung in the early years of the Christian Church. Let us read them again:

Philippians 2:5-11 "Have this mind among yourselves, which you have in Christ Jesus, who though he was in the form of God, did not count equality with God a thing to be grasped, but emptied himself, taking the form of a servant, being born in the likeness of men. And being found in human form he humbled himself and became obedient unto death, even death on a cross. Therefore God has highly exalted him and bestowed on him the name which is above every name, that at the name of Jesus every knee should bow, in heaven and on earth and under the earth, and every tongue confess that Jesus Christ is Lord, to the glory of God the Father."

My prayer today is that we can sing them as forcefully and confidently as the Christians of the first century, for indeed they do express in beautiful and profound language what Jesus Christ means and is, not only to those of us who bear his name, but for all those who will seriously consider our claim for his universality.

Sermon

42

THE MATURITY WE SEEK AS CHRISTIANS

*I Corinthians 13:11 When I was a child I spoke like a child,
I thought like a child, I reasoned like a child;
when I became a man, I gave up childish ways.*

Prayer: Draw near to us and bless us, Oh God, that thy ways may be known upon the earth, thy saving health to this generation through Jesus Christ, our Lord. Amen

Some of the Christians at Corinth were quarreling among themselves. Many believed that when they became Christians they would receive special gifts or graces. Some did receive the favors, but others did not, and those who had not received the favors became jealous, angry, and bitter toward the others. Paul heard of this predicament, so he wrote the Christians at Corinth a letter. In the 13th chapter he wrote, "*When I was a child I spoke like a child, I thought like a child, I reasoned like a child; when I became a man, I gave up childish ways.*" It seems strange that Paul would suggest to grown-ups to grow up, for he was not writing to children. These people were over 21 years of age, most had families, and were holding jobs. Yet, Paul tells them to grow up, to act their age, to stop behaving like spoiled children.

At once, then, we are reminded in the 13th chapter of I Corinthians that being an adult involves more than age, height, physical strength, the right to vote, the ability to speak well, knowledge or high I.Q. Paul infers that maturity for the Christian is concerned with qualities of the human spirit that he observed in the life of Jesus Christ. These are the characteristics that we seek as Christians.

The first attribute that we as Christians seek after is the capacity to be responsible for our own lives and the tasks we are asked to perform. We grow from being cared for as children to men and women who are able to care for ourselves. The less we take care of ourselves when we are able to function the less we are mature; the more we can make a go of it ourselves when we are able the greater is our maturity.

Sometimes, I think, our young people are mistaken about this business of what it means to be an adult. Youth frequently give the impression that to be grown up means to drive an automobile sometimes far in excess of the speed limit, to smoke cigarettes, to drink beer and hard liquor, to stay out until the late hours of the morning, to engage in sexual relations before marriage, to dress slovenly, or to be indifferent regarding the more serious issues of life. To be sure, these are some of the things that adults do and I suppose many young people are only copying their elders. But let us be clear at this point. An adult may commit these acts but these acts are not what causes the person to be an adult, for maturity is not a matter of doing something. Maturity means to be something, to be a responsible person, one who can be trusted and counted on to take care of himself, to carry out what he says he will do or has to do.

Surely, a youth of 15 or 16 cannot be expected to manage his life and his affairs as though he were a man or woman of 30 or 35. But he can be expected to act 15 or 16 and not 5 or 6.

A young person in his teens can be expected to do what he is perfectly capable of doing – keeping himself clean, getting up by himself and getting himself ready for school without being nagged and prodded, being on time for school, doing his school work as well as he can without anyone having to remind him, learning to make decisions and acting on his resources, appropriate to his age, assuring a reasonable portion of duties of the household. Such living is managing one's life at a particular level of development. The successful performance of such practices determine largely a young person's ability to move on to a higher level of responsibility when he has to hold a job or perhaps be a husband or a wife, a father or a mother. What we will be tomorrow is largely dependent on what we are today. It is important, therefore, that young people have a chance to practice responsible living that is, if they expect to reach adulthood as mature adults, not speaking, thinking, reasoning, or behaving as irresponsible children.

As one moves into adult life, of course, his responsibilities increase and a person handles these obligations to the extent of his inner maturity. The person who possesses a high level of maturity assumes a certain degree of responsibility for the good of his fellowman and strives to provide his children with opportunities for their intellectual, social, moral, and religious development. The man of a low maturity level lives only for this own pleasures; the man of high maturity level lives for the benefit of his family and for those who need what he has to offer. Jesus, who attained the highest level of maturity mankind has witnessed, challenged us to break the bondage of childish behavior and to become mature persons when he said, *"Let him who would be my disciple deny himself, take up his cross and follow after me."* In modern parlance, this statement is a call to responsible manhood and womanhood.

This brings us to say, then that the maturity we seek as Christians beckons us to a life of wholeness. This is a word that you can put in the place of the word *salvation* if you like. Paul writing to the Thessalonians asked them to put on for a helmet *"the hope of salvation"*. We could just as easily say, and in plainer language, put on for a helmet the hope of wholeness. This is indeed precisely the point of our argument this morning: when we strive or seek after maturity we hope that we may become persons who are put together in one piece, or integrated into wholeness.

At this point, we may ask, "Are we not one piece, one personality, united into one package?" "Surely," we say, "we are not several people, flying off into several directions, like the knight who ran out of his castle, jumped on his horse and rode off in all directions."

We may be one body and one mind but so many of us are many persons. Too often we are caught between two forces and we do not know which way to go or which one is us. Here is a young man who says, "I do not know which way to go, shall I quit school or stay in school?" The indecision causes him endless anxiety and frustration and causes him to burn up endless energy. Here is a mother suddenly realizing that she is ruining her daughter's life because of her constant suspicion of what she is doing when she is out on a date. The mother says, "I don't want to be suspicious, but I cannot allow myself to trust her either." The anxiety caused by her inability to decide whether to be trustful or mistrustful makes her anxious and restless. She, of course, becomes irritable with her daughter, her husband, and with the other children. The family naturally becomes tense, gets on each other's nerves, and everyone wonders, "What is the matter with us?" The trouble, of course is a divided spirit in the mother. She is not to be criticized but to be helped, for nothing is quite so destructive in life as a personality divided within itself, pulled in two directions at the same time, without salvation or wholeness. The spiritual problem of immaturity, expressing itself in a divided soul, was not only faced by Hamlet, but also confronts you and me, "To be or not to be, that is the question."

This matter of wholeness needs to be faced at another level; else we may be led astray in believing that maturity means to be free of conflicting feelings. When we speak of wholeness, a desirable quality on the road toward seeking maturity, we do not mean a blissful and exotic paradise of wine and roses. We all have our moments of anger and tenderness, even toward the same person, maybe even in the same day. People who love each other can tolerate the other's displeasure and resentment on occasion. We also experience those times when we are in a state of confusion and do not know whether to turn to the right or to the left. The difference, however, between the real adult and the childish person is that the adult centered person can live with his frustrations and is able to resolve them. If the conflict persists and cannot be corrected he is wise enough to seek counsel from a trusted friend or a professional person. It is not weakness to seek help. It is wisdom to realize that we need to correct the flow that disturbs our relationships with ourselves and with each other.

The last quality we shall mention that we seek as Christians is to live beyond and outside of ourselves. The child lives only for himself, unto himself, and with himself. Often we become irritated with young children because they seem so self-centered. They want their way and they conceive of everything for themselves. If an adult is talking and the child wants to talk, he has no hesitation about interrupting. If the child's mother is talking on the telephone and the child wants a drink of water, the child has no conscience about demanding a drink because his mother has no business talking on the telephone, for she exists to serve his needs. Children are completely self-centered and there is no such thing as an unselfish young child.

Such behavior is expected, of course, in young children and it would be completely unreasonable to expect unselfish behavior, for unselfishness is a quality of maturity, not of childhood. For self-centered behavior to be a part of adult life may be understandable but it is completely out of character and represents an arrestment of spiritual growth.

An obvious trait of living outside of one's self is generosity. Generosity does not necessarily mean being generous with money, for over-generosity with money may imply a stingy spirit that somehow must compensate for its guilt by lavishing people with gifts and favors. Generosity means giving of one's time to those who may need it. One may give only fifteen minutes a day to a friend who is lonely, but during those fifteen minutes he gives the time freely and graciously, listening carefully and earnestly to what the lonely person has to say. Generosity also implies taking time out to be what one is to those who look to him for what he is. A child looks to a father to give him direction and guidance for his life, to instill in him a sense of right and wrong, to set limits and boundaries for his life, and to help him achieve a sense of purpose and independence. A mature father provides this role with gratefulness and strength. Generosity also implies an openness to the opinions and beliefs of others and to accept new information, not because it confirms one's prejudices and opinions, but because it enlightens and offers new facts on which to base decisions, for maturity carries with it the implication of growth, not stagnation.

More than generosity, however, living outside of one's self also implies the capacity to live in a world of change, not reacting emotionally against it, but dealing intelligently with it. When we live outside, not inside, ourselves we do not become fixed, rigid, or immovable, but we are able to make adjustments and changes with the requirements that are placed upon us. Man's ability to adapt himself to most any type of climate, food, and condition is one of his unusual achievements, little known by the other creatures of the earth. The giant dinosaurs that once roamed the North American continent disappeared because they could not withstand the colder temperatures and drier climate that came on the earth in an early period. They had become too adapted to a particular climate and food supply so gradually they disappeared. This occurrence reminds us of those who can change their way of living and way of thinking to fit the time and circumstances. They can stand outside of themselves and perform what is required and demanded. The rigid, less adaptable person is closed in his little world and finds it difficult to ever advance beyond the world of the child.

Who can doubt that it is painful to allow one's self to grow and to seek maturity? One of the most excruciating of all experiences is to leave the comfort of one's little provincial world and to move out where the water is deep and the current is swift and to become a part of the teeming life of humanity. Yet, as Kierkegaard so forcefully reminds us, "To venture is painful but not to venture is to lose one's life." To find one's life then is to set one's face to the wind and the storms and yet not turn back to safety; to feel the pain and anguish of a new idea or a challenge and yet not to fear it but to welcome it; to feel the awful hurt that comes from new associations and from being embarrassed because of one's shyness in a crowd and yet to stay there until one feels comfortable and confident; to feel the terrible loneliness that comes to one who is left alone when others who mean much are gone and yet to stay at one's post and not to give up – these are the ordeals and the trials that come to one who is courageous enough to seek the maturity that Christ offers. The way of Christ is not the child's way, nor the way for the fearful or the coward. It is not the easy or the most profitable way but it is the most exciting of all ways and to him who seeks he will find and to him who asks it will be given, and to him who knocks the door will be opened. We may never attain the maturity of Christ but our lives can be made new by striving for it.

43

THE WAYS WE COME TO THE TABLE OF THE LORD

World Wide Communion Sunday

One of the earliest practices of the small Christian community after the death of Jesus was to observe the Lord's Supper. We have no record to tell us how the occasion was observed until about the year 58, almost 30 years after the crucifixion, when Paul, in writing to the church at Corinth, informed the Corinthians that it was the custom of the Christian communities with which he was familiar, for the faithful to meet in the evening, presumably on the Lord's Day, have a meal together, called the Love Feast or Agape, and conclude with bread and wine to commemorate the sacrifice of Jesus and anticipate his early return. In one form or another, the last part of this ritual, the taking of bread and wine, has been observed regularly and consistently by the followers of Christ through the years and around the world.

In comparatively recent years, because thoughtful Christian leaders have become acutely aware that the divisions of

Christendom are, in a sense, a denial of our Christian witness, many have sought to overcome our divisions and emphasize our likenesses, rather that our differences, by designating one Sunday a year when all Christians everywhere observe Holy Communion. This is that day and this church considers it a privilege to join with Christians throughout the world in observing World Wide Communion Sunday, a custom which has been heeded since 1940.

In recognition of this special day, I have decided that it would be well for us to give our attention to the various ways we come to the table of the Lord, for surely we are unable to appreciate our oneness unless we are thoroughly familiar with our differences. Let us look, therefore, at the several ways we as Christians observe the Lord's Supper. There are about five general interpretations of this supper our Lord asked us to remember in his name.

First of all, there is the belief that the bread and the wine change their substance when appropriate prayers are said over these elements by the priest and they become the actual and real body and blood of Christ. This doctrine is called transubstantiation, or change of substance. This doctrine is held by the Roman Catholic Church and the Eastern Orthodox Churches, only the Eastern Churches are not as literalistic about the change as the Roman Church. In recent years, many leaders in the Roman Church have pressed for a less rigid interpretation of this doctrine but recently Pope Paul rejected these relaxed views and reaffirmed the long held belief in transubstantiation accepted officially by the Church in 1215 and reaffirmed by the Council of Trent in 1562.

Roman Catholic theologians uphold this view by calling attention to the exact words of Jesus as quoted by the writers of the gospel and by Paul. Mark, writing in about 70 A.D. and drawing upon a traditional source, quotes Jesus as saying, *"This is my body."*

"This is my blood." Also Matthew, evidently copying Mark and writing about 90 A.D., gives the same statements *"This is my body." "This is my blood."* Luke had a different source and changes the account slightly. He writes *"This is my body,"* and *"This cup which is poured out for you is the new covenant in my blood."* Paul's account, which is older in time than either Mark, Luke, or Matthew, uses *"this is my body,"* but like Luke says *"This cup is the new covenant in my blood."* If a person accepts a rigid and literal interpretation of the biblical record of the Last Supper, he will have to admit that the Roman Catholics are, at least, consistent and have good grounds for their belief in transubstantiation.

It is important to mention, I think, the seriousness which the Roman Catholics and Eastern Catholics place on the Eucharist. It is the focal point of their service or Mass and occupies the place of greatest importance. When the priest turns the host and the wine to body and blood, he is sacrificing Christ all over again for the sins of the world. When he gives the communicant the host, he gives him the actual body of Christ and this physical element gives the person strength and grace. The person must, therefore, be as pure spiritually as possible when he takes Christ into his body; consequently, before he receives the presence, he must confess his sins and receive proper absolution. Also he must fast four hours before he receives the body. Only the priest can drink the blood. This was begun during the early centuries so as to avoid spilling the blood of Christ. Once the wine has been changed to the blood of Christ it becomes extremely sacred and holy and cannot be disposed of in any way except by being consumed by the priest. If it cannot be consumed, then it is placed on the altar and a lighted candle is placed in a red glass flask near by to indicate the presence of the Blessed Sacrament. This blessed wine or blood is, then, treated of course, with the utmost respect and reverence. When I was in the service and inspected chapels, I always was asked by Catholic chaplains when we entered a small chapel where a candle was burning and the Sacrament was being preserved to speak quietly and walk softly. I always followed their instructions, for I knew how deeply they felt about the Blessed Sacrament – they devoutly believed they were in the actual presence of Christ.

Another view of the Lord's Supper seems similar to that of the Roman Catholic, but is really quite different. This interpretation holds that the bread and wine are not the actual body and blood; nevertheless, the real presence of Christ is in the substance. The elements are still bread and wine, but in some mystical sense which cannot be explained, Christ is really present. This view is sometimes called consubstantiation. It has been held traditionally by that grouping of churches called Anglicans – the Church of England, the Protestant Episcopal Church in the United States, and the various communions in Scotland, Wales, Ireland, and British Commonwealth nations that are in the Episcopal tradition.

In the Anglican Church, only the priest can administer the bread and wine – both are received by the communicant. The sacrament is not preserved once it is blessed but is disposed of in a reverent manner.

During the past 50 years or so there has been a difference of opinion between Anglican leaders regarding who is permitted to receive Holy Communion. The rubric of the Book of Common Prayer of the Church of England of 1549 reads, "And there shall none be admitted to the Holy Communion, until such time as he be confirmed." Some interpret this to mean that it applies to anyone whether he is in the Anglican Church or not. In other words, a person has to be confirmed by a bishop before he is permitted to receive Communion. This is closed communion, only available to confirmed communicants. A growing group of Anglicans, however, contend that this statement in the rubric applies only to persons who are specifically identified with an Anglican group: if a person has been raised an Episcopalian, then, he is not eligible to receive communion until he is confirmed. If a person is a confessed believer, however, and comes from another Christian denomination, the rubric does not apply and he is welcome to the bread and the wine. The only condition for not accepting communion would be any hindrance a person imposes upon himself when he hears the invitation given by the priest, "Ye who do truly repent and desire to commune..." In 1946 Dr. Geoffrey F. Fisher, then the archbishop of Canterbury, in a sermon preached at Cambridge University said, "I love the Church of England, as the Presbyterians and the Methodists love their churches... What I desire is that I should be able freely to enter their churches and they mine, in the sacraments of the Lord and in full fellowship of worship that His life may freely circulate between us." Not all agree.

The third way Christians come to the table of the Lord is represented by the influential Lutheran bodies. They reject transubstantiation and consubstantiation. Their position is that the body and blood of Christ are not substituted for bread and wine (transubstantiation) nor is the real presence in the substance of bread and wine (consubstantiation). Rather, they maintain that the elements are real bread and wine but in some mystical sense, which they do not attempt to explain, the presence of Christ is "given in with and under the bread and wine." The observance or rite is, therefore, not a memorial but a sacrament, a means whereby divine grace is received by the recipient. Some Lutherans are stricter that others concerning the importance of receiving communion. Some bodies require that persons state their intention to receive Communion the day before the service; else they may not accept the bread and wine. This is done to insure that the person is sincere in his intention to commune with Christ and has prepared himself prayerfully and spiritually. He might even make a confession to his pastor if he felt such an act was necessary. Several Lutheran groups do not provide communion for persons who do not prescribe to their particular Confession of Faith. Those who do prescribe carry a card so they will be admitted to the Communion service of another congregation who holds to the same Confession. The minister giving the communion signs the card so that the person will have a record of his participation in Holy Communion.

The fourth way, for want of a better term, could be referred to as *irregular ways* for they deviate considerably from the large number of Christians. The Church of the Latter Day Saints, for example, or Mormons, observe Communion but they use bread and water and the service is open only to their adherents. The Church of the Brethren has an unusual observance which is a threefold Communion service, known as the Love Feast or Agape. This includes feet washing, symbolizing humility and service; the common meal, representing fellowship and peace; and the Communion, using bread and wine, which symbolizes communion with Christ. In all probability, this observance was practiced by many Christian Churches during the first century and has strong New Testament backing. If persons are interested in doing exactly what persons did as described in the New Testament, they should give serious consideration to this ancient practice of the Brethren.

Other deviations include the practices of the Society of Friends, or Quakers, the Unitarians, and the Christian Scientists. Neither of these groups observes Holy Communion, although they have different reasons for abstaining.

The fifth approach or way is that followed by the largest number of Christians who conceive of the Communion Service as a memorial to the life, death, and resurrection of Jesus. Some use bread and wine, others use bread and grape juice, but in either case, there is nothing unusual, mystical, or supernatural that surrounds the rite. It is done to remember Christ out of respect and appreciation for what he means to believers. Christians in this grouping are the Methodists, Baptists, Presbyterians, United Church of Christ, the Christian Churches or Disciples of Christ, and other similar denominations. We are indebted to the Swiss Reformer, Zwingli, for this post Reformation interpretation. It was April 13, 1525, that Zwingli held the first service when people were told that the bread and wine were simple symbols to remember Christ. This was a banner day in the history of the Reform movement.

Of course, each has its own particular emphasis within the larger circle of belief. Some Baptist congregations permit only persons who belong to that particular congregation to participate. This position has nothing to do with Communion but is an extension of their position on the nature of the Church. The church, many Baptists insist, is a particular congregation and only persons in that particular congregations can engage in the life and practices of the congregation, with communion serving only as one of the acts in which members can participate. Baptist churches usually have communion once every three months.

Presbyterians and United Church of Christ also have communion once a quarter, but there is nothing unusual in their beliefs, only a clergyman is required in most instances to initiate the observance. Methodists have communion once a month and only a minister may administer the bread and cup. Communion for Methodists and generally for Presbyterians is open to all who believe.

So we come to our own denomination, the Christian Churches (Disciples of Christ). The observance of the Lord's Supper has always had special significance for us, perhaps for two main reasons. First of all, one of the reasons Thomas Campbell left the Presbyterians when he was a minister on the frontier in Western Pennsylvania in the first decade of the 19th century was because he gave communion to Christians who were not Presbyterians. He wanted a wider association with other Christians and he felt an open communion service was one way to make his desires relevant. The Presbytery denied him this right and a fracture developed that later led to a complete break and to the formation of a new movement.

Another reason for the significance of communion to Disciples is that we observe the service every Sunday and make the bread and wine available to all believers. We do this because our founders, especially the Campbells, believed that it was important for churches to return to the simplicities of the church of the early part of the first century for the sake of bringing Christians closer together in a unified body. Because the early Christians observed the Eucharist or Communion each Lord's Day, he felt it would improve Christian unity if churches in his day followed the same procedure. Campbell was naïve in believing that weekly communion would restore unity to Christendom; nevertheless, we have been faithful to his practice and we observe the custom every Sunday. I am not sure weekly Communion makes us any better Christians than people in other denominations but I believe there is value in practices that link us with the past. In a sense, it reminds us that we are not our own; that we are largely what we are because of what has happened to us in the past. Also it symbolizes our belief in the dignity of each person and gives testimony to our common humanity with all Christians as well as non-Christians everywhere.

One warning, however, must be voiced. When a ritual is observed either frequently or infrequently there is a tendency for the ritual to become an end in itself. A salute or a pledge to a flag frequently becomes the end product and tricks us into believing that when we salute or pledge allegiance to the flag we are patriotic and good Americans. But this is not the case. Patriotic and good Americans serve their nation when they are needed, they pay their taxes, they treat all people – black, white, yellow, and red – with respect and as human beings, they give faithful allegiance to law and order, they insist on justice, not for a few but for all, not what we saw happen this past week in a so-called court of justice in Alabama. They make an effort to uphold the great traditions upon which our nation came into being to honor and respect. The salute or the pledge is merely to show that we underwrite these principles and promise to uphold them, not to live any way we want to.

The receiving of the bread and wine, therefore, each Sunday can so easily become a hollow mockery. If we think just eating bread and drinking wine is the final objective of our coming here each Sunday, we can forget it and stay home. Our objective is to become responsible Christians who are willing to bear the ethical and moral burdens of Jesus Christ. The Communion reminds us of these aims and reinforces our desire to accept the claims of Christ for our lives. When he had finished the meal with his disciples, He left the room, not to forget his solemn pledge but to make good his promise to die on a cross for what he believed was the will of God for his life. Perhaps a thoughtful but disturbing question to ask ourselves when we have received Communion today is this: Will we remain faithful to our pledge to live and to die for what we believe is God's will for our lives? If that question can be answered in the affirmative and the person who answers it really does what he says it doesn't make any difference which path he takes in coming to the table of the Lord, for the ultimate expression of Christian witness is not a way or a form, or a method, but a life that is honest, sincere and committed to Christ, who is the way the truth and the life.

Sermon

44

USING AND MISUSING OUR MEMORIES

I Corinthians 11:24 and when he had given thanks, he broke it, and said, "This is my body which is for you. Do this in remembrance of me."

There is nothing quite so marvelous as the gift of memory. It is the cord that connects today with yesterday, making it possible to finish each day knowing that tomorrow we shall be able to awaken from sleep and take up again where we left off. How poor life would be without this unusual gift. It permits us to renew old acquaintances, to feel at home in familiar haunts, to enjoy the treasures of reading, to perform creative work, to carry on conversation, and to do a hundred other pleasant tasks because the know-how, we once learned, is still a part of us. Life would indeed be enfeebling if each moment was separate to itself without any relation to every other moment.

Jesus was keenly conscious of the significant role of memory. He did not want his faithful friends to forget him. He so desperately wanted them to retain and live by what he had tried to teach

301

them during the short three years he was with them. He associated himself with a plain meal of bread and wine and made a simple request: When you eat together and break your bread and drink your wine, remember me and what I have taught. *"This do,"* he asked, *"in remembrance of me."* He depended on the power of memory to continue what he started. How essential memory is in undergirding our lives with meaning and richness. Without it our Lord would be lost!

But like so many noble qualities which human life holds in such abundance, memory is not only a blessing. It can also be a curse. There are some experiences we wish at times we did not remember. We make fools out of ourselves in so many ways in a lifetime, behave stupidly, say the wrong thing, pass up opportunities, use the wrong approach in raising our children – that we wish in recalling these things that there was no such thing as memory. It would be better to forget! Then there are frightening, terrifying experiences at one time or other that we have endured. Sometimes they are so vivid in the recesses of our minds that they cause us to sleep restlessly, dream fretfully, and we often wake up in a cold perspiration, shaking and afraid. "Will it never go away?" we exclaim, "Oh, if only we could forget!"

Memory then is a powerful force available either for our benefit or our harm. It can enrich or it can destroy. It is essential that we know how to use memory properly if it is to be a constructive force in our living.

Surely, then, in the first place, memory is able to cripple or assist in avoiding past mistakes. I say our recollections can assist us in not repeating our foolish errors of yesterday. These memories of ours can also cripple and damage us so completely that we find it difficult to make a go of it today. It depends on how we handle that past mistake whether or not it will be to our advantage or disadvantage.

Here is a young man who goes off to college with flags flying. He and his parents have planned and saved for the young man to get a college education and he is determined to make a success of it. But even the best plans sometimes do not succeed. The young man works hard at first but soon discovers there are more interesting things in college than classrooms and books. He finds the social life exciting, which is beneficial to him, but he spends too much time at it and not enough at his desk. The first year ends. The grades are rather poor, even some courses are not passed. He is disappointed. His parents are disappointed. "I am a failure," he cries in despair, "I am stupid in my studies. I'll never make it. The best thing to do is quit."

His old dad is, however, a wise man. He has been through this sort of thing himself. He was a boy once himself and he knows the temptations youth face. He has also tasted disappointment and failure many times in his life. So rather than severely criticizing the boy, he sits down with him and suggests they discuss the problem together. After the dejected boy spends several sessions with his dad and goes over what he did at college and how he spent his time that first year, he understands he isn't stupid, but he used his time and efforts poorly. His problem is not a matter of intelligence; it is a matter of self-control in budgeting his time and reevaluating what is important. Social life, yes; bull-sessions with other students, yes; sports, yes; studies, yes - but each activity must share his time according to its importance and not have one area take all of it. So the young man goes back to college his second year a wiser man – not in spite of his mistakes, but because of his error. He ends up after four years with his diploma.

Memory of our failures can cause us to give up in despair as the young man was first wont to do. It can also turn a failure into a victory. The difference lies in its use. There is no use *crying over spilled milk*. What is done is finished. The mark of wisdom is to capitalize on our recollections of a mistake and resolve to make an honest effort not to take that wrong turn in the road again.

It can also be said, in the second place, that our memory is a powerful instrument either for enfeebling or strengthening our lives. It can either destroy or enrich.

Our experiences are generally of two types: those that provide us with comfortable and deep satisfactions, and those that leave us uncomfortable, distressed, fearful, and anxious. The residue of these experiences is implanted within our spirits, becomes a part of our memory system, and is a determining factor in the kinds of people we are. We do not even always realize they are there. Most often they are hidden from our conscious memories, but hidden or not, they have direct bearing on our behavior and attitudes as the invisible strings in a puppet show move the puppet characters here and there on the puppet stage. We learn our lessons well when we are young and the remembrance of them lingers long.

It is those experiences that made us afraid and anxious, especially when we were young, that now clog our memory channels and cause so much damage to ourselves and others. When our bitter engagement on the battlefield with the North Korean and Chinese Communists ended in 1953, we were absolutely appalled to learn that 21 of our soldiers who were in the Communist prison camps did not want to return to their home country, but wanted to stay in Communist territory. We were even more astonished to hear later that one third of our servicemen in prison camps in varying degrees complied with the enemy. Studies of these staggering reports indicated that the servicemen who were the most serious offenders were young men whose early home and community life had been surrounded by unsettled and unpleasant conditions. Many were from homes where parents were separated or divorced. Excessive drinking was most always a factor in the home. All practically had no understanding of what it means to have affection and to be wanted as part of a family or group. Their whole memory system was terribly out of order. The life experiences of these young men were more in the nature of bad dreams than interesting living. It is no wonder they had no resources to draw from when they needed them most.

Good experiences in the life of the family create a reservoir of wholesome memories from which persons can draw spiritual water to provide them strength all the days of their lives.

Do you see why it is necessary that we do the best we can to provide our children the best kind of home life we possibly can? I do not mean a large or expensive home. Riches have little to recommend themselves at this point. *"Man does not live by bread alone."* I mean home life that is shared by persons who love, honor, and respect each other and in which children know and feel that they are wanted and that they are given responsibility for contributing to that home.

The church congregation, too, must be alert in providing the kind of atmosphere which is conducive to Christian growth and faith. Young people are quick to sense sincerity and love in the lives of those who direct the life of the church fellowship. They are also quick to sense hypocrisy, pettiness of spirit, and meanness of heart. Our job here is to provide a happy, friendly, warm fellowship for all who attend. This will do more than a thousand words, or reams of paper, or masses of diagrams to provide persons with staying power and faith as they face and participate in the ventures of life.

Now, we come to another observation concerning using and misusing our memories: memory provides an opportunity either for depression or joy. There is perhaps nothing quite so marvelous as to participate in significant experiences with a person you love and like to be with. We see this especially in young people. They enjoy being with each other at a party, hiking, eating, or just talking. Our house rocked and rolled the other evening with teenage fun and frolicking. I don't see how they stood it. I had to put cotton in my ears – but they like it, not so much what they did, but just being together.

On a deeper level, there is the happy time a young couple just married has in going off on a honeymoon together. It is a time when life is carefree with no one to whom they have to be responsible. They are together, nothing else really matters. Then on a still deeper level, there are those deep satisfactions derived from the joys and hardships of married life. Planning a family, paying the rent or mortgage, visiting and differing about in-laws, attending church, changing home and jobs, having children, enduring illness and sometimes poverty – these and a thousand other shared concerns are significant experiences that enrich life and make it worth living. It is so because they are shared with persons we love, cherish, and respect.

But these experiences do not go on forever. Life on this earth is transitory and partial. Age comes upon us, and its accompanying problems. Children grow up, move away, and form their own family ties. Illness incapacitates us or another; and those we love are sometimes taken away and we are left alone with only our memories. The woman composer of the expressive song *When Day is Done* and her husband lived a wonderful life together. He was taken away and so she expressed her sadness in her poem and music:

When day is done and shadows fall,
I think of you.
I miss your love, your tender kiss the whole day through
But I miss you most of all
When day is done.

Such memories bring a tear and a choke to the throat. It isn't easy to recall such happy memories that are over and done with. And we should never repress the feelings that accompany our memories. It is good to cry and shed a tear. But memory is misused if it is permitted to keep us in the doldrums and incapacitate us for living in the here and now. *"Let the dead bury the dead,"* said Jesus. Tragedy is real but must also be risen above and captivated.

The sure cure for sadness caused by a loss of happy moments and loved ones is gratitude. How poor our lives would be without the rich and beautiful experiences with persons we loved but are no longer with us! "It was better to have loved you dear and lost than never to have loved at all," is not bad advice. So for those who have enriched and have given meaning to our lives let us give thanks.

It was not easy for the early disciples to lose their Lord. So strong was their gratitude, however, for him and what he believed, lived, and taught that sadness was dispelled. The amazing fact of the New Testament is that there is no gloom connected with the death of Jesus Christ. It is a book held together by the thread of faith and joy, hope, and love. So grateful were they that they had been permitted to know and to be associated with him that their *hearts burned within them* whenever they felt his presence and Paul was able to transform his feelings into these stirring words, *"Thanks be to God who gives us this victory, even our faith, through our Lord Jesus Christ."* It makes a difference, doesn't it, the way we use our memories?

But one more point: memory can either kill or enliven the present and the future. It seems to me that about the saddest of all experiences is to visit a country or a town and hear a guide or a citizen of the place relate glorious legends and events of long ago, but to hear that there are no events or stories of today. The past in such a place is more real and vivid than the present. The people take pride in what once was and in what people of yesterday did, but they have nothing to commend in the present.

Now surely we ought to be proud of our traditions and to delight in the accomplishments of our ancestors, but to live only in the past and to permit the present to find its meaning in the events of yesterday is a misuse of our memory. God has given us memory not to anesthetize our spirits but as a gift to provide meaning for the present and direction for the future.

Even as we observe the memorial of our Lord's death and resurrection around His table each Lord's Day, there is a danger our observance can become an end in itself. We may become so intent on remembering our Lord that we shall forget to live in His Name each day of our lives. *This do in remembrance of me,* is not a call to contentment and withdrawal from the busy rush of the world. It is a clarion call to make for Him *a world of righteousness, from pride and despotism free.*

Let us take a tip from the early church. Their Lord was taken from them. At first, it seemed their world had come to an end. There must have been a real temptation to retreat from the world and to organize a monastic order to preserve his memory. But it all happened so differently. They did not decorate the Upper Room with wreaths and flowers. We have no record of special mourning clothes they wore. They made no effort to build a memorial to his name, wasting time in stones and mortar. They did not try to find the stable where he was born, make a shrine of it, and charge admission for people to visit it. No effort was made to find the coat he wore on the way to the Cross. They took seriously his teachings, *"Let the dead bury the dead."*

For those early Christians, memory of their Lord did not tempt them to worship him as an ancient god, nor did it cripple their lives. Memory ushered forth in dynamic action. *"He is Risen,"* they cried. Their marching orders in his memory were to venture forth to the ends of the earth with the proclamation that Christ is the Lord.

And to you and to me the words still pour in upon us strong and clear, *"Go ye into all the world and preach the gospel to every creature, baptizing them in the name of the Father, and of the Son, and of the Holy Spirit."* This is what we do when we place our memories of Him under the direction of his Lordship. This is the proper use of memory at all times and in all places: To channel our memories into constructive activities for life in the here and now.

45

UPROOTING AND TRANSPLANTING

Psalms 137:1-9

1 By the waters of Babylon, there we sat down and wept,
when we remembered Zion.
2 On the willows there we hung up our lyres.
3 For there our captors required of us songs,
and our tormentors, mirth, saying, "Sing us one of the songs of Zion!"
4 How shall we sing the LORD's song in a foreign land?
5 If I forget you, O Jerusalem, let my right hand wither!
6 Let my tongue cleave to the roof of my mouth, if I do not remember you,
if I do not set Jerusalem above my highest joy!
7 Remember, O LORD, against the E'domites the day of Jerusalem,
how they said, "Rase it, rase it! Down to its foundations!"
8 O daughter of Babylon, you devastator!
Happy shall he be who requites you
with what you have done to us!
9 Happy shall he be who takes your little ones
and dashes them against the rock!

Some months ago I happened to be traveling on an airliner, and chanced into a conversation with a young business executive who was sitting next to me. He told me that his firm had transferred him four times in the past seven years. He went on to say that he and his wife were concerned because of the effect the frequent moves might have on their children. He said also, that sometimes he felt like an uprooted plant that has no place to grow. He said, "I wish sometimes I could settle down and grow like a plant that is really growing in good soil."

The feeling of this business executive is not only his feeling, but it is also the feeling of millions of people today in our American society. Someone has called us a generation of gypsies, for one out of four American families change their address once every year. People not only move from town to town, state to state, from house to house in the same locality, but people are also moving up and down the economic and social ladder. The culture we live in as adults is not always the same culture we lived in when we were children. Now this uprooting of life leaves marks upon persons. Sometimes the mark is one of grief and sadness. When the Hebrews were carried by Nebuchadnezzar to Babylon in the year 586 B.C., many of them could not stand the shock and the pain of leaving the old home back at Jerusalem. They were disturbed, they were sorrowful, they were grief stricken, and one of the Psalmists caught up the sentiments of these Jewish people and expressed it in the 137th Psalm. One sentence, it seems to me, stands out above all the rest to epitomize this feeling of loneliness and of sorrow, when one is uprooted from his home. He said, *"How can we sing the Lord's song in a foreign land?"*

Is it not true today, that people who are uprooted are grieved and are sorrowful because they are not living back home? They find the school, and the community, and the people alien. They wish they had not been uprooted, but nevertheless, there they are and sometimes this experience expresses itself in grief and sadness. Then sometimes individuals make a kind of adjustment in moving to a new community or to a new home; they are not really in the place they are living, but part of them is back in the old home town. They have one foot here, but one foot is back home. A man, who has lived in Washington for 35 years, still has his residence in Michigan, and when he talks of home, he talks of the place where he grew up as a boy. For 35 years part of him has been in Washington, but the other part is back in Michigan. This often happens, doesn't it, to many of us who are not able to make an adequate adjustment when we are uprooted and have to move and live in a new environment? Then, sometimes, this predicament leaves its mark in the form of romanticizing the place from which people come. You hear people say, sometimes, there is no place like home. They feel that the place from which they came is the most wonderful place in all the world, and there is no other place like it. Sometimes people express this sentiment regarding their church affiliation. One woman related to me, this very sad experience, and it is sad, and I think that we should appreciate what people are up against when they have to pull up roots and move to a new place. She said, "I grew up in a little town in Indiana, and I hated to leave this home, but I had to move to Washington. I have lived in Washington for 20 years, and whenever I think of church, I think of that little church back home in Indiana. I was unable to move my church affiliation from the place back home to the place where I have lived for the past 20 years, because it seemed I was being irreverent, in a sense, I was being sacrilegious breaking my identity with the little congregation back in Indiana, but she said, after being away for 15 years I went back for a trip. I could not find the little church, for where it once stood there was an office building. I finally found the congregation, she said, in another part of town, but it was a new building, and no one knew me when I went to services on Sunday morning. No one ever knew that I had been a member of the church."

You see she was living, not in reality, but in fantasy. She was romanticizing about what she thought was the place where she belonged. Now, we have to be realistic about life. Wouldn't it be wonderful if we could recall and live the old experiences of childhood? But life is not like this, there is no moment but now; and so the healthy position, the only position that we can take if we are going to be positive, and productive in our living, and to be able to sing the Lord's song in a foreign land, is to transplant ourselves to the place where we now are. This is the way the Lord's song is sung, and when we use this phrase, what we really mean is, that we are living life at its best, and that kind of life is more rewarding and satisfying and abundant to ourselves and to other people. When we live creative, productive lives - *that* is when we are singing the Lord's song! When we transplant ourselves, surely what we are doing is identifying ourselves with the place where we are now living. We not only live in a house on a block, and send our children to a school in the neighborhood, but when we are transplanted, and are sending our roots down to become creative persons, then we become a part of that community. We identify ourselves with some church with which we can share our lives with other Christian people, we become involved in the voting of the community, we share in its problems, we carry the burden of the place where we live, this is transplanting ourselves and singing the Lord's song in a land that need not be foreign, but can be our home. You see, land is neutral, we only make ourselves foreigners. It's not up to the community to adjust to us, but it is our job to become a part of the community and to live in it. Now surely, we only sing the Lord's song by identifying with the place where we are, by sharing our lives with the lives of other individuals.

Did you know that some Americans that go to live in other countries, in Japan, or in Germany, or in France, or Austria, or eslewhere, live in little isolated American communities, and never learn the richness of the country where they are living? You see it's so much more comfortable and safe, to stay with those who are like ourselves. But it is so much more rewarding to venture out and dare to enter into the homes of the people of the new land, to eat at their table, to share their food, to hear their conversation, to learn other customs and their practices, and to share life with them. And when we do, we soon learn that really, the peoples of the earth are not really very different. When you boil this all down, we are pretty much the same kind of people. We have the same aspirations, the same dreams, and the same hopes. The only thing that keeps us apart are the artificial structures and barriers that have been erected to keep us behind and away from others. We only learn to sing the Lord's song as we learn to share life with people everywhere. Now this does not mean we become like the people, with whom we are living. I may live next door to a Jewish family, but that doesn't mean that I become Jewish, nor that they become Protestant. I may also live next door to a member of the Roman Catholic faith, but I do not become a Roman Catholic and neither do they become Protestant. But what I want to emphasize, is that when we live in a place we should learn to share life at its deeper levels with other individuals. Then we can begin to know, understand, respect and share the deep richness of human relationships.

It took Jesus to appear on the human scene to make people aware that there are no real barriers between us, if we have the courage to share in the life of other individuals, and they share also in our lives. Thanks be to God that a few people understood Jesus Christ, and made it possible for His interpretation of life to be part of mankind. An interpretation of life, that places us in contact, in communication, in relationship with places, and people wherever we live. This is what we mean when we say, that in Christ, there is no East or West, but one great brotherhood around the whole wide world.

In the name of the Father, and of the Son, and of the Holy Spirit. Amen.

46

WORKING ON THE SOURCE OF THE PROBLEM

Matthew 5:23-24 So if you are offering your gift at the altar, and there remember that your brother has something against you, leave your gift there before the altar and go; first be reconciled to your brother, and then come and offer your gift.

About a year and a half ago, my family had the unusual pleasure of having a flood in the basement of our home. If you have ever had that experience, I think you know what I mean, if you haven't, I do not wish it upon you. When the water first started pouring in through the cinder blocks above the floor of the basement, we tried to patch up the holes with a caulking compound, but the water kept pouring in through the cinder blocks above the floor of the basement. We finally had to give up and began to bail out the water, rather than trying to stop it from coming in. The next day an expert in water-proofing came in and looked over the basement, sized up the problem, and stated exactly what had to be done to stop the leaks. His solution was drastic and expensive, for it involved digging tunnels along the wall through the cement floor. Rather meekly I asked him if the holes couldn't be patched with a caulking compound or some other less involved and costly procedure. "No," he said, "to correct the problem you have to get at the source. You have to drain off the water under the basement floor to relieve the pressure, to keep it from coming up the walls and into the basement through the cinder blocks." I accepted his advice, paid the bill, and fortunately we have had no further flooding in the basement.

Now Jesus had a way of correcting human behavior problems in the same way that this waterproofing expert corrected the water problem in the basement of our home. Jesus did not believe in patching up the cracks and crevices in human character with a neat slogan, a magical formula, or a pill. He insisted that wholeness in a human life could be attained only by working at the core of the difficulty. Jesus suggested that persons had to go to the source of their predicaments before they could expect any relief from anxiety or mental pain. For example, he saw individuals who were suffering discomfort because of feuds and disharmonies between themselves. They thought they could get rid of the problem by saying a few pious words, offering a sacrifice, or placing money in the offering plate. These were acts of piety, beneficial in themselves, but they could never be employed to correct a problem involving interpersonal relationships. Here is what Jesus said,

"If you are offering your gift at the altar, and there remember that your brother has something against you, leave your gift there before the altar and go; first be reconciled to your brother, and then come and offer your gift."

Like the man who knew his business in stopping leaks in basements, Jesus knew how to assist persons in overcoming the pain and anxiety resulting from personal feuds. Work on the problem at its source!

For reasons not always understood, however, you and I find it almost impossible to work out our personal difficulties by attacking problems at their source. We possess an almost uncanny capacity not to work at the center of our predicament, but rather to dabble at the periphery. We find it easier and more comfortable to put on a patch rather than performing a spiritual overhaul. Here are some of the ways we indulge in patchwork.

One technique is to try to make the symptom of the problem go away by indulging our appetites. A person who experiences discomfort because he may feel uncomfortable around others may try to make the discomfort go away by eating more than is necessary. Another person may handle the problem by stealing, a procedure frequently used by children who feel inadequate around other boys and girls. A person with the same feelings of inadequacy who has plenty of money may go on frequent spending sprees buying what they do not need but buying nevertheless and concocting reasonable explanations for every purchase. The worst habit for getting rid of inadequacy, of course, is drinking. No one will ever know the amount of liquor consumed by persons who are trying to find some way to handle their personal inadequacies. Eating, stealing, buying, drinking, and other similar habits do relieve those awful feelings connected with inferiority temporarily just as aspirins temporarily relive the pain of arthritis. Unfortunately, however, aspirin does not cure arthritis and neither does indulging our appetites cure our inadequacies whatever they may be. They lack the power to get at the source of the problem. They relieve, but they do not cure.

Another popular way by which people solve their problems of living is by making a change. Many persons change jobs again and again because they grow dissatisfied on a job, don't like the people they work with, don't get ahead, or for any number of reasons. Somehow they think the problem they have, whatever it is, will go away. They will feel better, or they will do better if they can move on to another position. Sometimes, it does help to make a change whether in a job or in place of living or in another situation providing the problem does lie in the job condition, and is really outside of one's self.

A third method utilized by persons when faced with a thorny problem is to give it to another person. Years ago when I first started in the ministry I thought my job was to make the problems of other people my problems. Persons would come to me with a sad tale and I thought my job was to take the problem, work it out and hand back the problem with a solution, all tied up in a neat little package. It did take me a number of years to discover that I was more worried about the persons' difficulties than they were. They were handing me their problems. I was doing the suffering, they were going blissfully about their business, and I was doing them more harm than good and tying myself up in knots. Today I am not so eager to make the problems of others my own. My job, I feel, is to help others learn to handle their own problems, for this is the way persons learn to become adults.

There are other ways, of course, by which persons turn over their problems to others. Sometimes a couple who are not doing well in the business of marriage will have a child, thinking that a tiny baby in the home will somehow get rid of their childish behavior. No baby can solve an unhealthy situation perpetrated by childish adults. Again, a man who is a reckless philanderer thinks he can become a new person by marrying a chaste girl and she may think she can cure his drunkenness and waywardness by marrying him.

I suppose such situations do occasionally have happy endings, but I am inclined to think they occur more in story books than in real life. A peripheral solution can seldom solve a deep-seated emotional or spiritual dilemma.

Another way of working on personal foibles, and one that has been found disappointing, is wrapping up one's self in religious devotions and observances. Now, religious faith can assist in handling a religious problem but religious exercises cannot solve problems unrelated to religion; and to make an effort to do so only compounds the problem and causes it to become more serious.

A person sometimes comes to the ministry who has made a poor showing in another career. He hasn't done well in his occupation as an attorney, a bank officer, a military officer, or a business man. Somehow, he thinks that the ministry is where he belongs and that he can make a go of it as a clergyman. Perhaps, he can, but usually he deceives himself into thinking that by some peculiar quirk the ministry will solve his problems. Or again, a mother with a wayward child thinks that if the child will only go to church the child will become a different person. When I was a chaplain, I frequently had company commanders call me to tell me they were sending a poor undisciplined soldier to me so that I could straighten him out. Somehow, in desperation they felt the chaplain had some magic wand he could wave over a soldier's head, or a mysterious word he could say to him and the soldier would be a new man. These are all ways of trying to work at problems on the fringes or by doing a patch job here and there. Jesus never indulged in aspirin tablet remedies. He turned the attention of people to the source of their problems. He never used religious paraphernalia to cause individuals to hide from, gloss over, or to get away from the problems of living: *"First be reconciled to your brother and then come to the altar to offer your gift."*

This leads us to suggest then, the appropriate ways to get at our problems, ways consistent with the spirit of Jesus.

Here are questions thoughtful people ask themselves. What is it that is causing me to feel the way I do, to think the way I think, or to behave as I do? Why do I indulge myself? Why don't I get along well with others? Why do I feel so miserable when I am in the company of certain people? As one student who failed college last year recently said to me, "I seem to be smart enough. Why do I want to spend my time playing and drinking all of the time instead of doing my school work?" A woman who came for counseling asked, "Why do I try to embarrass one of my best friends when we're in a group?" These are indeed uncomfortable questions. They provoke pain and even bewilderment but they seem to be necessary to get at the source of our predicaments. These are not unusual questions for a person who discovers something new. Newton discovered the law of gravity by watching an apple fall to the ground. He asked, "Why?" And from this question he discovered the law of gravity. Why are we unable to sleep? Why don't we have proper digestion? There are reasons why we have these problems of the inner life, and the wise person is the one who makes an effort to find out the reason.

Another excellent step in working on the fountain head of a problem is to look for and to expect that the answer to our "Why?" may be within ourselves. Certainly, not all of our life problems are our fault. We simply are not so omnipotent. Yet, it is certain that many situations that cause us unhappiness have their source within ourselves and we should strive to discover if this is the case. If a person bounces from one job to another, in all probability, there is something lacking in his performance that needs attention. If there is friction between persons in a family each person contributes his share of the difficulty. The only way for better relations to develop is for each family member to look to himself for the reason. Shakespeare summarized the predicament about as well as you will ever find, when in *Julius Caesar*, he has Cassius say to Brutus:

> "The fault, dear Brutus, is not in the stars,
> But in ourselves, that we are underlings."

What is more anxiety provoking than to admit that perhaps we are the one who is responsible for our dissatisfactions and miserable condition. It is easy to see the beam in others' eyes, but so hard to see the speck in our own.

But once we do discover the source, we need to find the best way to correct it. We must first of all fit the solution to the problem. If a nasty disposition is the problem, a new necktie or new dress, or giving money to the poor, or saying a prayer is not the answer. The antibiotic to a nasty disposition is to practice becoming more pleasant and looking for blessings in life rather than hard luck. If the problem is self-centeredness, stubbornness or laziness, acts of kindness and unselfishness become necessary. If one finds no meaning in existence, then an understanding of what Christ has to say about the world is his answer. Here a religious solution is offered for a religious problem.

Finally, then, once a person believes he has found what it takes to really work on his problem then let him diligently and faithfully work on it. Intention is not enough, discovery and insight are not sufficient. There remains the capacity for long hard arduous labor to work one's way through and out of one's problems. We are helped in our endeavors to stay at the task by accepting the encouragement of others. So often we resist what others suggest just because another person wants to help. We burn up vital energy and incapacitate ourselves for quality living by always defending, resisting, fencing with those who seek to help us. On the other hand, when we do not resist but accept the support and encouragement of those who love us and are interested in us, we tap those rich spiritual resources that give us that extra power to solve our problems and learn to live with them and we move on to higher ground and the life of freedom and creativeness. How many men have finished a hard task because they accepted gladly the encouragement of a friend or a wife? Many times in the introduction to a book, I find the writer saying, "I could not have finished the manuscript without the constant help and support of my wife." We very much need, not to defy others, but to freely accept what they so graciously have to offer.

Most of all we need to be receptive to the graciousness of Jesus Christ and his pronouncements concerning life. He gives no shortcuts, no miracle cures, no magic formulas, no patent medicines in handling the perplexities and problems of living. Yet, he does offer what it takes to make us new persons and persons who are fit to live with. He offers no easy way out of predicaments; he insists we maintain a sense of responsibility for ourselves and for our society; he encourages us not to be afraid to look deep within ourselves for the problems that life presents to us and to keep at the everlasting business of changing ourselves, for he who would be his disciple must daily *be born again* before his life can be finally changed in the fullness and likeness of Christ.

47

THE ROLE OF THE CHURCH IN THE WORLD

Reformation Sunday

John 1:7-8 (Said of John the Baptist)
7 He came for testimony, to bear witness to the light,
that all might believe through him.
8 He was not the light, but came to bear witness to the light.

This is a day of self examination in the life of the church. Just before the start of World War II, the church was under fire by critics from all sides. Then following World War II, particularly during the 1950's, the scene changed. People began going to church that had not been in years. Church attendance soared to new heights and membership in churches in the USA jumped to 65% of the total population - the highest church membership in the history of the country. The last five, six or seven years have been a period of cooling off, both attendance and membership have dropped off. Enrollment in most all theological seminaries has declined. These signs, however, are not all bad, for church growth and enthusiasm have been replaced with something deeper: People within the church, clergy and lay people alike, are asking some penetrating questions concerning the mission of the church in the world. So today the church is in a period of critical self-analysis.

The question, of course, that is asked foremost is this, "What is the role of the church in the world?" Leading critics have compared the church to a country club, a knitting society, or ladies afternoon tea party, far removed, these critics affirm, from the leaven (or yeast in the bread) whose function is to redeem society. Other critics have said church going is merely a dull, monotonous routine people have gotten into that has no relationship to anything substantial or moving. One wit wrote concerning church going:

> They do it every Sunday
> They'll be all right on Monday.
> It's just a little habit they've acquired.

Well, church members who love the church see something in it of lasting value. They take seriously the comments of the critics and are now engaged in one of the most critical analyses of the church and its mission that the church has been subjected to since the days of the Reformation. This time, however, the criticism is coming from the top rather than from the bottom or the outside. Before the church, however, can be adequately evaluated it is essential that attention be directed toward its basic function or role in society. Today, therefore, let us examine its fundamental and primary role in society, not to explain or elaborate but only to stress the broad objective of the role.

Any number of texts could be selected from the New Testament to get at a biblical basis for the primary role of the church. One text that seems to present the matter about as well as we could discover is given by the writer of the Gospel of John. He writes concerning John the Baptist,

"There was a man sent from God, whose name was John. He came for testimony, to bear witness to the light, that all might believe through him. He was not the light, but came to bear witness to the light."

John the Baptist was not the truth but he came to bear witness to the truth. He was before the truth seen in Jesus Christ and he told about the truth or the light that was to come. The church came after that light that was seen in Jesus Christ and the church like John is not the truth but bears witness to the truth or to the light seen in Jesus Christ. There it is: the role of the church in the world is to be a witness to that truth, that light, that way portrayed in Jesus Christ. If we accept this assumption – the church as a witness to the truth of God known in Jesus Christ – then all sorts of conclusions present themselves in understanding the role of the church in the world.

One conclusion we draw from this assumption is that we have a perfectly clear explanation of why the Protestant Reformation occurred in 16th century Europe – the Roman Catholic Church had developed to the place where the Pope and the other officials of the church did not conceive of the church as a witness to the truth but rather they thought of the church as the truth. The church in that day taught that it had within itself the power of life and death over all who were a part of it. It condemned men to hell or assured them a place in heaven. When Pope Leo asked the faithful throughout all of Europe to contribute funds to complete the construction of St. Peters Church in Rome, he assured them that their gifts would purchase sufficient indulgences to guarantee a perfect remission of all sins. Of this event, Roland Bainton, in his *Life of Martin Luther* writes, subscribers to the indulgences

> "would be restored to the state of innocence which they enjoyed in baptism and would be relieved of all the pains of purgatory, including those incurred by an offense to the Divine Majesty. Those securing indulgences on behalf of the dead already in purgatory need not themselves be contrite and confess their sins."

In other words, a person buying an indulgence was given a guarantee by church officials that the spirits of departed members of his family would be released from the pains of purgatory and allowed to enter the paradise of heaven. Here is a jingle that was used to sell the indulgences,

> "As soon as the coin in the coffer rings,
> The soul from purgatory springs."

Evidently, modern TV commercials are not the first to use jingles to sell merchandise.

The church of the 16th century had indeed stooped to a low spiritual level. The period is regretted by all honest Roman Catholic leaders today and the Roman Catholic Church today is certainly not the church it was then. Yet, these practices just described and the position of the church of that day that it was the truth, that it spoke for God, were some of the basic reasons that Luther and the other reformers revolted and led a revolution within the church that shook Europe to its foundation. The Reformation occurred and the Protestant movement began largely because the church failed to comprehend that it was not the light but only a witness to the light.

The lessons of the Reformation, however, were soon forgotten. Persons who revolted against the claims of the Roman Church that the church was the truth soon thought of themselves and their pronouncements as the truth rather than interpretations or witnesses to the truth. Even Luther, in his later years, gave his approval to the persecution of the Anabaptists, a group of Christians in Germany who did not accept either the claims of Rome of the beliefs and practices of the Lutherans. They rejected infant baptism, the ministerial office, and refused to swear allegiance to the established government. These people were treated cruelly by the German states and Luther concurred in their death. He, the great reformer, forgot too soon that even he was not the truth but only a bearer of the light. Neither do we enjoy remembering that John Calvin, the influential Frenchman who did so much to advance the Protestant cause in Switzerland, had little patience with those who differed with his views. Calvin played an influential role in having Servetus put to death. Servetus was a devoted and sincere Christian leader in Switzerland who disagreed with Calvin. Calvin thought the views of Servetus heretical and he sanctioned his execution. The temptation to be God is most attractive and there are few who can resist. From the days of the reformation until now, and even today, denomination after denomination has claimed itself the truth, forgetting that its role is to bear witness to the truth and not to claim it is the truth.

One of the most promising signs in our times is the critical self-analysis to which most of our major denominations are subjecting themselves. Growing from these self evaluations is the insight that no denomination, nor any group of denominations is the light or the truth. Church group after church group is realizing that all each can claim for itself is that it is a witness to the truth that it has discovered in Jesus Christ; that every other denomination is also a witness; and that no witness can claim any greater validity for its testimony than any other witness. This is the fact of the present state of the claims of the various churches that compose the body of Christ.

Notice if you will the developments that are taking place to give evidence to this central fact in the life of the church today. The Vatican Council and Pope Paul have jointly declared that more stress will be placed on establishing points of contact with other Christians as well as non-Christians. Already, a common Bible is under preparation, shared in jointly by Roman Catholic and Protestant Biblical scholars. Other significant developments are the conversations now taking place to bring about eventual union in the USA among Methodists, the United Church of Christ, the Evangelical and United Brethren, the Protestant Episcopal Church, the United Presbyterian Church, and our own denomination, the Christian Churches. Churchmen participating in these discussions only recently reported that almost all points of major differences have been settled and soon a plan for union will be submitted to the churches for consideration. These are indeed significant days in the life of the church.

At last, we have begun to understand that what the writer of John was saying in effect centuries ago in his biography of Jesus – no person, no group of persons, no institution can be the truth that we know in Jesus Christ. The most that any of us can possibly accomplish is to make an effort to witness to that truth and to listen in sincerity to the witness of others, for in that way we learn and profit from the testimony of others. Reformation is not confined to the 16th century nor to any particular period of history. Reformation is a phenomenon that has to occur every single day in the life of the church in order for the church to be faithful to its role in the life of the world, to be led by the truth that we know in Jesus Christ, our Lord.

48

BUILDING ON FOUNDATIONS LAID BY OTHERS

I Corinthians 3:1-11

1 But I, brethren, could not address you as spiritual men, but as men of the flesh, as babes in Christ.

2 I fed you with milk, not solid food; for you were not ready for it; and even yet you are not ready,

3 for you are still of the flesh. For while there is jealousy and strife among you, are you not of the flesh, and behaving like ordinary men?

4 For when one says, "I belong to Paul," and another, "I belong to Apol'los," are you not merely men?

5 What then is Apol'los? What is Paul? Servants through whom you believed, as the Lord assigned to each.

6 I planted, Apol'los watered, but God gave the growth.

7 So neither he who plants nor he who waters is anything, but only God who gives the growth.

8 He who plants and he who waters are equal, and each shall receive his wages according to his labor.

9 For we are God's fellow workers; you are God's field, God's building.

10 According to the grace of God given to me, like a skilled
master builder I laid a foundation, and another man is
building upon it. Let each man take care how he builds upon it.
11 For no other foundation can any one lay than
that which is laid, which is Jesus Christ.

No one ever makes a discovery, accomplishes a task, or develops a concept by himself, for he who discovers, he who accomplishes, and he who develops always builds on the insights and efforts of others who preceded him. Sir Isaac Newton, who lived in the seventeenth century, is credited with formulating our current laws of gravity, however, Newton would be the first to admit, were he alive today, that he did not discover the laws of universal gravitation by himself. Rather Newton would admit that he was able to develop his theories because of the earlier observations and experimentations of men who preceded him - such astronomers and mathematicians as Aristarchus of Samos who lived as early as 270 B.C., Copernicus, Kepler, and Galileo and numerous other men of science. Newton accomplished his tasks because he could build upon foundations that had been laid by others.

When Paul was developing Christian communities in various towns and cities of the Greco-Roman world, he was aware that he was not promulgating a new venture. He knew that the Christian faith he was teaching and spreading was not his own. He had something to say and something to offer concerning the new faith he had accepted, but he knew he was not the author or the originator. When he wrote to the infant church at Corinth from Ephesus in about the year 54 A.D., he said:

"according to the commission of God given me, like a skilled master builder I laid a foundation, and another is building upon it. Let each man take care how he builds on it. For no other foundation can anyone lay than that which is laid, which is Jesus Christ." (I Corinthians 3:10-11)

Paul, therefore, sets the stage for the event which concerns us today. We are here to lay the cornerstone for a new building. This is a significant event in the life of this church. You have worked hard and long and many have contributed sacrificially to make the laying of this cornerstone possible. And you and others who will come after you will also work hard and long to complete this building and assist in making this church a creative force in this community. Your sacrifices and commitment are well known and you and your capable minister and leaders are not only to be congratulated, but also thanked for what has been done and what will be done here for the cause of Christ. But you would be the first to realize that you are indebted to those who have labored before you for what is happening here today. You are laying a cornerstone, but you are also building on foundations laid by others. Principally, however, you are building on a foundation that has already been laid, which is Jesus Christ. This church as it lays its cornerstone for its new building is faced with the obligation, therefore, not only of starting and erecting a new building, but also of living out in its life and work the task that was initiated by Jesus Christ. The building by itself is of small value unless the program contained within it and expressed in the lives of its members is consistent with, and faithful, to the foundation laid by Jesus Christ.

What then is the foundation laid by Jesus or the mission that you and I, and all Christians, are called upon to proclaim to the world? An analysis of the life and teaching of Jesus, as provided for us by his interpreters in the early church, provides us with a way of looking at life that may be expressed in four brief statements. We may call these statements the four corners of the cornerstone. They seem to exemplify the foundation laid by Jesus.

First, man must have a supreme loyalty outside of himself that gives meaning to his life. Jesus insisted that this loyalty is personal and he called this loyalty, God or Father. Such a belief and a proclamation was not a matter of proof with Jesus. It was a matter of acceptance. More urgently still, it was a matter of necessity.

It takes no great stretch of the imagination or a particularly brilliant mind for us to see that we have to attach ourselves to something or someone for us to stand existence. Kierkegaard, I believe it was who said that we are *thrust into life* and almost at once we yearn for someone to whom we can turn to help us feel comfortable. The baby is a lonesome, helpless creature and he cannot tolerate the feeling that he is stranded and alone. He needs the warmth and affection of his mother and the strength of his father as much as he needs milk and food and shelter. The attachment to persons changes as the little child grows and he moves out into the world and later becomes an adult, but the need for affiliation with others never changes. He selects other persons to whom he attaches himself to be sure, but his need for others remains constant. If he does not experience this cathexis (emotional investment or attachment) fully and lovingly from others, he fights for it. No wonder we face so many angry people who want to hurt and destroy others. They desperately want the affection which only another person can give. If they do not experience this emotional attachment with another, they become attached to things or they may strike out against others and join the host of delinquent and criminal people in our society.

But attachment to people, things, movements, and objects are transitory. They appear for a little while, and then like vapor, they vanish. Sometimes people we love and who give our life importance vanish through death. Worse still they vanish because they become corrupt and we have to disown them. They may also vanish because they turn on us, leave us, and we find ourselves afraid and lonely. Fame, fortune, good looks, a job, a political or social party – they all eventually dry up, disapppear, no longer need us, become corrupt, and we are left with nothing but desolation, disillusionment , and dry bones. Nothing in this world is really capable of everlasting permanence and stability and is worthy of our ultimate concern and supreme loyalty. Yet, we need such a loyalty; we cannot seem to stand without it.

Here is the real cornerstone that we as Christians offer to the world. We offer the world everlasting permanence, a God who loves us and who is capable of eternal devotion. He never dies, deserts, or leaves us. Even in death we can say, *"I know in whom I have believed."* Jesus sums up the case in an air tight compartment. *"Seek ye first the kingdom of God and all these things will be added unto you."* This pronouncement is the spiritual alternative to despair and futility.

The statement that occupies the next corner of the cornerstone we are called to represent to the world is that man lives at his best when he lives by contribution rather than by acquisition. Another way to state this proposition is that life is at its best when giving, not getting, is the moving force in one's life. Jesus said it this way – *"He who will find his life will lose it, but he who loses his life will find it."*

One of the real problems that face many people today is that they are living miserable, unsatisfying lives. They hold jobs, earn a high income in some instances, but still something is wrong. They cannot somehow get rid of their feelings of discomfort and stress. They try a pill, overindulge themselves in sexual escapades, allow their beards to grow long and shaggy, try LSD, sit before a TV screen, buy every new piece of clothing that comes on the market, clutter up the house with ornaments and knickknacks they don't need, they may even try the church or visit the doctor and the psychiatrist. Still somehow, they live in a state of frustration and unhappiness.

What is the trouble? I do not wish to simplify the problem but I can say without hesitation that one of the reasons is that these unfortunate people are much too concerned about themselves, how they feel, who is going to like them or not like them, whether they will be noticed or not noticed, if the minister will call or not call on them, if people will invite them to their parties or exclude them, worry about the slightest fever or pain, if I will have a good time, if I go to the party or stay home, if I am dressed properly. All such fears are merely variations on a very ancient theme – preoccupation with self. In psychology, we call such behavior egocentric. It wouldn't be so bad if it were not so destructive to human life. We cripple ourselves or we lose our lives when we are always occupied with ourselves or trying to find our lives.

Jesus maintains that this disturbance can only by cured by *being born again* or changing one's whole approach to life, until we think not in terms of what can I get or acquire, but what can I give or what can I contribute. Men such as Socrates or Jesus gave almost no attention or thought to their lives. When they had to choose between what others wanted of them and what they wanted for themselves, they gave up their lives. Socrates drank the hemlock and Jesus accepted a cross. No wonder people call these persons gods – they lived on a plane of selflessness, not self-centeredness. This kind of living is the foundation we build on and let each man take care how he builds thereon.

The third corner of the stone of our faith is authenticity. By authentic we mean for something to be what it is purported to be. By an authentic person we mean for a person to be what he claims to be or what he represents himself to be. Here is what Jesus constantly stressed in his attacks upon the Pharisees. They were not what they claimed to be. His most violent criticism of human behavior is recorded in the twenty-third chapter of Matthew where he reminds the scribes and Pharisees of the inconsistency of their behavior. *"Woe to you, scribes and Pharisees, hypocrites. You outwardly appear righteous to men but within you are full of hypocrisy and iniquity,"* summarizes succinctly his indictment.

Now when we turn to the person of Jesus what strikes us forcibly about his life is not the unusual events connected with his birth, the cures and healings attributed to his powers, or the description of the events after his crucifixion. What is so amazing and so divine about his life is the realness, the complete reliability, the authenticity of his being. He was what he claimed for himself. He spoke of love and he was loving. He spoke of faith and he was faithful. He preached self-abandonment before God and he abandoned himself completely. He spoke of sincerity, trust, and respect and these he revealed, almost completely. No wonder he could say – *"The Father and I are one."* He integrated, fused, and welded together what he believed and taught with what he lived and was. If we as Christians have anything at all to present to the world it is an authentic person who has the right to be given the title, Lord of Life.

This is *our* foundation. Do we dare to build upon it? Do we dare to improve upon it? No, we cannot improve upon it, we cannot lay another foundation, *"For no other foundation can any one lay than that which is laid, which is Jesus Christ."*

To build upon the authentic foundation given to us by Jesus Christ is indeed a tall order and I wonder sometimes how any man ever has the nerve to try it, for as Albert Einstein once said, "The mind of the Galilean is too great for us to emulate." Who can possibly do what he asks and be what he was? See how we have failed? We talk justice but we deny justice to persons who are not exactly as we are. We speak of sacrifice but we sacrifice really so little, at least, most of us do. We preach love but we show so little of it, even sometimes toward those who are members of our own families. One little boy said to me recently, "My mother goes to church every Sunday and she tells me I should love others as Jesus loves me." "But," he asked as he looked up into my eyes longingly, "Why doesn't she love me? All she ever tells me is how much she does for me and how ungrateful I am for her love. Yet, my Sunday School teacher tells me that if you love someone, you don't think of getting anything in return. You just like the person because of who he is." These are the words of a little child who is suffering from schizophrenia in its earliest form because he has been denied the affection that he must have from a parent who does not make him feel guilty or obligated because he was born or what is done for him.

Because we cannot ever hope to do our task as Christians, does not give us an excuse for not trying. What makes us real and authentic people is not that we try and succeed, and what makes us unauthentic is not that we try and fail. What destroys our authenticity is talking and living and behaving as though we are authentic but are really quite different. Perhaps it might be better to say with Iago in Shakespeare's Othello, "I am not what I appear to be." The pathway for us is to frankly admit that we believe in the way of life that Jesus lived and gave us, but we also admit that we do not or cannot measure up – yet we keep on trying. One man, who lives in another part of the country and is someone I admire, put it this way, "I know I should love a Japanese as my brother but I cannot, but I pray for forgiveness and ask that someday I can." This is not rationalization, hypocrisy, or sham. It is authenticity.

Well, we have a big foundation on which to build. It is not only large; it is also demanding and even sometimes frightening. Yet, we find the challenge both rewarding and exciting. Let us lay the cornerstone of the new building today with zeal, enthusiasm, and commitment. Let us also lay the stone with thankfulness for what others who have preceded us have done for us and be aware that we must be mindful and thoughtful of our business, *"For no other foundation can any one lay than that which is laid, which is Jesus Christ."* Let us be determined that we shall do our best to be faithful soldiers in his name.

Sermon

49

IS THERE GOODNESS IN ALL THINGS?

Romans 8:28 "We know that in everything God works for good with those who love him, who are called according to his purpose."

There are a number of statements in the New Testament that are hard to fathom. They somehow do not make any sense. One of these statements is nestled in the eighth chapter of Paul's letter to the Christians in Rome: "*We know that in everything God works for good with those who love him, who are called according to his purpose.*" It says *all things* that happen are good, not some things or a few things but *all things* contain goodness.

Is this possible? Are all things that we experience good? What about illness, injury, loneliness, failure, separation from loved ones, harshness, and death – are these occurrences good? Was the horrible torture of missionaries and white settlers in the Belgian Congo this past week by mad African natives good? Is there goodness in the massacre of Dr. Paul Carlson or George Clay of NBC? The answers to these questions would have to be *yes* if we accept

Paul's observation that there is goodness in all things. Let us this morning examine this hard comment of Paul's to see if it does contain good sense.

Surely, in the first place, it has to be said that the statement does not say that everything in every event is all good. There is a certain approach to evil which holds that misfortune, pain, illness, even death, do not really happen. They only seem to occur. Such experiences are not real but are merely pleasantness in disguise. In a sense, such a way of thinking would have us believe that misery and suffering are masks such as children wear on Halloween whereas that which is actual is behind the false face. Those who claim such an interpretation would have us think that the pain, torment or anguish we experience ought to not really occur because the stimuli which produce these feelings are only apparitions. They do not actually take place; therefore, we are really somewhat foolish, and are really playing tricks on ourselves to feel any hurt or sorrow.

Christian faith, however, does not know anything about such an interpretation of pain. Our faith frankly admits that accidents, murders, and massacres do exist and that these tragedies in human life do take place. They are real and no amount of mental effort to make one think they do not occur can remove their presence or the pain they produce. Paul would be the first to say that distress, persecution, and famine are with us in all of their rawness and nakedness. He would also be the first to say that these moments and occurrences of suffering which come to all of us are not all good. They can produce heartache, loneliness, desperation, depression, mental distress, even suicide and these feelings and acts are not good. The loss of Jesus to his generation in the prime of his manhood was not good. The burning of John Hus at the stake in the 15th century by the decision of the council at Constance was not good.

The murder of President John F. Kennedy by Harvey Lee Oswald was not good. The butchery of Dr. Carlson and others in the Congo was not good. The loss of a limb, the passing of a loved one, the torments of a sick mind are not good. A starving child, a deformed body, or a retarded child are not good. Christian faith never dismisses bad or evil things as insignificant incidents, as unreal images, or as events we can call good.

What Christian faith does say, however, is that God works in everything to permit us to bring some good out of every circumstance whether it is good or evil. Not everything is good but for those who believe and trust in God's action in every event, some element or factor of goodness can be found. Dr. Brightman used to say that "God is not the voluntary cause of suffering but he is able to bring value and meaning out of all human misery and pain." This is another way of expressing what Paul penned to the Romans: *We know that in everything God works for good with those who love him, who are called according to his purpose.*

Looking back, we can see goodness in the death of Jesus. That event which cannot be called good did, however, contain within it seeds of goodness. Men and women – those who loved their Christ and his Father and their Father – were determined to continue what he had begun. His death caused them to catch a glimmer of who He was and what He was. Although their understanding of him was not perfect – at times it was most imperfect – what they did comprehend made new persons out of all of them and gave an impetus to a new movement of faith that has meant salvation for millions from that time until now.

The martyrdom of John Hus, although not good in itself, had within it forces that produced new life in the church. It caused people to become aware of the deeper elements in Christian faith, and inspired persons such as Luther, Zwingli, and Calvin to lead the Christian movement out from under a monolithic, stale, and spiritually indifferent church to a more vital expression of faith. The reformers realized as Hus taught years earlier that abuses had to be eradicated and a new approach developed if Christ and his death were to make any difference in the redemption of society.

If it is true that some good things did result from the crucifixion of Jesus and from the burning of Hus then there is the possibility that we can discover some positive gain from suffering that comes to the lives of each one of us. A friend of mine told me recently of his brother who is slowly dying in a hospital in one of our nearby southern cities. While my friend was visiting his brother recently, he by chance began talking with the patient who occupied the bed in the same room with his brother. This stranger told my friend: "I know your brother is very ill and I am sorry that he will not live. Yet, I want you to know that his cheerfulness and calmness in the face of dying have been a great help to me. When I came here, I was sullen and angry because of my illness, for I will not make it either. But these months I have been associated in this room with your brother have taught me not only how to die but also the meaning of life." This is what we mean by some goodness in all things.

Now the crux of the matter is that a person has to have a desire to find something of value in painful experiences if any value is to be found. Goodness does not come automatically. It does not usually come rushing in upon us. Most of the time it breaks in upon one gradually, but it can only be seen or felt if one wants to find it. In other words, in order to see God at work in all things – in the painful as well as in the pleasant – one has to love God and to believe that he is faithful and sure. *"Ask, and what you ask will be given you. Search and you will find what you search for. Knock and the door will open to you."*

The problem, I think, with most of us, however, is that we fail to find goodness in all things for two possible reasons. First, we do not want to find any good in our misfortunes; and secondly, we don't want to see the goodness we do see. Let us look at these defenses we employ when faced with personal tragedy, pain, or sorrow.

We do not want to find any good in our misfortune because we like to hold on to our self-pity. We like to be sad because it causes others to feel sorry for us, to give us attention, and to tell us what a terrible burden we have to bear. Self-pity becomes a cherished possession and we hold onto it like a precious jewel, refusing stubbornly to let it go, for if we do let it go, we will have to change our pattern of living and become a new person. The only way, however, to see any meaning in any event that has caused us suffering is to want to see within it some possibility of goodness.

The other hurdle that interferes with seeing something beneficial in misery is not wanting to see benefit when we do see it. The reason we refuse to see it is because what we see is not what we want to see. We want things as they were before, not anything new or different. Sometimes when a woman loses a loved one – a husband, a child, or a parent – the bereaved demands almost, that she cannot be comforted or helped unless the deceased is returned to life and with her again. Since such a demand is impossible, then nothing else will suffice, so she holds on to her sorrow and shuts her eyes to any benefit.

Years ago I visited the home of a lovely woman who had lost her husband. When I visited the house, I did not know she was a widow. After we had been talking for a while, she mentioned her husband. She showed me a beautiful portrait of him on the wall, pointed out his favorite chair, told me of his accomplishments, and finally showed me his study and bedroom, arranged with exquisite taste and furnishings. Finally I asked, "Where is your husband? Does he travel?"

"Oh no," she said, "He has been dead for over 20 years." This is an extreme case, but it highlights what I mean by refusing to see anything new in tragic events because of an insistence to see only what once was, not any possibility of goodness.

When we, however, want to discover something of real value in a tragic event, we can find it and we can turn death into a resurrection. This is finding goodness in all things. Now goodness has many expressions. The highest good, however, is allowing unpleasant events to contribute to our spiritual growth and development. Dr. Victor Frankel tells in his book *Man's Search for Meaning* of the years he spent in a German concentration camp as a Jewish prisoner of the Nazis. He and others were reduced to a diet barely enough to sustain life. He was beaten, abused, and suffered privations that hardly seem possible for a man to bear. One incident in his book comes to my mind that has a direct bearing on our discussion this morning. It seems that on a particular day the men in his camp were made to fast because of an infringement of the rules by one of the prisoners. On the evening of the fast, the men were sitting silently, miserable, glum, tempers taut because they had not eaten all day. As bad as the food was, it was better than nothing. Dr. Frankel, a psychiatrist in civilian practice, sensed the situation and began to talk to the men in his hut. He reminded them of past memories they could still cherish. He recalled the resources that they had found available to keep them alive whereas others had died.

As he closed his short talk, he reminded the men that they must not lose hope but should keep their courage in the certainty that the hopelessness of their struggle did not detract from its dignity and its meaning. He also said that someone looks down on each man in difficult hours – a friend, a wife, somebody alive or dead, or a God – and that each inmate would not want to disappoint that person who looks down. He hoped that person, that God, would find the men suffering proudly – not miserably – knowing how to die. He also reminded the wretched men that they should seek to find some meaning in their sufferings, if for no other reason than to be worthy of one's sufferings – Is it any wonder that this dedicated doctor who today is practicing in Vienna is having such an impact on the best thinking in religion and psychiatry? He is reminding us all that God is working good in all things for them who love him and are willing to search for a higher meaning for their lives, even in the depths of despair.

Now surely not one of us would ever say that it is so easy, so nice to trust in God and find life sweet and pretty. That kind of talk is ridiculous and is nothing but cheap sentimentality and is an insult to the intelligence of brave and courageous people. To suffer is hell and is to be despised. God forbid that we ever call loneliness, pain and misery easy and sweet. The point, however, that Paul makes in his letter to the Romans is that when tragedy does come we do not shirk it or run from it. We take it, we bear it, we grind it out, we even go into the depths of pain, loneliness, misery, and fear but we come out of the pit, thanking God we have been able to endure, and then search for some meaning to it all and discover in it all some way to turn it into an asset for good. This is the Christian approach to evil.

50

BLESSED ARE THE DEBONAIR

Matthew 5:5 Blessed are the meek for they shall inherit the earth.
Heureux les débonnaires; car ils hériteront de la terre.

Translation of J.V. Ostervald Paris 1928

Some time back when I was teaching a course on the New Testament, a member of the class raised an interesting and important question about her uneasiness with the third Beatitude. She said, "I have always thought of Jesus as a strong and out-spoken person and in this beatitude, he seems to be exalting meekness as a virtue."

The woman did indeed raise an important question, for she saw an inconsistency between this teaching of Jesus and the way he lived his life. Jesus never hesitated to speak his mind or to take action when he thought it necessary. We recall that he did take a whip and drive the money changers out of the temple. So what is wrong here?

What is wrong is that the word *meek*, as in the King James Version of the Bible as well as the Revised Standard Version, was a suitable translation for Shakespearian England, but not for today. Even today, we do not have a good English word for the Greek word. Greek is the language in which the New Testament was written and from which our translations are made. The word *meek* in Greek has various translations but the one that captures the real meaning of the original is found in the French Bible which reads, *"Heureux les débonnaires; car ils hériteront de la terre."* (Blessed are the debonair, for they will inherit the earth.) When we think of the text in this manner – blessed are the debonair – the translation takes on an entirely different flavor. Rather than implying passivity, submission, and weakness, the translation of the text now emphasizes cheerfulness, a pleasant disposition, graciousness, kindness, and openness of spirit, attitudes that are consistent with the life and teachings of Jesus.

This afternoon, we will consider only one of these attitudes or dispositions of mind and spirit as to how cheerfulness of spirit can be useful to us in living an abundant life, letting each of us be a recipient of the Master's teachings, for he taught that he came that we might have life and to have it more abundantly.

First of all, I think that we need to keep in mind that cheerfulness – as we learn from the teachings of Jesus and from the way he lived his life – does not necessarily mean laughter or mirth. Rather, cheerfulness means a contentment, a peacefulness, a satisfaction, a gladness that a person manifests as he or she goes about the business of living whether at work or at play. When Jesus' parents found him in the temple exchanging points of view with the elders, he asked them why they inquired about his absence, *"Did ye not know that I must be about my Father's business?"* These words of Jesus are indeed serious; yet, they are spoken in gladness, with a heart that is cheerful in anticipation of the work that lies ahead for him. In his entire ministry, Jesus depicted a demeanor of confidence and deep satisfaction in encountering the people he met.

One fact seems certain: Jesus never expressed any *gloom and doom* in his life. Even when things were not going well for him, he never complained or indicated despair. Even as he hung on the Cross, he was not consumed by the tragedy of the event. Instead he forgave those who placed him on the Cross, thought of the robbers who were on crosses beside him, and offered his life without rancor or resentment. In a spiritual sense, he overcame those who spitefully put him to death and could say to his followers, as reported at a later date, *"Be of good cheer, for I have overcome the world."* That is what it means to be debonair! It is cheerfulness in its highest sense.

A debonair spirit enables us to rise above our misfortunes, and even to find contentment, rather than to be overcome. I like the story of the owner of a barber shop who lived in London during the terrible days when the city was being assaulted by German war planes. He came to his shop one morning after a heavy raid during the night and found his shop badly damaged but he could still do business. He hung a sign on his shop which read, "I have had a close shave. What about you?"

Misfortunes come to each of us in one form or another, none of us escapes them, raining both on the just and the unjust as the Scriptures remind us. The difference between us is not what comes to us but rather how we respond to the misfortune. The London barber responded to his misfortune by rising above it with good cheer, planning to make the best out of a bad situation. Another barber who faced the same situation might have been overcome by the damage to his shop, complained to his neighbors about his bad luck, and cursed the Germans, perhaps even going into a deep depression. It is no wonder that Jesus in the Sermon on the Mount blessed the debonair and said that they would overcome or possess the world of cynicism and despair.

I remember visiting an older woman some years ago who had become largely confined to her room and required assistance to move about, complaining bitterly about her condition and saying that hardly anyone ever came to see her. I inquired of the nurse if that was the case. The nurse said that people did come to visit her when she first came to live with them but that few ever returned because of her constant complaining. I felt myself feeling very sorry for this lady because she was defeating herself, driving people away when she really wanted them to visit her. A skilled counselor finally was able to break through her resentments and helped her to discover how badly she was hurting herself.

I think you will be pleased to know that her talks with the counselor led her to see the errors of her ways. Change did not come easily for her. The old ways had become deeply ingrained as all habits are and a person can learn the habit of finding fault as easily as any other habit, but with motivation and perseverance they can be changed. Because this lady was in need of others to come to see her, she gradually learned to be pleasant and grateful to those who returned to see her. In time, I am told, she became a gracious lady, a spirit she had somehow lost after she became necessarily dependent on others.

Blessed are the debonair! We are never too old to capture the spirit of Christ in our lives. We can learn to overcome the negative passions in our lives, so that we can say with the Apostle Paul, *"I have learned to do all things through Christ who strengthens me."* I assure you it is never too late to learn to live the kind of abundant life that he taught and lived.

51

WHEN COMMON EVENTS MAKE MOMENTOUS DECISIONS SEEM TRIVIAL

Christmas

Each day issues are discussed and decisions are made at higher levels of government that are so momentous in nature and design that they affect the lives of people everywhere. A battle rages in the United Nations regarding the role of the United States and Belgium in removing white settlers from the insurgents in the Belgium Congo. Our Secretary of State confers with the French government concerning the question of including an atomic fleet in the armamentarium of the North Atlantic Treaty Organization. President Johnson decides to push plans for a new canal in Central America replacing the old Panama Canal across the Republic of Panama. These and other issues are crucial and they have far reaching implications, even affecting possibly your life and mine.

Yet, at this season of the year such matters seem to drift into the background, and a common event, the birth of a child whose name was Jesus, is pushed into the foreground. Activity, in a sense, seems to stop. Committees are adjourned, work in factories halts, schools close, offices cut down on their activities – life pauses for a while to remember and pay homage to a child born of humble parents in the quietness and austerity of a stable.

Now, the wonder of the birthday of Jesus is not merely the remembrance of his birth. The wonder of it all is that the observance of his birth reminds us of what is most real, deeply significant, and vital in life. Christ represents what we most deeply cherish and what we most highly prize, and Christmas gives us once each year an opportunity to withdraw from study, work, large issues, business, and just the daily routine of living and emphasize what we most truly are.

For one thing, Christmas gives us an occasion to remember the children. Whatever else we may say about Christmas, it is an occasion for children. Persons are fortunate who have in their homes children who still delight in getting up early on Christmas morning and running downstairs to see the Christmas tree and what the good St. Nicolas has brought during the night. Those of you who have little children will probably wish you didn't have all of those toys to wrap on Christmas Eve and that you could sleep longer on Christmas morning but yet you know, know deep where it counts that Christmas morning is the brightest day in your life because you have been allowed one day in the year to be extravagant with your child or your children, and to see your children as merry and happy as a child can ever be. What parent would not like to be extravagant with his children every day; but we resist because we have been told it is not wise to spoil a child with too much. So we usually spoil in moderation most of the time. But, on Christmas Day, well, what we have taught as crucial to a child's welfare – frugality, moderation, restraint — seems trivial. On Christmas, we give out of the abundance of our hearts; we spoil them indeed, put them at the center of our affections, and do for them in abundance. Christmas is for children. It is their day. Yet, it is the parents' day too, for it is one chance to express through gifts what they feel genuinely in their hearts.

Again, Christmas provides us the chance to express to others how we most deeply feel about them. In our culture, we do not feel at ease expressing our affection for others. We have been taught that we ought to keep our feelings to ourselves, even when we would like to tell others how we feel about them. Now, I am not advocating that we should go around telling others how much we like them or how much we love them. We would probably be suspect if we did. Yet, the expression of feeling in wholesome and constructive ways is indeed healthy for the giver and the receiver of affection.

These are the values that are really the most important in our lives. These are the values that Jesus Christ emphasized. He reminded us of the supreme importance of human relationships, relations that make other values and events seem trivial. How essential is the observance of his birthday for us! It points us to that which is supreme in existence.

Christmas, then, in the third place, renews human relationships. All year we have been busy with taking care of our children, cutting lawns, taking care of our homes, working on a church building, serving on committees, trying to get ahead in our business, working to keep our heads above water, doing our best to stay up with our various responsibilities. These are the affairs that are immediate — these have to get done and for most of us we barely get them done. These are the important things. They demand our immediate attention.

Yet, we know there are people, even family members, we have known through the years, in one place, then another, who are now out of our circle of contact, but who are important to our lives. We don't keep in contact with them regularly, but that doesn't mean they are not within the affection of our friends. So, once each year, Christmas comes around. The things we have been engaged in are temporarily put aside and we take time out to send a card or write a letter to keep our lives in touch with those we once knew so well and to maintain the bond of affection and love.

What we are doing when we exchange cards, letters, and greetings with friends and members of our family of years ago is precisely, in a sense, what we do when we remember Jesus each Sunday in the Lord's Supper. We do this in remembrance of Him. And each Christmas we send a card, a gift, in remembrance of those we love.

I would hate to think what would happen if Christ had not come and there was no time in the year to celebrate his birthday, no time to extend our remembrance of him into the lives of others. No gifts would be sent, no cards would be written, no telephone calls made, no visits made – there would be no occasion to renew the ties with those whom we once knew so well and whom we do not ever want to forget. Let us never, never become so callous in sending our cards or exchanging our gifts that the exercise becomes tedious and meaningless. Let us be grateful that Christmas, though it is in a sense an intrusion into our daily routine of living, gives us an opportunity to maintain our ties of affection and friendship with persons we would never want to forget.

Sometimes, I hear the remark made that Christmas is such a bother. People sometimes say that they are glad when Christmas is over and they can get back to business and life as usual. I can appreciate these remarks, for sometimes we do go to an excess in our buying and find ourselves with bills after Christmas we don't know how we can ever pay. On the other hand, the person who believes that Christmas is a bother fails to comprehend what the event is all about. He probably sees it only in its secular aspects and fails to comprehend that Christmas is an extension into our society and into our human relationships of the spirit of love and affection. Every Merry Christmas is an expression of goodwill. Every present is a token of love and remembrance. Every card and every visit is a representation of what is deepest and most real in life – the affection and the love that each person has for another. Let us be grateful that there is a time each year when all the affairs of commerce, the decisions of state, and our own business activities are set aside and are considered trivial and we have a chance to give our attention to our relatives and our circle of friends.

52

THE JOURNEY OF THE WISE MEN

Matthew 2:2 Where is he who has been born king of the Jews?
For we have seen his star in the East, and have come to worship him.

The account of the journey of the wise men to the place where Jesus was born in a manger-crib is for many a disturbance. Those who are disturbed say that they cannot believe the historical details surrounding the story. For one thing, they show with accuracy that Herod died four years before the birth of Jesus, yet the narrative written by Matthew includes a brief description of an encounter between Herod and the wise men. Also, others point out that it is incredible that a star could lead anyone to a tiny spot on the earth – a star is too high in the heavens for anyone to tell what place it is over! Then, others who raise a doubt concerning the account as it is recorded ask this question, "If the visit was made by the wise men, why isn't it found in any other writing in the New Testament except in the gospel of Matthew?" Surely, an event of such spectacular importance, they say, would have been widely known and written about if it had occurred. These are indeed thoughtful questions and they do cause us to be disturbed concerning the accuracy of the gospel account.

On the other hand, a person misses the point of the narrative of the journey of the wise men if he focuses his attention on historical details and situational occurrences. Such matters did not concern the author of Matthew. His interest was to give his testimony and that of the early church regarding their belief in the supreme importance of Jesus for their lives and for the life of the world. The story is their gift to honor Jesus and to proclaim their everlasting gratitude for the contribution he had made to their lives. For Matthew and the Christians of the first century, Jesus was Lord of life and even the very wisest of men bowed down, worshipped him, and brought him gifts of gold, frankincense, and myrrh. There are few accounts of faith recorded in the New Testament that are told with such sensitivity, intimacy, and depth of feeling as one finds in the story of the journey of the wise men from the East as told by Matthew. Our Christmas observance would indeed be poorer without it.

This morning, however, we wish to go somewhat deeper in thought to discover what this dramatic portrayal of faith tells us about wisdom, for the story, after all is the response of wisdom to a new discovery. A new event had occurred, a new life had come into the world, and a new thing had happened, a new king, some dared say, had been born. What was the reaction of wisdom to this event?

First of all Matthew tells us that wise men are learners. They came to see for themselves what had occurred and to discover what they could learn from this unusual person who had of late come into the world. Here we find the difference between the man of bigotry and prejudice and the man of spiritual depth and insight. The bigot asks, *"Can anything good come out of Nazareth?"* The man of wisdom replies, *"Come, let us see this thing that has come to pass."*

Notice if you will the different ways that Jesus was received by the people of his generation. Those who were governed in their thinking by ties to political parties said, "Away with him. He is upsetting our social structure. He tells us to love our enemies. Such foolishness will make political parties unnecessary and we will not have a job. Let us not bother with this idealist. The sooner we get rid of him the better."

Those who were tied to race and clan also despised him. He ate with sinners and publicans. He talked to Romans and even praised second-class citizens by telling the parable of the Good Samaritan. Some super-patriotic Jews could not tolerate consideration for non-Jews and they too joined in the procession to destroy him.

Yet, Matthew tells us, men of mature judgment, balanced thinking, men of wisdom, came to worship at his feet and to learn from his lips. What a difference there is in persons who have something to defend or to sell, or who have an axe to grind, and those who are only interested in learning. One comes to learn some new thing that has emerged in the world.

This does not mean that men of judgment and men who are wise do not know anything and have nothing to offer or to tell the world. They knew a great deal. They have much to share. But they know that what they know is always tentative and subject to change. They also know that the final word can never be spoken, for the final word can never be known. It can only be sought, searched for, but never found. The story illuminates the point that wise men are learners.

Next, the story of the wise men so beautifully told by the writer of Matthew's gospel leads us to see that wise men search for wisdom wherever it may be found. Imagine men of profound scholarship coming to learn at the feet of a child born in a stable, an odd place to find anything of worth. Yet, they came and brought gold, frankincense, and myrrh and since that time the men of wisdom of all the ages have listened to Jesus, a person who was born in a stable, who was born of common parents, never owned more that what he wore on his back, never wrote a book - poor fellow, never traveled more than 500 miles in his whole life, and yet, his life and words have transformed the thinking and the behavior of millions.

Hear what wisdom has said - Mahatma Gandhi, "I cannot accept your Christianity, but I can accept your Christ." H. G. Wells, "Is it any wonder that to this day this Galilean is too much for our small hearts?" Abraham Lincoln, "I would gladly become the member of any church that had as its creed the basic teachings of Jesus Christ." Even Napoleon, in his moment of defeat when he spoke his wisest words said, "I have been a failure but Jesus Christ remains victorious." Ernest Renan, "Whatever may be the unexpected phenomena of the future, Jesus will not be surpassed." Wisdom does turn to a Galilean manger for inspiration!

This testimony of wisdom, not to be ashamed to look for life's most important assets in the most unusual places, is a lesson for all of us. We are at times so burdened by the sophistication of this age that we are actually too proud to look in humble places for the best that life can offer. We think that happiness can be found only in rich food, expensive clothes, obscene literature, crude jokes, and fast living. Jesus, however, turns us around and points to the gaiety of the child who knows none of these activities but finds his happiness in simplicity, trust, and getting the most out of each moment he lives.

Sometimes, we think that wisdom is congruous only with education. We look down our noses at the person who has not been so fortunate as to have had the benefits of extensive schooling. Yet one of the wisest men I have ever known could not write his name. On the other hand, he was one of the ablest farmers in Scott County, Kentucky, and had the strange capacity to know what was right in most situations. He had learned to think, to trust his intuition, and to live a life that was uncluttered and uncomplicated. He could figure out in his head the yield per acre of whatever crop he was growing. Those of us who were fortunate to share life in the community with him learned and profited from his style of life and his approach to matters of serious concern. Education is essential but it is futile without the maturity to use it wisely.

In the last place, the visit of the wise men tells us that men of wisdom have nothing to lose but everything to give away. Those men from the East are a strange contrast to Herod about whom the writer of the gospel tells us. Poor Herod. We see him anxious, on edge, fearful that someone might usurp his kingdom and take away his grandeur and his power. He tried to deceive the men from the East by insisting that when they found the child, they should return and tell him so he too could go and worship him. But the wise men were not deceived by flattery and slyness, by a kind of make-believe pompous piety. These men saw through Herod as easily as one sees through a child who tries to tell a fib. They merely returned to their homes by a different route after they had seen the child and did not return to tell Herod what they had seen. The wise men, however, were not anxious that a new man of wisdom had come into the world. They were glad that new truth could now be found. Yet, Herod is not glad, but afraid. He was afraid he would lose something of worth to him. They were glad they could find something of value.

This contrast in the feelings of wise men to Jesus and those of Herod is applicable to people of our age. At times, I think that those who accept the truth of Jesus for their lives and those who did not, differ in much the same way as the men from the East and Herod differed. The wise men bowed before the Christ child gladly. They accepted his wisdom for their lives. They felt they had nothing to lose, but everything to gain. Herod, on the other hand, had to protect his influence, his proud disposition, his self-importance, his place in the world. He felt something would be lost if he gave his life in unselfish and devoted services to his kingly task. His objective was to get everything he could from life – fame, wealth, power, and influence. The objective of the wise men, however, was not to get, but to give, to learn, and to share. What a difference there is in the life of a person whose sole motivation is to exploit the society he lives in and in the life of a person who is interested in improving his community!

This morning I wish to lift up for your consideration two paradigms or models. One is the model of Herod – grasping, controlling, conniving for power and control over others. The other is the model of the wise men – releasing power, seeking nothing for personal advantage or gain, searching for truth, and offering themselves for the good they can give. Which do you choose? What model do you prefer with which to identify your life?

The Christmas story of the wise men offers us the image of the wise men, for they are the ones that lift up and glorify Jesus Christ, the Lord and Savior of life. Are we afraid to commit ourselves to life as we understand it in him because we are afraid he will cause us to give up something we cherish and are trying to protect? If we are, we need not fear, because rather than taking away our identity, he gives us a cause to live for, a faith to believe in, and truth to seek after. A purpose for living is indeed the critical issue of our day. We have the things to live with but so many of us lack a truth to live for. Jesus Christ offers that truth and the prayer for this day is that we shall be wise enough to seek after, to find him, and to bow down and worship him as did the three wise men from the East. We need not be disturbed regarding the situational aspects of the story of the wise men, but every serious minded Christian ought to be disturbed about the ethical implications of the story for their lives.

Sermon

53

LIGHT IN THE DARKNESS

John 1:5 The light shines in the darkness,
and the darkness has not overcome it.

The last Sunday in the year is a fitting day for reflection. It is a time to look back over the year and to consider significant observations we have made and new lessons we have learned.

One observation I have made which I would like to share with you this morning is that we have lost through death during 1965 five highly influential religious leaders. One was Dr. Albert Schweitzer; a second was Dr. Anton Boisen; a third, Dr. Paul Tillich; a fourth, Dr. T. Hassel Bowen; and a fifth, Dr. Daniel C. Troxel. All of us know of the work of Albert Schweitzer. Some of us perhaps know of the distinguished philosopher, Paul Tillich. The other Three – Anton Boisen, Hassel Bowen, and Daniel Troxel – may or may not be familiar to most of us.

This morning I wish to acquaint you briefly with these men, not so much with what they did in their own particular fields of effort, but rather to introduce you to the resources which they employed to handle the central problems and complexities they faced in the human enterprise. Each in his own way brought the same ingredient to life – they were not overcome by the various vicissitudes of life but they managed to surmount life's obstacles and to bring light in the midst of darkness, although each demonstrated this quality in a special and different way. Surely, this divine quality – taking an obstacle, a misfortune, or a knotty predicament and rising above it, changing it in some way for a greater good – is what the writer of John observed in the life of Jesus and prompted him to declare that he was the Word that became flesh. John would say that Jesus was the Son because he caused the light or the power of God to shine in darkness. Men tried to extinguish that light but he was conqueror over the darkness. *"The light shines in the darkness, and the darkness has not overcome it."* Let us see what it was in the lives of the men I have mentioned that gave them the capacity to bring light out of darkness, hope out of hopelessness, meaning out of meaninglessness, and understanding out of ignorance.

First of all, Albert Schweitzer brought light out of darkness by giving his best to persons who were ignorant, sick, and despised. He was severely criticized by his friends for using his unusual talents in service to people who neither cared, nor had any appreciation, for his tremendous intellectual power as a thinker or his creative talents as an artist. His friends told him he was wasting his talents. They insisted that he should remain in academic and cultural circles speaking, teaching, writing, and interpreting the many fields in which he was so outstandingly competent. Schweitzer often said that his most vexing problems were not so much with the Africans or with the privations of the African bush country as they were with his friends. He found it difficult to explain to them why he felt he had to go to Africa as a doctor, without appearing overly righteous or downright stupid. It was during this trying period of explaining his reasons for going to Africa that Schweitzer discovered the meaning of the words of Jesus, *"A prophet is not without honor except in his own country and in his own house."* Anyway, Albert Schweitzer went to Africa. He brought light out of darkness by using his gifted and unusual talents for those of an unfortunate station in life. He did not define or defend his faith. He lived it. He was faith in action as that faith is known in the Lordship of Christ.

The next man, Dr. Paul Tillich, had a different way of turning an obstacle into a thing of meaning and purpose. He was not a reformer, crusader, or a man who served directly in unpleasant situations. He was foremost a theoretical philosopher and theologian. He was born and educated in Germany, the son of a Lutheran minister, and came to this country during the early years of Hitler's regime at the age of 47 to teach at Union Theological Seminary. He painstakingly learned the English language and emerged as perhaps the most creative and influential thinker in philosophical and theological circles of this century. After teaching at Union, he went to Harvard, then to the University of Chicago, where he died at the age of 79 on October 22nd while still in active service.

One of the main problems with which Tillich wrestled during his lifetime was how to bring the vast differences in theological interpretation into one system where people could conceive of their differences, not in terms of division, but in terms of unity. He felt that if Christian leaders could think big enough concerning God and Christ, their interpretations could be seen as merely manifestations of the same phenomena, only explained in different ways. Another problem with which he constantly dealt was how to make theology sensible to the secular philosophers, anthropologists, psychologists, and scholars in the other behavioral sciences as well as how to incorporate the insights of these secular disciplines into theology. He was acknowledged as the *universal thinker* by leading Protestant, Jewish, and Roman Catholic theologians as well as by men from the non-theological world. His books and vast writings are read and quoted by all men and women who are interested in the intellectual problems of religion and their relationship to the world of secular knowledge.

Many have even credited Tillich with being the leader responsible for breaking down the traditional intellectual barriers between Roman Catholic and Protestant thinkers by forcing them to think of themselves, belonging not to a different faith, but to the same faith. Tillich brought light out of darkness by not being dismayed by the apparent insurmountable intellectual problems in religious faith but by staying at the task – studying, reflecting, thinking, insisting, that no man has all of the truth or no truth, but that pieces of truth belong together if one is wise enough to put the jigsaw puzzle together. Tillich may not have finished the puzzle but he certainly put enough pieces together to help us see that the pieces belong together, that we live, not in a multiverse, but in a universe.

The third man is Dr. Anton Boisen who died October first, within a few days of his 89th birthday. Boisen is little known outside of circles interested in relating the insights of psychiatry and religious faith to one another. Boisen was a deeply sensitive person who, as a young Congregational minister, suffered a severe mental illness; he called it

a plain and unmistakable variety of catatonic schizophrenia. He was hospitalized when the first attack came on – he had several other episodes – and was out of contact with reality for several weeks at a time at various intervals. When he regained his composure, he began at once to study the cause and the meaning of his illness.

This curiosity led him to an interest in the capacities of religious faith in assisting persons with mental illness to regain their mental health. His life work, previously unclear, now began to take shape and ushered in the movement of educating ministers to work with mental patients and to emphasize the pastoral function of the ministry in the light of recent insights developed by psychology and psychiatry. The work of Boisen has had considerable influence on the training of the ministry, causing seminaries to rethink their approach in educating the minister. Furthermore, he helped us to see that mental illness may be an effort on the part of the person to find himself rather than to lose himself, for in losing one's self, the person may be finding himself, providing, according to Boisen, that the person has sufficient religious resources to handle the attack and fight it through.

A man of lesser degree would have become embittered because of a mental breakdown. He might have succumbed to his feelings of personal inferiority and given up, humiliated and ashamed of his condition. He might even have hid himself, afraid for anyone to know about his sickness. But the greatness of Boisen showed itself. Rather than decrying his illness, he accepted it, acknowledged it, learned all he could from it, and used the experience for the larger good of ministers and the task of the church. This is bringing light out of darkness.

The fourth man, Dr. T. Hassell Bowen, passed away the 28th of August at his home in Lexington, Kentucky. For over a quarter of a century, Dr. Bowen was minister of the First Christian Church at Harrodsburg, Kentucky, and taught for 35 years at the College of the Bible, now the Lexington Theological Seminary, in the field of Christian Doctrine and Systematic Theology. He was my teacher and the one who gave me my start in theological thinking. Dr.

Bowen was foremost a problem raiser rather than a problem solver. He raised a question and gave his students the task of studying the problem. He believed that a person should never accept anything without critical inquiry. He insisted that one think through his problem and find a position, not necessarily an answer, but a position, that he found intellectually satisfying. He wanted a person to find a reason for the faith that he held, and at the same time, to keep an open mind.

Dr. Bowen taught in a day when theological students raised serious doubts regarding faith, at a time when the debate between science and religion had not been adequately settled. This was the darkness he found and he helped students to discover a way out of the darkness of doubt to the light of a reasonable interpretation of Christian faith. Few men helped more Disciple ministers in finding a firm intellectual undergirding for their faith as did Hassel Bowen and we will sorely miss him.

The last man whom I shall mention this morning in our recollections of the past year is Dr. Daniel C. Troxel, who, for twenty-seven years, taught New Testament at the Lexington Theological Seminary, and died on November 30th at the age of 82. Dr. Troxel was also my teacher. He was an inspiring professor and exalted the ethical teachings of Jesus. He had little patience with a faith that was oriented toward ritual or centered on form. For him, religion was life and the purpose of religion was to ennoble and enrich the arena of human living. He also insisted on sound and responsible scholarship.

The most important contribution of Dr. Troxel to religion, however, was that he gave religion a radiant expression in his own life. To use Dr. Fosdick's phrase, his faith was *not a creed but a force*.

He not only taught faith, he lived it. He had three children and a lovely wife. His son died at a young age in a fire and one of his two lovely daughters died in her early twenties from leukemia. Mrs. Troxel died several years ago of cancer. He had more tragedy in his life than few people are asked to bear. He experienced many times what Georgia Harkness called *the dark night of the soul.* Yet, during all the years I knew Dr. Troxel, and I saw him frequently over the years, I never knew a person who was as kind, as humble, or as genuinely helpful to others. Never did I hear him express one word of complaint, one sentence of self-pity, or one ounce of bitterness. In fact, his thoughts were never about himself; his only concern, it seemed, was the welfare and good of his friends, especially his students. He was another of the great men whom we have lost this year who had the rare capacity to turn the darkness of night into the light of day.

Now, the conclusion of these recollections of five men of religious faith, whom death took from us this year, is that you and I also are called upon again and again to enter the darkness of night. Each of us suffers pain, loneliness, failure, the agony of perplexing problems concerning life and faith. It is not that some of us are hurt and others escape pain. We all are battered and torn in one way or another. The crux of the matter is that some are beaten by misfortune, while others learn from misfortune and emerge from their predicament the better and wiser for it. How well are you utilizing the resources available to you in this business of making the most out of what life brings and demands of you? Are you, as did our Lord, turning darkness into light? If so you have learned the true meaning of the birth and life of our Savior whose birthday we celebrate this holy season.

54

THE ETERNAL PRESENCE

Luke 2:25-32

25 Now there was a man in Jerusalem, whose name was Simeon, and this
man was righteous and devout, looking for the consolation
of Israel, and the Holy Spirit was upon him.
26 And it had been revealed to him by the Holy Spirit that
he should not see death before he had seen the Lord's Christ.
27 And inspired by the Spirit he came into the temple; and when the
parents brought in the child Jesus, to do for him
according to the custom of the law,
28 he took him up in his arms and blessed God and said,
29 "Lord, now lettest thou thy servant depart
in peace, according to thy word;
30 for mine eyes have seen thy salvation
31 which thou hast prepared in the presence of all peoples,
32 a light for revelation to the Gentiles, and for glory to thy people Israel."

In the gospel reading for today, we are introduced to an unusual person whose name was Simeon, unusual because, for reasons we cannot possibly comprehend, he saw, represented in the infant Jesus, the eternal presence. Simeon was so overwhelmed by this revelation that he exclaimed, *"Lord, now lettest thou thy servant depart in peace, according to they word: for mine eyes have seen thy salvation, which thou hast prepared before the face of all people; a light to lighten the Gentiles, and the glory of thy people Israel."* Simeon might have said, "Behold, the hope of the world!"

Other unusual persons – with powers to pierce the eternal presence – have followed in Simeon's footsteps, although not always in the same manner nor in the same way. During the middle of the seventeenth century, Sir Isaac Newton, we are told, was sitting under an apple tree and saw an apple fall. Now, he had seen apples fall many times before. On this particular day, for reasons we are unable to explain, Newton saw this apple fall differently than he had perceived it fall on other days. The notion came to him that the apple did not drop to the ground haphazardly nor drift off into space.

For the first time, he saw that the apple fell precisely straight down. When he saw the next apple fall, it seemed to fall at about the same speed as the previous apple. From this unintended experiment, Newton identified the law of universal gravitation and named the force that pulled the apple down to the earth, gravity. The eternal presence operates in a multitude of forms, each of which we identify by separate names but each is a part of the same divine presence.

Good eyesight, beyond the physical senses, is a necessity in knowing the eternal presence. When Helen Keller was two years old, she became afflicted with a crippling disease that left her unable to see, hear, or talk. For five years, she lived in fear, anger, and frustration. At the age of seven she was placed in the care of Anne Sullivan who also had suffered a severe illness when very young that had left her blind. Miss Sullivan recovered her vision by a series of eye operations. She continued, however, to perfect her communication method and to teach it to the blind.

Helen Keller became her most difficult student. After months of resistance, even rages, from Helen, Miss Sullivan finally broke through to Helen and taught her, at first, the names of objects. Then in time, when she had taught her to express herself in terms of ideas and in sentences, Miss Sullivan introduced her to the concept of God. Almost at once, Helen signaled back that she had always known that such a presence existed. Helen possessed a bright and inquiring mind, and she also had profound spiritual insight, at a depth – for reasons we do not know – that few possess.

Many centuries before Helen Keller lived, a young Jewish man, with a depth of spiritual insight similar to hers, discovered peace, strength, and courage from his faith in the goodness and dependability of the eternal presence. He expressed his confidence in these magnificent words:

The LORD is my shepherd; I shall not want.
He maketh me to lie down in green pastures. He leadeth me beside the still waters.
He restoreth my soul: he leadeth me in the paths of righteousness for his name's sake.
Yea, though I walk through the valley of the shadow of death, I will fear no evil: for thou art with me; thy rod and thy staff they comfort me.
Thou preparest a table before me in the presence of mine enemies: thou anointest my head with oil; my cup runneth over.
Surely goodness and mercy shall follow me all the days of my life: and I will dwell in the house of the LORD for ever.

Psalm 23

Centuries later, we meet the Apostle Paul who like the ancient Psalmist found within himself the unseen forces of the eternal presence. As the leader of the Christian movement to the Gentiles, Paul traveled to Rome. Here the mad emperor Nero accused him and his companions of setting the city on fire. Nero had probably had the fire set by his own soldiers. Paul was thrown in prison. Even here God gave him the resources to deal with the demands and challenges of leadership.

While in prison, Paul wrote letters of encouragement to various churches he had established, for many of them were also in danger of persecution. Drawing upon his own experiences as way of bolstering the church at Philippi, Paul wrote:

> ...I have learned, in whatsoever state I am, therewith to be content. I know both how to be abased, and how to abound. Everywhere and in all things I am instructed both to be full and to be hungry, both to abound and to suffer need. I can do all things through Christ which strengtheneth me.
>
> (Philippians 4:11b-13)

Let us come now to the present and become acquainted with a man who like the Psalmist and the Apostle Paul, came in contact with the eternal presence and found resources to enable him to handle the demands and challenges of his life.

We meet this man through Dr. Larry Dossey who was his physician. In his book, *Healing Words* (1993), Dr. Dossey reports a conversation that he and this patient had on the day before he died of lung cancer. As Dr. Dossey sat with him, his wife, and his children, the dying patient – choosing his words carefully and speaking in a hoarse voice — told him that during his illness he had learned to pray.

Dr. Dossey was surprised by the patient's statement, for he knew that he was not a religious person. The doctor inquired of the man what he asked for when he prayed. "I don't pray for anything," he replied, "I wouldn't know what to ask for."

Again Dr. Dossey was taken back, so he asked, "If you don't ask for anything, then why do you pray?"

Faintly but firmly, he answered, "I pray so I will not be alone."

The ways to discover the resources of the eternal presence are varied and many, available both to you and to me.

Dick Cheatham with his baseball bat in the 1920's

Dick and Louise Cheatham in California before he left for the Aleutian Islands

Chaplain Cheatham in front of the Chapel
on the island of Attu in the Aleutian Islands
Winter of 1944-45

The Attu cemetery referred to in the sermon ON REMEMBERING THE DEAD.
Memorial Day 1945

The Post Chapel on Attu 1944-45

Sightseeing in Berchtesgaden, Germany
From left to right: Morris Schollenberger, 'Hansel', Lola May Schollenberger,
Chaplain Richard Cheatham, Louise Cheatham

Chaplain Cheatham in Germany with his two children Lynn and Richard

Visit to the 7th Infantry Division Memorial Chapel on
American Armed Forces Day, 17 May 1958
From left to right: Madame Rhee, Wife of President of Republic of Korea
Mrs. Dowling, Wife of American Ambassador to Korea
Syngman Rhee, President of Republic of Korea
Lt. Col. (Chaplain) Cheatham, Division Chaplain 7th U.S. Infantry Division
Ambassador Dowling, American Ambassador to Korea
Major General Sands, Commanding General, 7th U.S. Infantry Division

Chaplain Cheatham in his robe - Louise helps him hold a picture

Chief of Chaplains Frank Tobey and Louise Cheatham pin "eagles" on
Chaplain Cheatham after his promotion to Colonel at the Pentagon 1961
Rich and Lynn Cheatham at left

Dr. Cheatham in California

Dick and Louise Cheatham at Patriots Colony, Williamsburg, Virginia

24901138R00221

Made in the USA
Charleston, SC
09 December 2013